Mothering Our BOYS

A guide for mums of sons

MAGGIE DENT

Pennington Publications
PO Box 302, Gerringong, NSW 2534
Website: www.maggiedent.com

Published: October 2018

Title: Mothering Our Boys: A guide for mums of sons

Edition: First

Author: Dent, Maggie.

Date of Publication: 8 October 2018.
Reprinted November 2018.

ISBN: 978-0-9945632-7-9

A catalogue record for this book is available from the National Library of Australia.

Layout and design: Katharine Middleton, Ink Box Graphics

Cover & back cover images: Samara Wheeldon (www.samarawheeldonphotography.com)

Author image credit: Tony McDonough/Telethon Kids Institute

I wish to acknowledge and pay my respects to Australia's first peoples and to the traditional custodians of this amazing land. I especially pay my humble respects to the Noongar peoples of South West Australia, the custodians of my homeland – the country of my childhood, which I carry deeply within my heart every day of my life. The ancient knowledge and wisdom that our Indigenous elders have known and shared for thousands of years still has value for our modern world. May we all find ways to walk gently and compassionately on these ancient lands, and come to a place where all children ever born are respected and have a strong sense of belonging deeply.

DEDICATION

To my dear boys – my sons Michael, Ben, Alex and James.
Fate, destiny or the divine
blessed me with you
when your tiny bodies and bright souls
were placed into my care as your mother.
Such a responsibility it felt –
to nurture and care for you as you grew
from babyhood to boyhood
and finally to manhood.
I trembled so many times
as we came to a new door in your lives.
I held your hands and encouraged you
and then watched as you walked through alone.
A tiny piece of my heart would break
as you met each new change and challenge,
as you stepped further and further from me.
Every part of my being
wanted to keep you close so I could protect you
and keep you safe, and to shield you
from the world's pains and heartaches.
But I know from deep in my heart
that you must walk your own journey in this life
to make your own choices
and to find your real self.
Always know that I love you
more than you can ever imagine.
I believe in each one of you and
I know that you will make our world a better place
because that is what you have been raised to know.
From the bottom of my heart
I thank you for choosing me to be your mother.
It is and always will be an incredible privilege and honour,
and the greatest gift I could ever receive.
All my love always and ever,
Mum.

FOREWORD

As a psychologist supporting children and their parents, and as a mother intent on giving my two gorgeous boys the very best, I read most newly published parenting books. If it happens that you have ended up holding this book in your hands then let me just say, you are so very fortunate.

This is a book the world needs more than ever right now. A book that should be a mandatory read for every parent of boys, and indeed, any other big person who has either a direct or indirect role in the raising of boys. As I read this book and went from tears (five pages in!) to laughter to vigorous nods of approval, it occurred to me that if all the big people in the land knew what is contained in these pages, we just might change the world.

In this wonderfully informative guide for mamas of boys, Maggie Dent has brilliantly woven together the science and heart of raising your sons, provided a wealth of information on additional resources, and all of this with a refreshing dose of practical, immediately applicable advice. If I know one thing for sure, never has there ever been a more important time for all of us big people to really step in and step up in how we understand and grow our boys. And here is why.

In my clinical work we see over 400 children come through my office to work with myself and our team every month. The majority are boys and there are two primary referral issues which, when you understand the connection between them, will bring you to your knees. The first is the younger boy, usually less than age 6, who has been referred because he has become behaviourally very challenging to his teachers and/or parents. The second is the older boy, often aged 12 years or older, who has been referred because of anxiety, depression, self-harm, self-medicating (substance abuse), and suicidality.

What is the connection?

The connection is that the young boy was sadly misunderstood. There wasn't anything at all "wrong" with him. He had a hard time listening, he struggled to obey the rules, he couldn't sit still, and he hated all those stupid crafts. He was also "overly" aggressive, even with the kids he called his friends, and engaged in "socially inappropriate" behavior like farting, burping, and fondling his genitals, despite constant reminders to stop.

Diagnosis? XY. He's a boy. A beautiful, intelligent, normal boy, born to do and see and play and experience. However, in a world where the typical developmental patterns of girls have been preferred over those of boys, and where classroom environments often cater to the same, he became a normal boy who was very misunderstood. The more misunderstood he was, the more protective he had to become. And so defiance and acting out behaviours increased while quietly, on the inside, so too did his questioning of his own self-worth.

Now imagine this toxic brew of misunderstanding as the daily environment in which your precious boy is marinated. It is perhaps little wonder then that when you fast forward seven or so years, he will be much more vulnerable to becoming anxious, depressed, and/or so full of shame that he considers his only option that of ending his own life. This is what I see playing out in my clinic. This is what brings us to our knees.

But, what if I told you all of that could be quite easily avoided? There is another option and one that you can get after right now. That is the option of really seeing and hearing your boy. Of really getting him. Of observing and responding to and interacting with your son in a way that truly has him knowing you have his back. You have him. And nothing, not anything, will ever get in the way of that. This book tells you exactly how to do that. Brilliantly, as you have all of that come alive for you in your relationship with your son, I would not be at all surprised that you might also find it comes alive for you with all of the men in your life – your husbands, your fathers, your brothers, your coworkers. So powerful is this book.

That is Maggie's gift to all of us in these brilliantly written pages. As you read, you will hear the retrospective voices of men who Maggie surveyed talking about what they so valued in their mothers. You will hear funny stories and anecdotes that keep it all real. You will benefit from the incredible wealth of knowledge that is Maggie's alone, gathered through years of experience as an educator, a counsellor, and a mother herself to four lads. With her common-sense approach, you will find yourself immediately empowered to confidently stride forward in the raising of your boy. Maggie's direct, soft, witty, and wise voice will leave you feeling like she is sitting right beside you, encouraging you along the way. Like you somehow were lucky enough to be sitting down to a warm cuppa with her.

Thank you Maggie for this book. Thank you for your soul on this earth. Thank you for all that you do for kids and their people everywhere. To quote you, as there are really no other words that fit my sentiment so perfectly, ***"I love you more than every star in the night sky. I love you more than every grain of sand on every beach in the whole wide world. And I love you more than all the hairs on all the bears."***

And now, I'm off to love on my boys, inspired in all of it.

—Dr Vanessa Lapointe
Registered psychologist, British Columbia and author, *Discipline Without Damage*

CONTENTS

BACKGROUND

> "There's not just one thing. Everything that she had done for me has deeply influenced my life and me as a person. She's made me the man I am today. Although we are separated by distance, she's always there for me, my wife and my kids." – Men's Survey 2017

Before I launch into this book, I think it will be helpful if I give some background as to where I've come from and why I became a passionate 'boy champion'.

My childhood was spent growing up on a farm in the Wheatbelt in Western Australia, near a tiny town called Wandering. I am the fifth child of six siblings. One of the best things about being a farm kid is that you can hang out and spend lots of time with your dad, and I did. I have so many memories of helping Dad with my siblings, whether that be shifting sheep, checking the lambs, going for rides on the tractor or in the truck, picking mushrooms, burning off, or playing hide and seek in the shearing shed. As the older siblings left, I was lucky to be able to spend lots of one-on-one time with my dad who was educated as an agricultural scientist, who read widely, and who had a strong social conscience and a really good sense of humour. My dad was also a master farter! So, in a way, I was able to learn how to communicate in 'man language'.

On top of that I was also a tomboy or maybe tomgirl — basically, I disliked girly things particularly dresses, dolls and anything pink. In my primary school years I was often found on the oval playing football with the boys rather than spending time with the girls. In our family we had three girls and three boys and my younger sibling James and I had a wonderful free-range childhood in so many ways.

When I graduated as a high school English teacher, my first posting was to Albany Senior High School and I very soon came to realise that a lot of boys disliked English. I had several male students in my class with incredibly low levels of literacy, and this bothered me a lot.

While I was teaching, I was also coaching boys' basketball teams because I am a bit of a basketball tragic. I learnt a lot about boys from those basketball days as well as my classroom experiences.

Following the arrival of my four eagerly awaited, fabulous sons, during my years as an at-home mum, I took a break from teaching and became a volunteer at a local hospice. As a bereavement coordinator I worked closely with families whose loved ones were coming to the end of their lives. Many of these were men and the stories that they often shared over a quiet cuppa touched me deeply. Many men saw that death was a form of failure and that, in some way, they were letting their families down by dying. Many shared deep regrets that they hadn't been the husband or father they wished they could have been.

We had a beautiful 10-year-old boy who we cared for and he taught me so much about life and living. Again, it was in the quiet moments when no one else was around that he would often share the little things that were difficult to share when there was too much else happening. This was where I learnt about holding a quiet space – for much longer than most females prefer – and to allow boys and men a safe place to explore emotions and situations that are vulnerable, frightening and sad.

I went on to work part-time in a local funeral home as a funeral director's assistant. This meant, among other things, helping to transfer deceased loved ones, preparing the body, driving either the coach or the stretch hearse, and assisting with the funeral ceremony. As I was already an authorised marriage celebrant I began conducting funerals as well. This was a time when I worked closely with families and, again, I found an ability to draw stories more deeply from the men in the families I worked with. In some quiet moments I heard husbands share their deep love for the wife they had just lost and their regret that they had been unable to share those same words with their wife while she was still alive.

For a time when my sons were in primary school I also worked as an announcer on ABC radio in Albany. There were times when during an interview with a man I could tell he was struggling with some deep emotions around the story he was telling, and yet he was determined to force them down inside himself. I could see how difficult that struggle was and yet, at the same time, how important it was for him to squash those big feelings to conduct the interview. I began to question where men had learnt this emotional suppression.

When I returned to teaching, I had an epiphany one day that teaching adolescents to write paragraphs and essays was something that most English teachers could do. However, my innate ability to connect with, support and convince troubled teenagers not to hurt themselves or take their lives stood out to me as something of far more importance. Again, I felt I had a particular rapport with my male students, and it was so often the boys who ended up staying back to talk with me. So I completed a postgraduate diploma in counselling and stepped out of the classroom in 1998 to become a full-time counsellor with a special focus on self-esteem and resilience. Often I would be working with families to help resolve conflict, rebuild confidence and to offer support to them when the going got tough for children and teens. Many boys crossed my threshold in those early years and then, quite unexpectedly, older men began turning up in search of answers.

Drawing from all of these experiences, in 2003 I published my first book, *Saving our Children from our Chaotic World: Teaching Children the Magic of Silence and Stillness*. Soon after, I began running professional development sessions for teachers and seminars for parents and I have continued to run these all over Australia for the past 15 years.

My passion for resilience on all levels – individual, family and community – has seen me visit many rural communities around Australia after natural disasters like floods, drought and bushfires. Many years ago, I was invited to come and speak to a shed full of men in a rural community in Western Australia as part of a rural suicide prevention program. Since then I've had the honour and privilege of speaking to many men at seminars. Some men have told me that I make more sense than any other woman they have listened to. Some have said I helped them see the world the way their women do, and that this has helped them to better understand rather than react with frustration. I have a common-sense, pragmatic style of communication that's also a bit cheeky – much like how many men communicate. I joke that I'm bilingual: I can speak woman or man speak.

> *While I do call myself a boy champion, I am just as concerned with supporting girls and women to flourish. Just as I have run the men's seminars mentioned above, over the past 15 years I have also run many women's nights and weekend retreats — and 90% of my seminars are about raising both boys and girls to be happy, healthy, strong, kind and resilient.*

My strong social conscience definitely came from my dad. I am passionate about building understanding, personal and community resilience, and stronger, more connected families. Human relationships can be complicated and difficult, however, they also keep us alive and thriving.

I have had the honour of meeting, getting to know and becoming friends with people in many parts of this world. Despite this my closest girlfriends are still women I've known for 40 years. My extended family – including my 'good bloke' (my husband Steve), my siblings, nieces, nephews and all of my non-biological family – all matter enormously to me, and I love being a part of their lives. My former husband is also a man I still respect and care for deeply even though it's been 24 years since we were a committed couple. We both love our four sons and our extended family deeply, and we work closely to ensure we stay connected.

I am an incredibly blessed older woman. I believe in authenticity and share my mistakes and failings openly, including wearing my clothes inside out occasionally, getting lost and having endless battles with chin hairs that seemingly can grow during a two-hour seminar.

My four sons have made it to adulthood and have chosen strong, loving women as their partners in life. Grandparenthood has arrived – finally. My grandchildren have given me a renewed sense of purpose in life and I eagerly look forward to teaching them to cook some of Nanny's favourite dishes, to grow vegetables and flowers together, to build cubbies and sandcastles, to play basketball, and to fart well and laugh lots.

I hope this helps you understand a little more about how I became a boy champion.

– Maggie Dent, May 2018

> "Having them fight to have their own rooms and then finding them cuddled up in the same bed most nights." (Dear Boys 12 and 14) — Happy Mum

AUTHOR'S NOTE

Throughout this book, you'll notice two things featured in each chapter. Firstly, there are quotes from the Men's Survey 2017, such as the one at the beginning of the Background section preceding this Author's Note.

The Men's Survey was an online survey I conducted as part of my research for this book. I asked men, 18 and over, about their relationships with their mothers, including:

- **What would you say is one of the best things your mum has done for you/that has influenced you?**
- **In your life, what is one thing you wish your mum hadn't done?**

I had more than 1600 men respond to the survey, offering me some valuable insights into the mother-son relationship, and I have shared some of their comments in the book.

The second thing you will notice is the odd 'Dear Boys' quote from a mother, sharing a funny anecdote about parenting boys.

You'll see an example of one of these at the end of the Background section which precedes this Author's Note.

I asked more than 200 mums in my community: **"In 50 words or less, please share a brief anecdote about something your boy has said or done that has made you laugh"**.

The reason I sought funny reflections is because one thing I have learnt as a mum of only sons, is it's really important to lighten up.

In sharing these lighter moments, I asked the mums to nominate the ages of their DBs (Dear Boys) and to give themselves a pseudonym describing what kind of mum they are. So I am very happy to be able to share some of their joy with you.

Thank you again to all the men and women out there who did contribute to this research. It was a great honour to have you share your hearts and your humour with everyone reading this book.

INTRODUCTION

> "My mum taught me to never give up and to do what makes you happy and to be brave." – Men's Survey 2017

Boys in the Western world are in a form of crisis. Statistically they are struggling with transitioning into school, doing well at school, completing school and even the brightest of our boys are now failing university at higher levels than before. Boys are three times more likely to struggle with learning difficulties, ADHD and ODD – and boys' general disengagement from school is becoming more and more of a concern for parents and teachers.

In this digital world we seem to be losing many of our boys to their passion for gaming, which often becomes an addiction or at least an incredible distraction from living in the real world. The digital landscape is also a world that is unfettered, without the healthy boundaries needed to keep our boys safe. Images of violence, rape, child molestation and pornography are all at the fingertips of our precious, highly impressionable boys. They don't even need to search for pornography because it comes looking for them. Many innocent boys who enjoy watching funny cat and dog videos on YouTube will stumble innocently across highly disturbing images and video clips that can shatter their innocence very quickly.

For young lads on the journey to manhood who watch porn, it can be very difficult when their sexual awakening happens during adolescence to know any other way of experiencing sex and intimacy. We hear stories of girls ending up in emergency departments physically injured by boys who have been practising 'porn sex' rather than respectful, mutually enjoyable sex. Slapping, choking and forcing, regardless of concern for the girls, is a sure sign that a boy has learnt his sexual behaviour from pornography. Given that boys are generally highly visual, repeated exposure merely anchors in their minds this sexually exploitative behaviour. In recent times there have been reports in the media of some very disturbing and hurtful misogynistic behaviour. In a way, the digital world has increased sexually predatory behaviour for many teen boys and young men. I believe that with guidance, especially from the mums of sons, we can ensure our boys learn about the gifts of being in love – in safe, respectful, enjoyable relationships in the real world.

In another disturbing recent phenomenon, young boys – some as young as eight – are being diagnosed with eating disorders and in a recent study that included Australia and the UK there has been an alarming increase in the number of boys who are self-harming. What is particularly concerning about this is that many of these boys are only eight to 10 years old.

The world has changed in many unhelpful ways. Parents are much more fearful about letting their children have freedom to explore their neighbourhoods, local creeks and streams, or even to climb trees and build cubbies with their friends. This constriction of children's wild freedom to roam has seen a massive shift in boyhood in particular, and it has come at a cost that I will explore later. Rather than explore and experience life in the real world through their senses and experiences, many children now explore the world through a screen. This shift in societal norms is especially damaging for our boys who are still biologically wired to learn through experience – through testing themselves with real challenges with other people while learning to negotiate, construct, create and destroy! Remember that moment of jumping on top of a sandcastle that had taken all day to build? Now that's a moment to remember.

Adolescent boys on the journey to manhood are also struggling. Their boyhood has not given them a strong foundation to negotiate the massive shifts in testosterone, physical growth and brain changes – nor has it given them the social and emotional awareness to manage the complex, ever-changing school environment. The 'schoolification' of early years' care and education, and the growth in benchmark testing across the Western world, has put a strong over-emphasis on marks, grades and how students compare nationally. Supposedly this approach was introduced to revolutionise education in this country, as in the US and the UK, and improve the academic outcomes of all students. Sadly, it has done the reverse. Literacy and numeracy rates have not improved. In Australia there has been a huge increase in the number of 4- to 5-year-old students being suspended and even expelled – mostly boys. In many ways we are punishing boys who are developmentally not ready for a curriculum that has been pushed downwards. I fully support parenting author and psychologist Steve Biddulph's belief that most boys benefit from starting formalised schooling a year later than girls.

According to the annual Mission Australia Youth Survey, the three top issues of personal concern for young people are consistently **coping with stress, school or study problems** and **body image**.

Boys who are biologically wired to work with their hands and bodies as well as their brains – who often excel in trades or construction industries and engineering – often form the crippling mindset from a young age that they are in some way dumb or useless and that school will be a waste of time. Boys who struggle to find something they are good at can become angry and even aggressive.

Most of us will also be aware of the disturbing statistics around violence against women. Abuse can be verbal, psychological, financial, social, damaging property, stalking and harassment, and obviously physical. In Australia an average of one woman a week dies at the hands of a current or former partner. In the UK between 2013 and 2016, 70% of all victims of domestic homicides were women. In other parts of the world these numbers are much higher. Sometimes violence against women is a learnt behaviour from childhood, however, sometimes it happens when the emotional volatility for a man becomes too much and he snaps. I believe that with more emotional coaching in the early years of life, maybe we can prevent these disturbing statistics from continuing in the future. We need to teach our little boys how to manage big, ugly feelings and how to self-regulate in heated moments, rather than resort to aggression.

I also believe that with connected mothering, which understands boys better, we will avoid some of the deep wounding that can happen to our boys – often unintentional wounding at that.

On top of these grim realities, the depression and suicide rates, particularly in Australia, are the highest they have been in a long time. It isn't always obviously vulnerable young people from dysfunctional homes who struggle with mental illness or who die by suicide either. It can be our top students – the ones most likely to succeed. The pressure to succeed can sometimes be simply too hard to bear for an adolescent who is trying to work out who they are, do they matter and are they worthwhile?

> **"Men's mental health issues play out at a high level right across society. Statistics of suicide, premature death, accidents, violence, crime and addiction are dominated by men. Then there's the domino effect. Men who have been victims themselves tend to hurt others in the form of physical and sexual violence, other crimes and antisocial behaviour, marriage breakdowns, alcohol and drug abuse and moral bankruptcy."**
>
> – Georgina Barker, 'Lost Boys', *Scoop*, (Vol 65, Spring 2013).

People who work in mental health have started to identify that suicide can be linked not only to depression, grief, addiction and heightened stress, but there seems to be a linkage to deep loneliness for many men who have died by suicide. So often women are the social connectors in relationships and after a separation or divorce it seems many men struggle to connect, or to build new friendships. This is why I dedicate a whole chapter to exploring how to help our boys build and nurture friendships.

In my previous books I have strongly linked my writing to evidence-based research. In this book I still do that somewhat but I have changed my approach because, quite frankly, research can't explain everything. Over the years as a high school teacher, boys' basketball coach, counsellor, bereavement coordinator in a hospice, a celebrant who has conducted over 1000 weddings and over 250 funerals, a community bereavement educator, a suicide prevention facilitator, and a parenting educator who has run many 'dads only' and men's seminars — I have heard the voices of so many boys and men. So much of what I write in this book comes from my observations.

I also surveyed 1600 men for this book asking them what their relationship was like with their mother as grown men and, as I mentioned in my Author's Note, the best things their mum had done, plus the thing they wished she hadn't. Predictably, 85% of the responses came from Australia and the rest came from the United Kingdom, United States, New Zealand, Canada and Germany.

The good news is that of the men surveyed, 46% reported having 'respectful and loving' relationships with their mum, almost 20% reported they 'generally get on well' and a further 16% reported that their relationship is 'challenging however still worth it'. Of the rest, 13% of the men surveyed 'only relate out of obligation' and the remaining 5% reported that they were 'completely estranged' from their mother. Throughout this book I will share many of these men's responses so we can better appreciate the things that help, hinder or hurt in this primary relationship.

This book will rest not only on my experience as a daughter, a mother of sons and a counsellor, it will also rest on the voices of the good men who responded to my survey, as well as being informed by my years of reading and research around the raising of boys into good men.

As this book will have a strong anecdotal approach, the identity of the boys I write about will be protected. Most boys have a strong resistance to public disclosure and prefer their stories to be kept private. So to do that, a boy will be described as DB (8) — Dear Boy (aged 8).

We all carry various scars from our childhood — and that is because parenting children is not a perfect art. For some of us, our 'mother wound' may have been what challenged us in life. For others it may be a father wound. For some who had particularly challenging childhoods, it could be both.

Something I have discovered in listening to the stories of boys and men, is that sometimes the mother wound that caused them to struggle in life — particularly around self-worth, independence and in intimate relationships — could possibly have been avoided. Often that mother wound came from a place of misunderstanding rather than intention because we mothers and sons are, quite simply, different genders.

Even though we live in a time where we are recognising that nothing in gender is fixed, it still remains a fact that the influence of a mother on her son is massive. We all have masculine and feminine attributes and we are conditioned and influenced by the experiences that we have in the environment in which we grow up. This in no way disrespects the incredible importance of fathers or father figures in raising children. In an ideal world children need healthy connections to mother and father figures — even if they are not biological. This applies to whether partners are same-sex, married, divorced or otherwise — children benefit from the influence of men and women in their lives.

I am writing this book for mothers of sons — and women teachers of boys — and all those mother figures that exist in our boys' worlds. I offer you my views and experiences with the fundamental aim to help build understanding, empathy and compassion for our boys. If we can build a strong foundation based on unconditional acceptance and love, our sons will navigate the journey to adulthood with less suffering. Mums have so much to teach their precious sons so that they can learn emotional and social competence to align with their physical strength and 'warrior' tendencies.

Little boys can be easily influenced by others who have extreme views that are distorted or based on misogynistic values, which are no longer relevant or acceptable today. The best way to fight these sexist attitudes is to create change by modelling, using compassion and love through the education of the next generation of men. This starts from the moment of conception.

Boys are influenced, not only by their own mothers, but by the mothers of others. That is why this book is about boys, not just sons. So many men have shared with me how important a caring, older, wiser woman was in helping them find themselves and a better way of being in the world. Please invest your love and nurturing of your sons to the sons of other mothers and let the metaphor 'it takes a village' become reality again.

Mothering Our Boys is especially for mothers who either had no brothers or maybe they had a cold, distant, even dysfunctional relationship with a father figure. These mammas seem to be the most confused.

Here are some questions commonly asked by confused mammas:
Why doesn't he listen?
Why doesn't he do as he is told?
Why can't he sit still?
Why doesn't he clean up?
Why is he always touching things?
Why is he always hungry?
Why does he do so many dumb things without thinking?
Why doesn't he wear a jumper when it's freezing cold?
I will answer these — I promise!

I believe if we can see the world through boys' eyes a little better we will make different choices in the way that we mother them. We can learn to be the safe, loving base they seek when the world seems cruel. We can teach them that even though they may feel they need to be fearless, brave warriors, it's OK to feel fear, pain and sadness just like everyone else. We can teach them the values and morals of being a decent human being and that the most precious things you can have in life are a conscience, and a good moral compass. We can teach them skills that will help them manage their lives when they leave home, especially how to conquer failure. And we can teach them about valuing and respecting women, especially the one they choose to commit themselves to if that's a choice they make one day. We can teach them about unconditional love rather than the conditional love that many children experience.

To start us off, I'd like to share just a few of the things that men have shared with us in the survey, reflecting on what their mothers taught them. There are still so many more to come.

"My mum worked three jobs when I was growing up and, as a single mother, she instilled a great work ethic."

"My mum taught me to forgive and go forward in my life. Learn from unexpected outcomes and look towards the future."

"My mum inspired me to champion justice and equality."

— Men's Survey 2017

Mothers of sons know that there is often so much to laugh about when you have lads in your home or classroom. As I explained in my Author's Note, that's why I also asked mums to send us their funniest anecdotes to feature throughout the book. Enjoy these.

Also, I will apologise now if my humour offends anyone who reads this book. It is not my intention to offend – ever.

This book will particularly explore the creation of a sound foundation that mothers can build – day by day – before their boys reach puberty. The shaping of little boys' mindsets impacts the mindsets of older boys, teens, young men and even adult men. Poor behaviour is the consequence of poor choices – and mums have such a powerful influence in helping boys learn how to make better choices without hitting, hurting or shaming them. After puberty, boys begin the next stage of transformation – a form of knighthood – and it is a time when mums need to make some serious changes to the way in which they parent their sons. While this book will be fairly useful to mums of adolescents, I recommend all mums of sons also read Celia Lashlie's book *He'll Be OK*. It captures many of the messages I would share with mums of adolescent sons if this book was covering that age group in more depth. I also recommend Dr Arne Rubinstein's book, *The Making of Men* as a must-read when your son is around 10. And, of course, you will still have Steve Biddulph's *Raising Boys in the 21st Century* for further counsel.

So, come on mums of sons, dive into my guide to help you be the firm and loving mum your sons need.

> "My dear boys have invented a new wrestling game 'butt on head'. The winner is the one who literally puts his butt on the other's head (often, my husband and boys gang up on me and force me to play). Extra points if they fart!" – Lucky Mum

CHAPTER ONE

GENDER explored

> "My mum taught me that sometimes it's best to keep my mouth shut and let people believe what they want." – Men's Survey 2017

When my third son arrived, I started noticing something interesting. I had people, mainly women but there was the occasional man, come up to express their sympathy and deep disappointment to me because I had had another son. Having more than two boys appeared to be a pathway that deserved sympathy and solicited a well-meaning and yet patronising expression of impending doom! One person told me she had cried for me and another said she'd offered me some special prayers. Quietly I found this a little sad, as I was absolutely thrilled with the arrival of another healthy baby. One day, after one of these interactions, my 6-year-old son turned to me and said, "Mummy, why is that lady sad that you had another baby boy?"

How do I explain to a 6-year-old boy that some people think boys are in some way deficient to girls? Or maybe that they think boys are going to be much harder work than girls? Indeed, when I gave birth to my fourth son I was expecting bereavement cards! The same thing happened again. What surprised me was that some people expected me to agree with them because somehow I had missed out because I didn't have a girl. We need to be really mindful of how we speak around families who only have boys because this is where little boys start to realise that there may be something wrong with them. In a way it was a little bit lucky that my fourth son was born five weeks early and that I was quite unwell afterwards, because people were much more gentle with the whole "aren't you disappointed?" messages.

When we are talking about gender, it is really important to stress that both genders are equally fabulous and that they have more similarities than differences. However, these differences, which seem to stem from biological drivers deep within our DNA, need to be recognised because they can cause some parents and educators some confusion. As you read this book, please know that no one size fits all. Some of what I write about boys could possibly help you with your 'rooster' daughter, such as the 'tomboy' I was. It is widely believed that around 70% of boys have very common characteristics – this is a statistically significant number. However, our gentle, sensitive boys are often not like the stereotypical energetic, boisterous boys. Some of our sensitive boys express more traits that we think of as feminine – they are often gentle, thoughtful, nurturing and quite capable of chatting – like most girls. They are not **less than** boys – although sometimes people see them that way and want to toughen them up. They are just different and they still need to have the same loving guidance to help them become mature, responsible men one day.

The difference between a classic boy and a rooster girl is that your girl does not have a penis or the surges of testosterone that boys do. However, your sensitive, gentle son does have a penis and surges of testosterone.

As you read this book, please just take from it what may be helpful for you and leave the rest. Boys will grow to become men and some of them will be straight, some will be gay and others may be bisexual, transgender or otherwise. I think each of us wants for our boys to become caring, worthwhile members of our community who are capable of being present in loving, respectful relationships. We especially want them to be resilient and capable of overcoming adversity, no matter how it turns up in life, without needing to resort to aggression, addiction or profound disconnection.

As the #MeToo movement has shown us, we live in a time where women are no longer staying silent when they have been treated disrespectfully and inappropriately. That's why it is more important than ever that we are aware of how we can help our boys avoid becoming a product of the old 'male code', where men were tough and had a sense of power and entitlement.

There is definitely a grey area between playful teasing and flirting, which has no intention to hurt or harm, and the sort of behaviour that can be perceived as sexual harassment and completely inappropriate. We need to help our boys navigate this and think about how their words and actions may be perceived by others – and we need to help them clearly understand consent.

Gender needs – and is indeed witnessing – a shift from both sides of the spectrum, where men can now be more openly loving and caring, while women can be seen as strong and fit and brave. Having equity in pay, job opportunities and true equity in front of the courts is slowly happening in many countries. Essentially, raising our boys to be respectful of people who deserve to be respected, and those who are in positions of authority – regardless of gender, culture, disability or religious and political differences – is definitely a challenge. However, it is a challenge that parents of sons and teachers of our boys need to recognise as being important. It is not so much that our boys need extra guidance and education that worries me, it is how we teach this in a way that is beneficial and respectful of how boys learn best. We will explore that in more depth later.

> "I wish my mum had not put herself and her interests and needs so far behind everyone else's." – Men's Survey 2017

Gender stereotypes exist strongly in our society. Frankly, I think if we don't at least seek first to identify and understand what our general societal beliefs about boys and girls are, and what possible biological factors might be at play, then we cannot work towards parenting our children equitably and creating more harmony in our families and our world.

I have seen mums breathe big sighs of relief when they have heard information that reassured them that their 5-year-old son was probably acting very typically for a boy his age. This was something they did not realise when comparing him to his 3-year-old sister who was counting to 20, speaking in full sentences, colouring within the lines and able to sit calmly for much longer. Both boys and girls display some typical gendered strengths and challenges as they grow older. This book is written simply to build understanding, to get you thinking about how you see your children and to give possible solutions to challenging moments you may have in your home — from a different viewpoint — one that you didn't see before. Gender identity is not fixed and we are more 'soft wired' than 'hard wired' into having more 'masculine' or 'feminine' traits. As I have said before, you may very well have a girl who has a lot of masculine tendencies and vice versa.

> *So always keep in mind, I am more about questioning some of the messages that come from our conditioning — from our childhood, from the experiences we have had and from the continued socialisation that we have experienced throughout our life — rather than just identifying them.*

Once we give them light, we then have a chance to change them.

Do you remember how I shared how people felt sorry for me when I had my third son? This is a good example of how embedded gender stereotypical beliefs can unconsciously influence what we say and what we do. These good people meant no harm to me at all. They were just responding in a way that they had obviously heard before or that was based on a perception that they'd hung on to as a consequence of some experience they may have had. There was no malice intended, and there will be many times in this book that

I will challenge some of the things that we say and do. I have no intention to offend, upset or disrespect anyone who reads this book. However, I believe that by teasing out gender stereotypes and putting them under the lens of respectful observation, we may be able to shift the negative connotations that have shaped behaviour towards boys and which have caused deep, invisible harm. With understanding, comes knowledge and new choices.

> "One night at dinner DB (11) announced that they were doing Sex Ed at school and he knew ALL about sex — 'It's very unhygienic.' I nearly choked on my food laughing." — Happy Mum

I was a high school teacher for almost 17 years in co-ed schools and what I *generally* noticed most about girls, compared to boys, in my classrooms was:

- They could follow instructions better.
- Their concentration span was longer.
- They sat on their seats a lot more with less squirming and fidgeting.
- They tended to remember details better.
- They were easier to engage in activities.
- They needed less reminding about assessment dates.
- They thrived in group situations better than most boys.
- They came to class expecting to work.
- They had better organisational skills.
- They seldom needed to fart or burp in public.
- They spoke more quietly than boys.
- They tended to be more punctual to class than boys.
- They remembered their manners more often than boys.
- They used fewer swear words and profanities in class.

Given that I was teaching adolescent students – complete with swirling hormones and poorly functioning brains, and who were just beginning their sexual awakening – the above characteristics tended to happen in classrooms with students aged from 12 to 18.

We now know, thanks to advances in neuroscience and neuropsychology, that much of adolescent behaviour is dictated by developmentally driven brain changes. Puberty now seems to be happening as early as eight or 10 years of age rather than the previous age bracket of 12 to 14. However, there are various stages throughout a boy's life where his hormones or biological drives might impact his behaviour. I'll explore these throughout the book (and I've summarised them in a blog on my website called '5 Tricky Times in Boyhood That Every Parent Needs to Understand' if you'd like a cheat sheet!)

In my seminars about boys, I encourage parents and educators to see their 14-year-old boys in a similar way to 4-year-old boys. There is a strong drive for power and autonomy in these age groups that is coupled with massive surges of testosterone, impulsivity, often hyperactivity and badly behaved penises that they have very little control over. They have also got a strong egocentric view of the world, which can be annoying, however, it is developmentally important. Funny, yes?

> "I have to pause and reflect on the things I often hear myself saying. I only have sisters, so most of this 'boy stuff' amuses me. Today's was particularly interesting. 'Boys, stop comparing penises. It won't make them grow any quicker.'" — Mum of DBs (2 and 4)

Biological differences run deep

When we lived in traditional kinship communities or tribes, life was a lot less complicated and confusing, and the pathway to walk the journey from boy to man was clearly defined. Gender roles were very specific and that was because survival was dependent on this conformity. The gender that was physically strongest was responsible for keeping the rest of the community safe and well fed. The rest was up to the women.

Quite simply, little boys spent their whole time with the women in the tribe and all the other children having fun, playing in nature, and being loved and pampered by the circle of women. Around the ages of eight to 10, boys were removed from their mothers and the women, and were guided, educated and mentored by the men until they were initiated into manhood through a powerful ceremony. Around the age of 10, boys experience a massive surge in testosterone – so we can see why this may be a sensible age for boys to be shifted to the wild, open spaces with the men. Movement and risky play release testosterone naturally!

Every boy's journey was unique and different, and manhood was something you had to earn and learn. You certainly didn't become a man by spending years gaming in your bedroom slaying make-believe dragons, learning how to hack or finding out about sex from pornography.

About a decade ago, I knew a DB (14) who was a self-taught hacker, living in a country town. He had been able to hack into his parents' bank account and the police department's computer system, and eventually he completely crashed his high school's network. He is a good example of a boy who found a different context to being the more physically powerful gender. This partially explains the fascination with violent gaming for many of our boys.

In traditional cultures, there were clear rites of passage that defined significant life milestones, and things were clear and marked by ritual and ceremony. I wonder if the more contemporary rituals of getting a full-sleeve tattoo, sculling a yard glass at your 21st or doing burnouts on the local football oval are worthy ways of marking the threshold to adulthood? One of the most encouraging shifts that is occurring, particularly across Australia, is the return to rites of passage for both boys and girls. I acknowledge and pay my respect to two of the leaders of this movement, Dr Arne Rubinstein, CEO of the Rites of Passage Institute, and Andrew Lines from The Rite Journey. My dream would be to see these programs as a part of every high school in Australia and, an even bigger dream, in other countries in the Western world. They are powerful, positive and transformative, and our teens need these rites of passage as they step into adulthood in a confusing world.

There is great debate about whether men's brains are different to women's brains and, from my reading, the core differences seem to come more from our hormonal differences, and the social, cultural and biological drivers. There are also the instinctual behaviours that may be imprinted on our DNA from the time we lived in indigenous kinship communities. Men and women tend to interpret and process information a little differently at times but I'm not convinced this is a fixed reality, more like a tendency.

I respectfully acknowledge the work of Steve Biddulph, Michael Gurian, Dr William Pollack, Alison Armstrong and others in getting the big picture about some of the differences between men and women, and sharing them with the world – especially the differences that cause confusion and conflict. We are meant to be different to some extent, because we are driven by different biological and social drives. Yes, we do see the world through different eyes and our unique maps of the world are often different. So, let's explore these basic differences that come from our ancient ancestry and see how this can explain some of the confusion that exists in many heterosexual relationships.

Michael Gurian, author of *The Wonder of Boys* (1996), *The Good Son* (1999), and *Saving Our Sons* (2017), writes that the amygdala – the primary aggression centre in the brain – is larger in males than females and this could be linked to the creation of more aggression in males. When this is combined with massive surges of testosterone, it may give us a clue as to why boys seem more wired to like risky behaviour and 'warrior' behaviour. The effect of the neurotransmitter vasopressin has also been linked to tendencies of territorialism, competition and persistence. The biggest challenge we have in parenting boys is to work with these tendencies so that they can learn how to channel them in healthy and positive ways. Generally, little girls have different hormones and tendencies in their brain development (and social conditioning) to little boys. This does not mean that little boys cannot learn how to contain their impulsive behaviours, especially when they impact others. Of course 'boys will be boys' is still a phrase commonly heard when boys are being warrior-like or highly physical. However, these boys need to learn, while they are still little boys, that they need to be respectful of other people – but we need to do this without demonising their natural tendencies and seeing them as something 'wrong' or 'bad' that needs to be stopped.

If their behaviour negatively impacts other children or grown-ups, they need to know that that is unacceptable and inappropriate. They need to be guided to behave differently. Importantly, we can do this without hitting, hurting or shaming our little boys – more on that later.

Gurian believes that the invisible drive at the biological core of manhood is the pursuit to prove self-worth. No one can give a man his self-worth – he has to give this to himself. To find this place, boys and men often seek external ways or experiences to demonstrate potency, victory and independence, and this is what helps shape their search for meaning and purpose in life from a very early age. This is the warrior unfolding from within. Boys seem to be generally competitive, active and constantly in search of moments to prove their worth and value. Little boys are seeking the same evidence of worth from their experiences, so they can feel that they have done well. We might think of this as being like a 'self-worth barometer'.

When boys are happy with what they have achieved, they feel good about themselves. If they have failed to achieve what they set out to do or, even worse, they have upset Mummy, it really hurts inside. Even from a very young age, little boys will attack themselves for not being good enough or for failing. We need to keep in mind this emotional barometer of self-worth that exists within every little boy and man, and learn to treat it with respect and understanding.

For mums, understanding how sensitive our little boys are around this emotional barometer of self-worth can be incredibly helpful. Let's be honest, mums are conditioned to take good care of their homes and families. This likely also comes a little from the cave woman who exists within us as a biological drive. We like having things clean and tidy. It gives us a sense of doing well. How often do you get your little boys to pack away all their toys when it's time for dinner or bed? Have you ever considered that your little boy may have had a plan for what he would build with that Lego or indeed those Matchbox or Hot Wheels cars? A plan that you have now dashed and sabotaged for the sake of cleanliness? He never reached the level of achievement he had set for himself and he will feel disappointed, let down and even sad. He, of course, is unable to articulate any of this.

Following one of my seminars, a lovely mum of two sons emailed me to tell me how hearing this had been a profound realisation in her life. She went on to tell me that before school her 4-year-old and 6-year-old sons, who were not allowed to watch TV or use technology in the mornings, would build Lego. Every morning as they were ready to leave the house, she made them pack it all away. The day after the seminar she said to her sons:

"If you haven't finished building what you want to build, you can leave it there and finish it after school."

On the way to school her 6-year-old son said from the back seat of the car, *"Mummy I am so excited!"* When his mother asked him why he replied:

"Because today is the first day in my life that I'm going to be able to finish building what I started to build in the morning".

This mum was so grateful for that insight.

There is a pragmatism to boys and men that we women can sometimes struggle with. I suggest strongly, Mum, that you really listen to your son when he is trying to explain to you why he is doing something differently from what you want.

If you have a son who enjoys toast after school and you have growled at him for not cleaning down the bench after he has made his toast, listen to him. I had a similar discussion with one of my lads once and he said:

"Mum, why would I clean down the bench after I had my first toast when I know I'm going to come back in an hour and cook some more toast? It really is a waste of effort!"

On any given day, how was a son supposed to know how many pieces of toast he might need to cook – given that boys get hungry very quickly, especially after physical exertion? The same goes for a mamma's passion for using a plate when eating said toast – well, a boy may see his hand as an incredibly sensible alternative to a plate (and look at the washing up saved!). Just let it go and save your energy for the big battles.

I needed to see a new perspective through my son's eyes and realise that I was creating tension and conflict where I could simply let it go. Given I had four sons (equally as hungry), I could see it was a battle that wasn't worth fighting. Choosing the battles that are worth fighting and letting go of the ones that can wait is very much a part of mothering sons positively.

> "My DB (8) told me he had found a dead rat in the backyard. When I asked him what he had done with it, he told me he threw it to the neighbours'. I was horrified but couldn't help myself laughing." — Conflicted Mum

There will be many times when you are extremely confused about something your son is investing his time and energy in. You may notice from your kitchen window that your son is dragging his body around the lawn in a very specific way, over and over again – an act that makes no rational sense to you at all. Please be reassured that it will be making perfect sense to your son. It is absolutely OK for you to ask yourself, "Why is he doing that?" If possible, however, avoid asking your son until he has completed whatever unfathomable thing he is doing. I can assure you that, when a boy is intensely focused on something, **it matters to him**.

He may be learning something about the world or about himself. He may be testing his abilities or a hypothesis. He is learning and growing and, in that moment, he is taking an active role in his growth and development.

There were once three sons, DBs (6) (8) and (10), who announced to their mum that they were going to build a bear pit in the vacant block next door to their home (in Australia). Fortunately this was an experienced mum of sons who knew better than to question the need to build a bear pit in a country where there are no bears. She simply helped them find the necessary tools for this big job. Over the following week, several of the boys' friends turned up to assist in this mammoth task of building a bear pit. This was no small bear pit because in their conversations they realised that bears could be very big so the pit had to be very big. They spent ages negotiating what was needed to succeed in this important project! Every night, when they came in from the digging, they were absolutely physically wasted and totally committed to completing their task. When it was finished, the pit had a camouflage of long sticks and branches over it – so the unsuspecting bear would not see the pit until he had fallen into it. The boys were unbelievably proud when their bear pit was finished and then they promptly forgot about it. The project was done, the target was met and they simply moved on to something else. What is really funny about this story is that many years later when these little boys grew into young lads, DBs (18), (20) and (22), they had another encounter with their long-forgotten bear pit. One evening, when walking home from a local nightclub, they took a shortcut through the vacant block of land next to their house and, you guessed it, one of the boys fell into their bear pit. Needless to say, the following morning they were quite excited to take their mum out and show her how successful their bear pit had finally been.

> "Unloading our new bull with DB (3) son in tow ... husband always had a cycling cow ready to greet the new stud, so as to check that all the tackle 'worked' ... after some mandatory lip curling the bull mounted and did the job!!! Apprentice cattle farmer looked at me and said, 'Did Dad do that to you?' What could I say?" — Honest Mum

TOP TIPS

- ✓ Both genders are equally fabulous.
- ✓ There are some significant biological differences between girls and boys.
- ✓ Males and females tend to process information differently.
- ✓ Understanding these differences can improve relationships between mums and sons.
- ✓ Boys and men have an emotional barometer that measures their self-worth, based on experiences.
- ✓ Boys and men have a tendency to be pragmatic and they can make choices based on what they consider to be common sense.
- ✓ Mums will sometimes be confused by the things their son chooses to do – this is OK.
- ✓ Support your son when he decides that a project is important – even if it makes no sense to you.

CHAPTER TWO

UNDERSTANDING the main BIOLOGICAL drivers of MODERN-DAY cave MEN and cave WOMEN

In days gone by, as in my father's generation, boys had the freedom to roam, unsupervised on adventures that allowed them to be massively engaged in pursuits that helped them learn and grow using life's greatest teacher – experience. It was not unusual for boys to ride their bikes up to 10km to go fishing by themselves or with a group of other lads. Nowadays, these same boys would be driven by their parents to go fishing and an adult would probably be present for the whole experience. Our modern-day phobia that the world is unsafe is creating an environment where boys are finding it more and more difficult to find that place of self-worth through external moments of potency and success, and this may be contributing to creating a generation of frustrated and angry young men. There seems to be three traditional roles of mature men that have their biological beginnings inside the DNA of every little boy ever born. I again wish to acknowledge and respect the work of Alison Armstrong as several of these terms come from her excellent work in understanding the differences between men and women.

Ancient biological drivers for boys and men

1. The mammoth hunter role

The first, biologically driven role of mature men is to ensure the safety and protection of the tribe or community, especially those more vulnerable members of the group. This drive exists to ensure the continuation of the tribe/species. Essentially, when there was any threat to the tribe's safety and wellbeing, whether that be a rampaging mammoth or another hostile tribe, men took up arms and went to destroy the enemy. This meant the men needed to know how to kill and annihilate the threat whether with clubs, axes, arrows or any other means. To be really competent at using weapons, when there was no threat to the tribe men spent their days practising to use weapons (which is a bit like the role of sport in our modern world). Those of you who have been brave enough to watch the TV show *Game of Thrones*, even though it is only fantasy, will have a fair idea of how tough and bloody the job of protecting women and children may have been in days gone by. Being a mammoth hunter or a heroic warrior had a noble intention behind it – the protection of those most vulnerable and dear to them. This warrior instinct still exists within our boys and men today. While we don't have any mammoths to slay in our modern world, we have plenty of 'wars'. Some of the wars that men get drawn into as modern-day mammoth hunters are on our football fields, in speeding cars, and sadly on our streets at night with a bellyful of booze. To be a competent mammoth hunter, men needed to be able to focus on just one thing at a time – killing the mammoth. Until that mammoth was dead or had been removed as a threat, a man's job was not complete. This single-mindedness or single focus plays out today when men can't find the milk in the fridge or a shirt in their cupboard.

My old, wise friend Julian Krieg who was a pioneer of Wheatbelt Men's Health in WA explains the perceived differences between men's and women's thinking as:

> **"Women's minds are like she can be in every room of the house at the same time – rapidly linking and thinking many different happenings and realities at the same time. On the other hand, men are in one room at a time totally focused on one task at a time."**

Pastor and motivational speaker Mark Gungor has a great way of explaining the differences in the way men and women think. Search YouTube for 'Men's Brains and Women's Brains', 'Mark Gungor' and 'Nothing Box' and you will laugh and learn.

Let me give you an example of how this different way of thinking can work. Let's say a woman tells her male partner before work that his mother is coming over for afternoon tea later and they would like him to join them (i.e. could he come home early?). That information has been given to this man at home and then he drives off to work and that information is not in the 'work room'. The chances of him completely forgetting the afternoon date are very high. A woman, even if she had to go to work, would very likely still think about this appointment during her work day.

A poignant example of this came from a dad after one of my seminars. This is his story:

> **"Maggie, I knew it was our 10th wedding anniversary when I left home in the morning. I knew it was our 10th wedding anniversary at lunchtime and I had plans to get some flowers and chocolates on my way home — her favourites. And then that afternoon we had a fairly serious crisis at work that needed my full attention to resolve. When I walked in the door that night I realised that I had forgotten all about our 10th wedding anniversary. There was no way I could convince my wife that I had indeed remembered our anniversary most of the day. I felt like such a dickhead. I really love and adore my wife. So I really understand about the single focus."**

Evolutionary biologists claim that the biological drive to protect and defend is still fundamentally strong inside today's men. It is also present in our little boys in an embryonic way. And there are still modern-day mammoth killing tasks that men feel driven to conquer. Elite sport, mountain climbing and surfing all create these opportunities in a healthy way, most of the time. Good men turn up after natural disasters as mammoth hunters, driven to help conquer Mother Nature's devastation by working hard in terrible conditions to restore order from the chaos. Starting a new business, building a house, travelling, racing cars or motorbikes, or working in high-risk jobs like firefighting, sea rescue, scaffolding, deep-sea diving or in the State Emergency Service (SES) – these are all modern-day mammoth-hunting pursuits.

For some men, a trip to the camping store or Bunnings can seem like a modern-day mammoth hunting opportunity! Mammoth hunting is really about conquering challenge, removing threat and creating certainty. It also brings a sense of achievement, self-respect and that incredibly important thing – self-worth.

> Sadly, in our world today there is a strong individualistic, competitive pressure to win at all costs. There has been a rise in narcissistic-type behaviour among a large percentage of men that may have a quietly disturbing negative impact on our boys. Rather than the collective striving for the greater good that happened in prehistoric times,

individual success seems to have taken priority. Today, benchmark testing, some online gaming and even body image concerns are putting undue pressure on our boys to be better than others. This means those boys who have an additional challenge like a learning disability, or who have ADHD or dyslexia or maybe struggle with anxiety, often see themselves in a far darker light than just 'different'. Feeling bad or like a failure creates a mindset that can shape how a boy sees himself for life.

Mums have a powerful role to play in teaching our boys that everyone is unique and different, and that we are all on this earth to use our unique gifts and talents to make the world a better place in some way. This builds an understanding that living a life of meaning matters, even when you are not winning prizes or competitions. This message will help our boys see that gender equity also matters and that men and women are capable of being valued not just for what they do but for who they are and what they offer the world. It will help them see that a career pathway that does not respect the greater good may feel meaningless in time, even if it earns you lots of money. When the biological drive to win and kill the mammoth is a man's primary drive and purpose in life, a huge challenge can be created when that does not happen.

Indeed, if the reverse occurs where a man has lost his job, his licence, his woman, his money, his relationship with his children or any other significant failure or loss, he may see himself as a failure and feel shame and disgust at being "weak as piss". For many men, this is where the invisible bucket of anger and rage hides and it doesn't take much, a tiny trigger, and this rage comes surging out, irrationally, powerfully and destructively. Much of this anger and rage is directed at himself. His self-worth barometer is empty and this can feel incredibly painful. Again, when boys and men feel emotionally wounded and in pain, they often use anger and aggression or withdrawing and hiding as coping strategies. In a strange irony, for a few moments, the angry man who acts on these feelings may feel he has killed the mammoth. Unfortunately, he has killed another part of his own soul. The cycle continues as the search for self-worth goes on.

"I wish my mum had not sided with my father when he abused me."
– Men's Survey 2017

Young mammoth hunters, boys under eight, are seeking experiences that give them the opportunity to conquer, win, overcome or succeed – whether that's in sport, climbing a tree, play fighting, playing an online game or having a power play with Mum. When we deny boys competitive moments in childhood, how are they supposed to feel good about themselves if they are wired to need external evidence of their ability to win? I am deeply concerned about how we have sanitised play in Australia.

I am sure that my sons were considered to be feral and that I was seen to be a lax mother because my boys ran freely in nearby bushland, on the beach and (God forbid!) often went without jumpers or footwear. Maybe it was growing up on a farm that gave me the wisdom to know that such free-range childhood antics are innately what every child yearns for.

There were times as a mother I had to pause and consider some of the thoughts I had around protecting my sons – like when they wanted to dive into puddles and streams in the middle of winter. The first voice in my head told me they would get a cold and get sick if I allowed such ridiculous antics. However, my second voice said, "let them experience this", and they did – many, many times in their childhood. I still chuckle at how their tiny penises almost disappeared into their tummies because of the freezing water. When they jumped into the family vehicle afterwards, I saw little warriors who had conquered the world and although they were shivering and cold – their faces shone with pure delight. They were also wrapped warmly in the spare towels and blankets I always kept in the back of the car, just in case such an opportunity for experience arose.

> *May I suggest that you always keep spare towels, undies, a football or tennis ball and bat, a container full of little cars or trucks and packets of dried savoury biscuits in your vehicle at all times if you have sons. Many a day I have needed all of these things unexpectedly.*

The same drive exists all through boyhood and manhood. Sometimes when men retire, and stop mammoth hunting through their work, they can feel worthless, useless and struggle with their lives. All humans need a sense of meaning and purpose and men especially need to find that in the transitional periods of life.

Retirement needs to be seen by men as a new form of mammoth hunting. Men's sheds and sporting clubs that value the presence of older men in voluntary capacities help men continue to hunt mammoths, create projects, give women their space and have a laugh or two. As time marches on, the main threat men need to kill is the threat of poor health, boredom, apathy and worthlessness.

2. The deer hunter role

If the primary role of protecting women and children was taken care of and there was no imminent threat, then the secondary role of men in traditional communities was to hunt meat for food, hence the metaphor of the deer hunter. This is the incredible, instinctual drive men have in order to provide for their families – a drive sometimes misunderstood in our modern world because, let's face it, women also hunt deer now. Indeed, some women are considered 'better' deer hunters than their male partners because they bring home a bigger pay packet. On some deep level this can cause men confusion and a sense of feeling emasculated. This is a good example of how the male map of the world and female map of the world can differ and, without good communication, reassurance and combining abilities for the familly's betterment, some men struggle. A man's map of the world around being a deer hunter is largely influenced by his father's journey and, unconsciously, many men simply play out their dad's map without questioning whether it is appropriate for them in a totally different relationship, at a totally different time. Society, too, has laid down these stereotypes. One positive aspect of these changing times is the increasing number of at-home dads we are seeing. These are men who share the deer-hunting duties in their family. We are starting to see relationships as being more about teams and individuals working in specific roles. Does it really matter who is the deer hunter?

> "It's really, REALLY hard not to have a favourite child when the baby is sitting in his bouncer smiling winsomely, while his older brother (DB 4) is shoving whole Nutri-Grains up his nose, then pulling them out and eating them. (Fingers crossed that that's the grossest thing that happens here this week!)" — Bemused Mum

Traditionally, when men brought home the kill or the deer, they laid it at the feet of the women who were the organisers of the tribe. (Today, women sometimes get called control freaks instead of organisers.) The women then prepared the meat with the vegetables and berries they had gathered for the main meal (while taking care of the children and the elderly, and collecting the water and firewood). Men then often sat in front of the fire because their primary jobs of defending and providing had been taken care of, so there was nothing else to do but rest and chill out. To many men, at the end of the work day, that fire is now called a TV. No, that does not mean a man is lazy, disinterested or a slob, he is simply a man who has got the main jobs covered – there is no threat to anyone's safety and the deer has been delivered – the day's work looks done and it's fire time. Understanding where this need to chill, rest or regroup comes from can save a lot of bitching and whingeing in a committed relationship. However, in our modern world, especially when most women are also playing the role of deer hunters, this yearning to chill out in front of the TV (or screen of choice) needs to be reviewed. For many women, their time to chill out usually occurs after all the work has been done. This conflict of needs simply requires honest communication with understanding about our innate and individual differences so that harmony can prevail. One couple told me that since coming to my boys' seminar, every now and then they will remind each other lightheartedly when they are being a cave man or cave woman.

> "Driving with my mum and boys (DBs 3 and 4) we were talking about my cousin getting married and my DB (4) says, 'I'm never getting married'. I asked, 'What if you meet a really nice girl you want to be with forever?'. 'Nah,' was his reply and after a short pause, 'but I'll still make children'. Mum and I lost it with laughter!"
> — In-love Mum

So how does this second drive (to act in the deer hunter role) play out in our little boys' lives? Being a deer hunter can mean more than just bringing home food. A deer hunter is also someone who can solve family problems, provide solutions and fix things, especially things that require physical strength. So often in early childhood little girls have a superior ability to organise, structure, negotiate rules and to be the problem-solvers. Generally, they think better and communicate more effectively so, often, little boys are sidelined as being ineffective. Sometimes they learn to be quiet and to avoid contributing. Little boys love helping their mums because it feeds this second biological drive. We need to create meaningful tasks where they can feel really useful and that they are contributing as deer hunters. When we become overly confident as mums (or we're in a hurry!), we often do things for our sons that they can do for themselves. Often they don't complete many of our cleaning tasks to the standard we'd like, and their idea of tidy is not the same as ours. Please be mindful that for the developing psyche of our boys it is really important to keep them contributing. This is also really important during adolescence.

> "I wish my mum had not done so much for my brother and I when we lived at home. When I eventually left home, I really didn't have any idea how to cook, clean or do my own washing, etc. Being a young bloke, it's easier to let Mum do everything for you." – Men's Survey 2017

As I mentioned earlier, boys and men love projects because they are an outward expression of their ability to be really good deer hunters, and a display of how they can make a positive difference for the people they love. Given that I spent much of my childhood at my father's side, I am really capable at fixing things and undertaking jobs that might usually be considered work for men. Sometimes, I have consciously stepped back and let the boys and men in my life do these things even though I could do them. For me, this has been about respecting the need for our boys and men to do things that fill that self-worth barometer and to give them a sense of value in the relationships that matter and in our home. So, please, mums don't be too capable and confident. Let your son help contribute to how the family operates. Chores do matter and they need to be not negotiable and preferably not paid for. This helps our boys when they become partners and/or fathers to know that contributing to the family team is important and it's the right thing to do.

3. The man mentor and teacher

The third biological, instinctual driver of men is to help shape boys into being good men and capable warriors who will take over the key roles of male leadership within the tribe. In traditional cultures, when the boys were removed from the women and taken on their boy-to-manhood journey, they were taught the key life skills required to keep the tribe safe, fed and self-sufficient. While practising these life skills during hunting, fishing, swimming, tree climbing, stargazing and rock climbing, much fun was had by all, even though many of the pursuits were risky.

Boys need men in their lives to be able to process how to be a man. In his book, *Saving Our Sons*, Michael Gurian stresses the importance of the presence of an active, loving father in a boy's life, even after a divorce. Fatherless boys tend to struggle in life. These men do not need to be their biological dads. However, they do need to be good men, not abusive or toxic men, and men who have grown up to be mature, not adolescents in growing men's bodies.

Traditionally, in indigenous communities around the world the boys spent much of their boyhood around the women until aged around eight to 10. This is an interesting time in boys' development as there are serious surges of testosterone as puberty begins – it is almost Mother Nature's way of saying that it's time for the boys to be with the men.

There is no question that a positive relationship with a father improves every little boy's outcomes in life. The research is very supportive, however, of the notion that fathers need not be biological. What is required is the presence of a positive father figure, so if good men step forward when there is not a positive male figure available, little boys can still grow to be good men. I often hear people say that the 'crisis' for boys in the Western world has a lot to do with how few men work in early childhood or primary school anymore. That is only partly true. Some men who are still working in our primary and secondary school systems are pretty 'old school' and they still shame and emotionally wound our boys. I have also found that female teachers who really understand boys can positively transform a boy's experience at school and indeed at life, as much as a male teacher can. Boys are just incredibly sensitive to being valued, accepted, respected and understood in our homes and our schools. That needs to be a priority, not simply putting men in our primary schools.

> "I am so grateful to my mum for embracing and accepting my sexuality, and including my long-term partner in the immediate family."
> — Men's Survey 2017

Let's be honest — conflict often happens between men and women over how to raise children. Women regularly tell me that their children's dad is 'too tough', 'lacks empathy' and 'sounds grumpy'. Men tell me their children's mother 'worries too much', 'fusses too much' and 'does too much'. This is a classic example of the different styles of nurturing that tend to come naturally to men and women. Women's higher levels of oestrogen and oxytocin may mean they are soft-wired more to gentle mothering and protecting. Males have higher levels of testosterone and some studies suggest more receptors for vasopressin, which I mentioned previously, and which has been associated with territoriality, hierarchy, competition and persistence, as well as the capacity to bond. This may play out as men being more soft-wired to build capacity and resilience in children by having them meet challenges.

There is a middle ground and, to be perfectly honest, when that works well, the children — with the loving nurturing of the mother and the courage-building nurturing of the father — will grow up to be competent, caring, capable and they will thrive as independent adults. (Remember, sometimes this balance is in reverse in families where Mum is the tough-arse and Dad is the softy — but it still tends to work when these masculine/feminine traits are in balance, regardless of who is displaying them.)

Women's biological drivers

It is helpful for us to see what the key biological drivers for females are because this can help us figure out why sometimes we struggle to understand our son's behaviour. It is simply that we see it through a different lens, which is a bit like they speak French and we speak English.

Before we explore the key drivers, it might be helpful to see what instinctually led our cave-women counterparts. Once again, I acknowledge that not all men or all women will fit within these sweeping generalisations. I'm merely using these as a way to build understanding. Role reversals can and do happen.

1. Women as breeders and nurturers

All humans are biologically driven to reproduce to ensure the survival of the species. Indeed, this is the number one biological driver – keep the species alive – and it is deceptively powerful. To ensure this happens, one of the genders needs to be capable of conceiving and carrying into the world the next generation.

Enter stage left – the hormone oxytocin! This hormone is associated with not only maternal nurturance, but also verbal emotive connection and empathetic bonding. Men have very little oxytocin. This hormone helps explain much of the need for women to want to 'have a talk' and why they often need a lot more loving and cuddling before they are ready for sexual intimacy. Remember, hormones are powerful things and need to be understood and respected if both men and women are to enjoy each other's company and bodies. The massively swinging hormones when a woman is premenstrual are not intentional or planned – it happens without her permission, her knowing or her agreement! Why would we want to get bitchy? Why would we want to become impatient or moody, needing a full block of fruit and nut chocolate to save our sanity? And why would we want to have to put up with that every month for almost 40 years? We have no say – it's Mother Nature's way of ensuring that we're available to breed to sustain the species.

Not all women are wired to be wonderful, nurturing mothers, just the same as not all men are wired to be warriors and mammoth hunters. Thankfully, the vast majority of women are driven to care and nurture for babies and children. In traditional communities there was very little monogamy, and men and women came together in couplings in order to produce offspring so the species would continue to grow. There were very few committed relationships, so men had it a bit easier as there was no Valentine's Day or anniversaries to remember. The circle of women would collectively take care of all the babies and children in a supportive and loving environment. There was always a pair of arms, a breast or a lap for every child. These communities were high touch and often co-slept and so the basic needs of all the children were met.

> "I am so grateful for my mum for the massive support when I found out I had diabetes at the age of nine. I was extremely close to passing away and she wouldn't take no from the doctors and rushed me to hospital. I grew up and learnt to take ownership and control of my life from a young age." – Men's Survey 2017

Sadly, in today's modern world this loving, supportive circle of sisterhood has diminished drastically and many women appear to be doing it alone or in competition with each other, instead of being caring and supportive. The breakdown of the sisterhood has created enormous stress, exhaustion and guilt among many mums. It is important to encourage all mothers to have close contact with some supportive sisterhood. Apparently the healthiest men are married, and the healthiest women have significant, loving female friendships. No surprise there, eh?

Mother Nature is a very powerful thing. When a woman wants to become pregnant, her hormones make her even more beautiful and desirable than ever. Once the baby arrives, many men can struggle with a sense of being abandoned by their partner and, without good communication, they can flounder as to how to best love and support their family.

In a way having a baby is like the game of the relationship has changed, the goalposts have moved and there are no new guidelines in place. With a man being terrified of failing and yet still needing the external mammoth-hunting conquests to feel he is worthwhile, he often turns to his work to find success and self-worth, which can be challenging if work/life balance gets wonky. The enormous emotions that occur around birth can make men feel very vulnerable and out of control, and that can be frightening. Again their ability to communicate these big emotions can be a challenge for many men. In recent times, more light is being shed on the issue of postnatal depression among men, so we know that some of them struggle with this enormous change in their life.

"I actually wish she didn't ALWAYS put us boys first and herself second (or fifth as it would be) because sometimes it has been at the cost of her own wellbeing." – Men's Survey 2017

2. Women as organisers and berry pickers

The second biological drive that can create tension for boys and men is women's instinctual drive to be the organisers. If we step back into our tribal roots for a moment, women were responsible for taking care of the elderly, the sick, the pregnant and all the children while the men were away hunting deer. Women also had to search for the food to go with the deer like yams, or seeds and grains that could be turned into unleavened bread. They also searched for berries and fruits, and small things like protein-rich insects or lizards to add to the menu. While the women and children were searching, the women needed to ensure the children were safe – that they didn't eat poisonous berries or pick up a poisonous snake. They had to be hyper-alert during these times. They were also responsible for ensuring that the bloodlines of the tribe were kept clean and clear, so they kept an eye on which young boys and girls might be a good match for each other. Further, they were responsible for observing the changes in Mother Nature because they needed to prepare the tribe to move to a better location when things became unsustainable. Women were the ones who would weave the baskets or prepare animal skins to keep everyone warm. They were also responsible for creating medicines, and for treating wounds and illness; and of course they were the midwives, both of the living and the soon-to-be dead. Women had to multitask and be extremely good organisers or the community would simply disintegrate.

This is why, generally, today's woman can easily find the butter in the fridge, know where her son last had his school jumper on, balance the budget, meet her work deadlines, know whose birthday is coming up and where the library books are and when they're due. This ability means that women's thinking can appear to be very scattered as they are trying to see and do and attend to everything that they think is important to keep the family healthy and safe. Frequently, a woman wants to have the tidiest house, the neatest yard, the cleanest car and the best-behaved children because she is worried what others think about her – but maybe also because she is worried about what will happen if order is not maintained. This ability to multitask can sometimes be a burden for women because they can overthink, and over-worry. I have had mums tell me that they have been awake at two o'clock in the morning worrying that the children didn't eat broccoli the day before or that they missed having a bath.

In traditional societies, every woman wanted to get the very best berries for her family. Women are still instinctually wired this way today. Women are very good at guessing and being intuitive and picking up on hints, however men could save a lot of bother by asking specifically what it is she wants. My dearly beloved and I have had a few clashes about what cream he buys when I ask him to buy cream. There are many different creams and some simply don't work in some of the recipes that I love to cook. It is now a running joke between us when I ask him to buy cream. Sometimes, clarifying our needs and wants can improve our man and woman communication and our relationships. If our little boys see us communicating in this way with their fathers and father figures, we are setting them up to communicate in a similar, respectful way when they become adults.

Maybe it is due to these primal survival drives that, generally, women still have better memory storage capacity than men, mainly because of their need to be the prime organisers in the cave communities. They need to remember where the best berries are, where the bees are, where the ants' nests are, which trees will have fruit at what time of the year, and to remember who has 'mated' with who up to five generations ago to avoid inbreeding. This may be why women sometimes bring up events in relationships – painful events – for what seems like forever. Maybe?

This tendency to excel as either a multi-focus or a single-focus person is a key trait to remember as a mother of sons.

> "I wish my mum had more down time. She worked full-time (in retail) for a number of years and only retired at 65. Holidays were few and far between." – Men's Survey 2017

3. Women and the need to talk

Before we explore this topic, let's remember our biological beginnings with men as mammoth hunters and women as carers and gatherers. If you were hunting a mammoth or a deer, being silent or quiet would be an enormous asset, as would the ability to use non-verbal communication and silent signalling. Now consider the gathering activities, where women needed to continually keep track of the children, be mindful of hidden dangers and hazards in nature, and keep an eye on the weather. Verbal communication would be an important part of being an effective gatherer and carer. Many activities that women did in women's circles – like grinding grain, weaving baskets, making jewellery, tanning hides and preparing carcasses – required women to talk. In traditional communities, boys were surrounded by conversation, endless singing and storytelling, which gave them a fabulous opportunity to develop verbal language.

It is interesting that, due to the fact that I spent so much time surrounded by male company as a child, I often feel a sense of overwhelm when surrounded by women who do use a lot more verbal language than most men. Sometimes, I can struggle to keep up in a gathering of women because it is exhausting trying to keep track of the many conversations happening at the same time, and often they don't even all seem to relate to each other! I have been known to glaze over and sit quietly, hoping there will be a space soon where I can grasp what the heck is the main point of the conversation. I also struggle with long conversations on the telephone.

These biological drivers will have more relevance as I explore ways to improve communication between mums and sons – also it will help with understanding why, when you send your son into his bedroom to get his socks, he often doesn't return. Yes, it's incredibly frustrating, however I will decode why this happens.

Trust me, I have been there. One of my DBs (9) came to me one morning asking where his socks would be. I took a deep breath and replied, "Babe, we have had the same sock drawer since you were born. I would possibly look there first!"

Mums of sons have a huge job teaching their little warrior mammoth hunters that they cannot be a warrior without a heart – without developing the capacity to care for and respect themselves and others. We need them to come to a place of understanding so that the gender differences that cause misunderstanding can be bridged, and nurturing and strong relationships can be built with understanding.

TOP TIPS

- ✓ Ancient biological drivers can still influence behaviour today.
- ✓ Gender differentiation was essential for survival in cave man and cave woman days.
- ✓ Men and women today can still respond according to ancient biological drivers.
- ✓ Understanding these tendencies can improve relationships between genders.
- ✓ Traditional ideas about gender tend to be more fluid than fixed today.

CHAPTER THREE

Boys are not **TOUGH**, especially **LITTLE** ones

One of the most significant stereotypes that needs to be challenged is that little boys are in some way stronger and tougher than little girls. We need to also challenge the stereotype that says that little boys need to start practising how to be tough and how to freeze their emotions early in life in order to become a 'real' man.

Just last year, I was in an early childhood centre where I witnessed an educator shaming a little boy who was crying after he had hurt himself. In frustration, she finally said to him: "Go and stand in the corner until you stop sniffling".

Needless to say, it is lucky I am an emotionally mature woman because my first instinct was to shout at her. Can you imagine the educator speaking like that to a little girl?

I have had many grandmothers come up to me after my seminars telling me how their daughter-in-laws speak much more harshly to their sons than they do to their daughters, seemingly unaware that they do it.

Research has shown that parents treat their boys and girls differently right from infancy. For example, infant boys are touched more frequently and handled more roughly before the age of three months. Also physical punishment is applied more significantly for boys than girls in many Western countries. Also people have been found to label children's emotions differently based on the child's gender (i.e. seeing anger in an expression when they think the baby is a boy and fear when they think the baby is a girl).

One primary school teacher shared with me a story about a Year One teacher, who obviously believed that boys were stronger than girls. Apparently on very hot days she was known to tell the boys to stand like tin soldiers in the sun while the girls went inside to the cool, air-conditioned classroom. I think possibly this teacher may also have had a psychological issue around boys and men that needed some therapy to resolve!

So, the first take-home message from my book is that we need to take much better care of our little boys – emotionally, psychologically, physically and socially. We need to stop shouting at them, hitting them, shaming them, speaking harshly to them and simply being mean.

The stereotypical belief that the only way to get boys to do the right thing is by hurting them or being hard on them needs to be challenged every day because it is so deeply embedded into the psychology of our society. The scars this creates in early childhood fester deep inside like a cancer and are often the source of future irrational rage and aggression. This does not mean we do not discipline our boys or make them accountable for their choices. It means we need to consciously choose the same warm discipline that we tend to use around girls. Simple.

> "When my adorable son was about four, he had a stutter. It was Christmas time and we were all singing carols. Matt wanted to sing 'Away in A Manger'. He sang 'away in a manger, no crypt for his bed, the li li li little lord Jesus lay down his sweet head'. I can't hear that carol now 30 years later without laughing. When he was three, he rushed into our bedroom early in the morning to tell us that the kitchen light wasn't working ... 'you know (he said), like a kookaburra not laughing'." — Blessed Mama

So how come boys are not tough?

Male vulnerability in terms of health and wellbeing has been well-researched. This research continues to bring forward evidence that little girls develop faster and more thoroughly than little boys from conception. Even before I became a mother of my four awesome sons, I spent a childhood with my little brother who was much gentler and often less brave than me. Maybe this helped me to realise that boys are not inherently tough, even though they have a larger amount of muscle than girls. Physical strength is one thing but mental and emotional strength that can impact cognitive abilities and linguistic capacities is something else.

The sensitive nature of boys is something that I had intuitively worked out well before research confirmed it. Twenty-five years ago, Steve Biddulph wrote his first book about boys called *Raising Boys* and, by then, my eldest son was on the journey to manhood, but I still found Biddulph's work to be the best parenting book I'd read (actually, I have to admit, it was also the only one at that stage). Biddulph explores the same notion that there is a fragility, especially in little boys under five. Statistically, boys die in utero at a higher rate than girls; they die at birth at a higher rate than girls and they die in the first 12 months of life at a higher rate than girls. This situation continues through life, however, there are lots of other reasons why this discrepancy happens so let's start at the very beginning of life.

Technically, every embryo starts off female and sometime in the first 12 weeks of life, the massive flooding of hormones stimulates the embryo to either stay female or become male. Fascinating information to start with. In Steve Biddulph's latest, updated edition of his book, *Raising Boys in the 21st Century*, he explores a 2017 review of empirical research from highly regarded neuropsychologist Alan Schore, which suggests that the marinade of testosterone in utero seems to slow down the growth and development of the male baby's brain.

On top of the influence of hormones and social experience, Schore presents evidence that something else is happening in our baby boys' development. His groundbreaking work has shown that the delay in brain maturation makes boys more vulnerable in the long run to social stress (attachment trauma) and physical stress via endocrine disruptors or toxins in the environment. He goes on to say this "negatively impacts" their right brain development. Basically, this impacts our boys' social and emotional functioning, and their capacity to cope with stress.

> **"The testosterone effects in the womb and the first year of life slow their brain development (especially in the right hemisphere) so much that they are far more vulnerable than girls to anything that goes wrong."**
>
> – Steve Biddulph, *Raising Boys in the 21st Century* (2018).

The first thousand days from conception to the age of two are an incredibly important window and we need to nurture all babies and care for them as lovingly and calmly as possible. For our boys, though, it seems they are even more fragile, especially when it comes to attachment and bondedness – which influence our primary driver in life, human connectedness.

Belonging is another way of explaining attachment, which is the relationship between a key adult and a child, and then their wider community. Babies, toddlers and children need to have 'big people' they can trust to nurture and care for them. These people help guide and teach them all that they will need to know in life so they can become independent, capable adults who will hopefully in many cases find mates, breed and ensure the survival of the species.

> "I wish my mum had not been as critical and harsh as she was when we did not meet her expectations." – Men's Survey 2017

Primary attachments are the big people of central importance to a child's life – typically parents or close family members or caregivers. It is helpful for parents of babies and toddlers to have a circle of caring adults who can share in the raising of children. This allows for support, guidance and respite, which helps every parent, especially tired mummies, cope with this intensive time of life. For children who are in long-day child care, the early years' educators who form a loving, caring connection to them are technically a source of primary attachment, often called secondary attachment figures. If you take a look on YouTube at videos from the Center on the Developing Child at Harvard University, they explain the concept of 'serve and return' interaction between a child and their significant adults, where children reach out for interaction and, when adults respond, it assists essential brain wiring to occur. The Center also has an excellent video called 'The Science of Neglect' which shows how detrimental it can be for young children when this interaction doesn't take place.

Attachment is the 'super glue' that holds a child in close proximity to a parent/caregiver. A child is meant to pursue **proximity**, which means being close to their big person so that they feel safe and are safe. Attachment is as important to healthy child development as eating or sleeping. Indeed, in much of the most recent research, strong attachment and bondedness can be shown to be the most significant influence on emotional wellbeing, mental health and physical health for life and so if our little boys have a tendency to be more prone to the damaging effects of poor attachment, then this needs to be the number one focus of all mums of new baby boys. Maybe this needs to be spoken of in the prenatal classes given that we know the long-term negative consequences of this in our sons' lives.

This new review of interdisciplinary research by Schore supports the major premise that Biddulph made 25 years ago, where he wrote that he believed our young boys were more prone to separation distress and anxiety, and that they could become emotionally shut down as a result of feeling abandoned. This is also supported by research that shows that male adolescent violence is now strongly linked to neglect in early childhood, particularly a lack of physical and emotional nurturing (and, indeed, a lack of play). These are things that we can fix with awareness, knowledge and, most importantly, action.

> **"When an infant receives too little direct loving contact this can cause the area of his brain that regulates emotion, self image and beliefs about relationships to become atrophied with serious, long-lasting — often permanent — consequences for behaviour."**
>
> — Robin Grille, *Parenting for a Peaceful World* (2013).

Early mothering really matters

Maternal attachment has traditionally been the dominant form of attachment in the first few years of life for all children. Indeed, in traditional indigenous communities all boys spent around the first eight years of their lives solely in the company of the women, including the grandmothers and the aunties. In a way this is where they learnt 'women's business'. There was always a warm, open pair of arms and a soft breast anytime a little boy may have felt vulnerable. In no way was he expected to be tough or a brave little boy. He was seen just as the little girls were – a unique miracle who deserved to be reassured, cherished and loved deeply. There are some who argue that this window of maternal nurturing and comfort helped to build the neural pathways of being caring and loving later in life. Without this essential 'maternal' love, a person can grow up to be hardened and less capable of giving or receiving love. Certainly, research has linked postnatal attachment trauma to being predisposed to a range of personality and psychiatric disorders.

Every baby ever born is conceived and grown in the womb of a woman. There have been times in counselling sessions when people have recalled emotional memories from before birth or at birth. Indeed, I have witnessed people expressing deep sadness that they ever had to leave the womb – and in some way every little boy will have an unconscious memory of feeling safe inside his mother's body. This incredibly deep bond of connection is the beginning of a boy's relationship with his mother, and possibly the core of his sense of being. From the time that a boy leaves his mother's womb, he is on a gradual journey of distancing himself from the safest place imaginable. Many men have expressed to me that their mum was the safest person in their world and that, no matter what age they were, they could always turn to her and she would be there. This sacred, primal and unconscious connection is always present. There have even been stories from the battlefield that when some men face death, they call out for their mother.

> "My mum gave me unconditional love ... total and utter unconditional love. She is a true safe harbour that never shifts and I feel warm and cosy anytime I visit her home (which so feels like my home still)."
> – Men's Survey 2017

Sally Goddard Blythe is the director of The Institute for Neuro-Physiological Psychology in the UK and her main area of work is with children experiencing specific learning disabilities (dyslexia, developmental coordination disorder, attention deficit disorder, under-achievement, etc.). She believes that our modern world is making it more and more difficult for babies and toddlers to spend significant time with their parents, where she believes the healthiest 'mothering' can occur. On reading Goddard Blythe's book, *What Babies and Children Really Need*, it turns out that what they really need – time – is what many modern mothers cannot provide, simply because we live in a society that does not allow for it. I tend to agree with her. There is enormous pressure on today's mums to be everything – to look slim and ageless, to be fit enough to run marathons, to have a spotless house, to be a master chef in the kitchen, a goddess in the bedroom, run your own business, as well as being a good-enough mum. The former Governor General of Australia, Quentin Bryce – herself a mother of five children – said that, indeed, we can "have it all, but not all at the same time".

The first five years of life are incredibly important in terms of growth and development on all levels. The good news is that it is now socially acceptable for dads to be far more involved, and more and more of them are sharing the work/parenting load, some becoming at-home dads who support their partners as they continue their careers. In my book, *9 Things*, the first 'thing' that I explore is connected mothering and I argue that it is the *art of mothering* that is vitally important, rather than who does the mothering. The more mother figures the better. Research is quite clear that strong attachment can be formed with non-biological caregivers – it simply needs to be consistent, warm and loving.

> **"With emotionally responsive parenting vital connections will form in his brain enabling him to cope well with stress in later life, form fulfilling relationships, manage anger well, be kind and compassionate, have the will and motivation to follow his ambitions and his dreams, experience the deepest calm, love intimately and be in peace."**
>
> – Margot Sunderland, *The Science of Parenting* (2007).

Again, Schore points to research that indicates that infant boys are even more reliant than girls on their mother's input to help them regulate their emotional responses to stress. The ability to linger when feeding a baby, whether by bottle or breast, to gaze lovingly into a baby's face, to smother a baby's brow with endless gentle kisses and to make soothing low sounds of reassurance while a baby is being changed, dressed or settled is being undermined by the pressures and distractions of our chaotic world. There is research that shows that boy and girl babies in the first six weeks of life tend to do something very different when you lift them up out of a cot. Girl babies are much more likely to focus on a face, whereas boy babies are much more likely to focus on something beyond the face, like a mobile or a picture on the wall. Given what we know about the importance of 'mirroring' and mirror neurons, this different tendency – if left just to nature – might see a delay in the capacity for a boy baby to feel connected to the key caregivers, especially his mother, and to even learn to smile. Now we know this, we can ensure that we capture boys' little faces directly when we feed them or change them. Given the new phenomenon of 'brexting' or texting while breastfeeding or bottle feeding, we have some work to do to inform mammas of newborns how critical this first 12 months of life is to ensure boys in particular are attached deeply. We simply cannot leave this to chance. This is a really important first step to avoiding the beginnings of the 'mother wound', which I will explore in Chapter 12.

Many mums of young babies and toddlers tell me they feel they are drowning under exhaustion and stress. The first 12 months of a baby's life is when parents have the most disturbed sleep, and sleep deprivation is one of the biggest stressors of being a parent. This was why the tribal approach to raising children was pure magic. There was always another woman who could give you respite – which in modern terms could mean time for a little nap, to have a shower and wash your hair or drink that cup of tea while it is still hot.

Tired and exhausted mums and dads are often unable to meet the needs of their babies and toddlers with calmness and unconditional love. It is very difficult to be joyful and patient when you are completely sleep-deprived and exhausted. Healthy attachment needs human connectedness that is saturated with warm, loving interaction, respectful and child-centred care, and an unhurried, calm environment as much as possible. This is impossible 100% of the time and parents, particularly mothers, need to stop beating themselves up if they have days when things don't work out well.

Given how important this window of building strong attachment to our sensitive boys is, I need to clarify something here to avoid confusion later. Smothering our baby boys with tender kisses, attention and loving touch is incredibly important, especially in the first 12 months of life. This must not be confused with smothering them later in life by being over-invested in everything they do, and being too dominating. As our little boys become active – and toddlerhood is the beginning of that – they will naturally distance themselves a little from our loving tenderness. We need to ensure that we are still able to meet those needs for independence and nurturing in our little boys. I have devoted a whole chapter to exploring how boys feel loved to ensure there are plenty of suggestions on how to fill their 'love cup'.

> **"The parts of the brain concerned with regulation of emotion and deeply held attitudes to human relations are particularly dependent on human contact in order to develop. A mother's joyful interactions with her baby actually provide an essential building block to these areas of the brain."**
>
> – Robin Grille, *Parenting for a Peaceful World* (2013).

Emotional vulnerability

When boys are struggling with emotional vulnerability, they will do one of two things. They will come out fighting – acting out their emotions through angry outbursts or with irrational behaviours towards other children and their parents, or they will simply withdraw and seek isolation. One of the key things to always remember with boys is that:

> *Any time there is a significant change in a boy's behaviour he is usually struggling with something in his world that is overloading his nervous system and troubling his mind.*

While he is struggling, he may not be sure what it is that's causing the sense of overwhelm and distress. I have worked with boys who became very aggressive suddenly and the apparent trigger was a disaster that happened in another part of the world, which they saw on TV. I repeat my previous plea to all parents of boys and especially to mums of boys – avoid seeing your son as 'bad' or 'naughty'. Know that, in some way, he is struggling to cope with our world and he needs our help. This reframing around little boys' sometimes-irrational behaviour is imperative if we are to stop little boys staying confused around strong emotions.

I once worked with a mother of a 5-year-old son who had transitioned into preschool really well. Suddenly, he became physically aggressive towards other children, shouting and pushing, and he had even held a young boy in a headlock. He had also thrown a truck at another boy in the sandpit.

This behaviour was most out of character and the mum was desperate to find out what was behind it. I questioned her as to what things may have changed in her son's world that could have caused him distress and may have overloaded his nervous system. The first thing she could think of was that her mother (his granny) had been really sick in hospital. Apparently his granny was now at home, however, her grandson did not know that and this was the first thing on his plate of worries that contributed to his behaviour. I still felt there could be something bigger than that for such a sudden, dramatic change in behaviour from this little boy. Finally, the mum said, "I know what it is". The boy's much-adored preschool teacher had just left on maternity leave. He was struggling with grief and sadness, on top of the worry about his grandmother. Being unable to express this verbally, he expressed it through his behaviour. The new teacher in the preschool was made aware of the situation and made a concerted effort to build a bridge of connection with the little boy over the next few days. That little boy's behaviour returned to normal.

> "We were at the park having a great time, when my DB (9) comes running up to me and yells, 'Mum I think I broke my bum!!'" — Amused Mum

I have often found that when boys' behaviour is particularly aggressive and irrational, it is often linked to the more vulnerable emotions like fear, sadness and feeling dumb or inadequate. The same behaviour can keep happening in manhood and that is why we need to spend considerable time and energy in the first five years of a boy's life to help him navigate the confusing world of emotions, feelings and moods.

Boys need to feel that they can be loved, especially when they make impulsive poor choices as their biology often encourages them to do. In the chapter on ***"Mummy, do you love me?"*** I will explore the ways that boys prefer mums to show their love for them – and I will explore lots of ways of building loving connections with them, especially love bridges. We need to ensure that boys feel very secure in their world because this reduces the inner turmoil that can come from them being not as emotionally competent as our girls at dealing with conflict and high emotions.

Neil Farmer in his book, *Getting it Right for Boys*, writes that young boys tend to:

1. lack language skills
2. be less emotionally developed
3. be physically 'unjoined up' and often express emotions through action.

Decoding boy behaviour after school

Time and time again I have witnessed little boys who are unable to express how they felt so they used physical action, often inappropriately and without even realising what they had done. Take, for example, the little boy who comes out of his classroom and, on seeing his mother for the first time in hours, after a really stressful day, runs at her really fast and almost takes her legs out from under her. Some can see this through the lens of a silly or naughty boy. Much more likely is that this little boy wants to express just how much he missed his mum and how glad he is to see her. However, in the emotional volatility of the moment, he simply expresses it physically, reconnecting strongly and powerfully.

The same experience often happens when little boys finally reach the family car after school. Often there is a massive meltdown and they can become physically aggressive or verbally aggressive or collapse in tears, and it can happen quite suddenly. This can be really confusing for parents. For little boys, being away from Mum is still a challenge and being away from her in a sometimes confusing and busy school environment is a bit like going to war. All day he has had to be on guard, trying to be a good little boy and not get into trouble. Children try really hard to remember the rules and to do their best to navigate the confusing landscape of the social dynamics in the playground. It is exhausting and draining and, by the end of the day, most little boys are overloaded with the stress hormone cortisol. This means there is no goodness left in his little emotional bucket.

Your son will need some help to fill that emotional bucket with more positive feelings and emotions and the best way to do that is by helping him create positive neurotransmitters – namely serotonin, dopamine and some endorphins. The quickest way to move the cortisol is through food and we know that boys tend to get hungrier much quicker than girls so this is the first need to address after a big day at school. Make sure that the food you give him is not full of sugar – nothing beats a good quality sandwich or wrap. If you don't have food on hand when the meltdown occurs, there are other things you can try. I encourage all mums to be prepared by having some 'props' always available in your car. If you can see his face starting to darken, try putting on a brightly coloured wig, or a pair of flashing glasses or maybe some fangs! Anything that can suddenly trigger novelty will immediately lighten up your boy's mood. If you are unable to fart easily on demand, I suggest you invest in a whoopee cushion because there is nothing like a well-timed fart to make a boy smile. If you are lucky to attend a school that allows children to have a play after school, this will also fill your boy's goodness cup before you get to the car.

One thing to avoid in the car if you have boys:

Please avoid interrogating them about how their day went.
How was your day?
Did you eat your lunch?
Who did you play with?
What did you learn?
How was your teacher today?

Most boys have no idea about any of these things – they certainly can't remember them on command as soon as they leave school. This is one of the hardest things for mothers of sons to do. We women love an instant update of everything that happened since we last had you in our sight. A boy is just recovering from a highly stressful experience on the war front. He needs some transition time. By all means hug him, stroke him gently or tickle him, but hold back the questions. Simply tell him you missed him.

Bath time and bedtime are great times to chat about his day. Somehow, his memory kicks back in as he relaxes in his home and he is close to his key caregivers. This is a habit I encourage you to form with your little boy – having a quiet chat, still not an interrogation, now that he is in a calmer place. Bath chats, pillow chats in the dark or chats while playing a game – these are all situations where he feels less threatened and more open to connection. This ritual will help you later when you need to have a chat with your boy about poor choices, failure and, yes, that broken window or the unflushed poo you found in the toilet!

Speaking of poo, the vast majority of our boys do not defecate at school! The reason is quite logical. As I have said, the school environment is like a war zone and highly stressful. Boys and most men need to feel really calm to be able to download their poo. This is one of the significant differences between genders. Most women tend to go to the toilet when they feel it is the right time, do the job and come out. Men tend to take ages and, since the arrival of the smartphone, some men take an obscenely long time in the toilet. To recognise that stress definitely impacts performance in this department, we can see why boys can take longer than girls in toilet training. Performance anxiety is a real thing and it seems it starts early. No boy ever wants to poo in his undies or pants as that is considered a form of failure.

Back to the school environment, given that boys do not poo at school, try to avoid lingering when you collect your son just in case he needs to go. I have heard of little boys who have suddenly started kicking their mother when she stopped to have a chat to someone after school. Again, they find it difficult to find the words to inform you that they have a poo that is due, so their actions are an attempt to communicate this. Another suggestion before you stop to talk with someone is to quietly lean over and see if it's OK for you to have a chat. This is a form of code, checking out whether it is really urgent, mildly urgent or still brewing. When my lads were young, arriving home after school with four boys and only two toilets was quite stressful for me as a mother.

Another suggestion is try to avoid taking your exhausted son after school into a shopping centre without filling up his cup with lots of positive neurotransmitters. Essentially, you're setting him up to fail in such a highly stimulating environment with things that he'd love to have or touch. Please be mindful of this, even if it's not after school, as large shopping centres have so many risks and stressors for our little boy warriors. Remember, they have shorter attention spans than girls – a bit like a gnat sometimes – so we need to be careful that we are not setting them up to fail in a highly public environment. The same goes for coffee shops that are not boy-friendly until your young lad has mastered his moving body, his confusing emotions and his very poor self-regulation. It is often better for mums and sons to get a takeaway coffee and head to a park or a wide open space. He will gradually get better at developing his ability to manage highly stimulating social environments ... just give him some time.

Anger and emotions

> "My mum has always been my inspiration. My moral compass when learning. And my fall-back, always." – Men's Survey 2017

Partly due to the inner struggle between hormones, brain chemicals, social conditioning and the pressure for boys to appear powerful and successful often at any cost, boys struggle emotionally on many levels.

There is a mistaken perception that boys and men don't feel emotions as much as women – they do. They just process them and often communicate them very differently. It seems that boys need more time to be able to work out what big, ugly feelings are really all about, whereas girls tend to move from experiencing the emotion to interpreting the emotion much quicker. When boys feel emotionally vulnerable they tend to have a default setting that takes them straight through to anger, which is a very acceptable warrior emotion but often not acceptable in everyday settings.

- Sadness becomes anger.
- Fear becomes anger.
- Feeling misunderstood becomes anger.
- Feeling rejected becomes anger.

- Feeling ignored becomes anger.
- Feeling disrespected and invalidated becomes anger.
- Feeling dumb becomes anger.
- Uncertainty becomes anger.
- Forgetfulness becomes anger.
- Frustration becomes anger.
- Disorganisation becomes anger.
- Feeling unloved becomes anger.
- Having no friends becomes anger.
- Grief can come out as anger.
- Fear of failure becomes anger.
- Confusion becomes anger.
- Being unable to communicate his needs becomes anger.

Here's another interesting thing about boys and how they're different from girls. As I wrote earlier, girls generally have better verbal processing skills. Michael Gurian writes about how males and females tend to process emotion differently in the brain. He writes that males tend to move emotions very quickly from their brains into their bodies. They also tend to sense the emotion but then shift it to areas of the brain that will work to solve the problem causing the emotion. Females, on the other hand, tend to quickly shift emotions up into the brain's limbic system and to the 'word centres' of the brain. What this really means is that a woman can get emotionally upset swiftly and easily – and often from an unintended, incorrectly perceived moment in the life of her sons or male partner.

Her default mechanism is to verbally express her unhappy feelings quite quickly – and in her volatility she may express these feelings in ways she may later regret. Most boys and men feel blindsided by these outbursts and may have no idea what's triggered it – they may be working to solve the problem but appear to have shut down emotionally to the woman. I usually suggest to men and boys to avoid taking these outbursts personally. Most adult men learn to avoid defending, or buying in to the volatile emotions, however, our young boys and adolescent boys can find it frightening and scary. They genuinely hate to upset their mum. They hunger for her acceptance and love. Being typically pragmatic boys, they often feel they are responsible for their mother's anger or unhappiness.

Mammas, if you have an irrational, emotional meltdown in front of your son take yourself for a quiet walk outside and calm yourself down. When you are calmer, please return to your son and apologise that your big, ugly feelings ran away from you and it was absolutely not his fault. Even if he has done something that's upset you, remember, boys find it difficult to differentiate between you being angry at what they did and being angry at them.

As you read this book, if there are times you realise that some of the choices you've made in the past have made things difficult for your son, simply tell him – apologise and tell him you're going to try to be a better mum. Seriously, he will forgive you in an instant. Daughters don't forgive so quickly. Indeed, they often save it up and give it back to you possibly many times throughout life! I say that with my tongue firmly in my cheek, but I do think boys tend to forgive more easily than girls.

> *The stronger a boy feels emotionally connected to his adult allies, the safer his emotional world becomes and the better his behaviour will be.*

It is a bit sad that, due to their inner warrior, our boys often make more mistakes, break more things, forget more things and are often the ones who bear the brunt of our discipline much more than most girls.

Boys who do not get the emotional support and coaching to understand big, ugly feelings and how to manage them tend to have the following:

1. increased misbehaviour
2. increased anxiety that can impair development
3. weakened relationships with key caregivers.

It seems that little boys and, later, older boys are more emotionally vulnerable than girls and when they feel threatened by poor attachment or lack of deep emotional bonding, they can become emotionally shut down. Quite often the strong frustration that boys display, which does turn into anger and aggression, is quite simply to do with feeling misunderstood and unheard. Given that little girls' capacity to communicate verbally is so much more advanced, is it any wonder that boys can get really frustrated?

> **"Boys speak their first words later than girls and their speech does not become 99% comprehensible often until they are four years old — a full year later than girls. A preschool girl has a large vocabulary, has better grammar, and forms longer sentences than a boy of the same age."**
>
> – Ruth Hanford Morhard, *Wired to Move: Facts and Strategies for Nurturing Boys in an Early Childhood Setting* (2013).

The Longitudinal Study of Australian Children also shows clearly there is a gender bias in how well our boys transition into the early years. Much of that has to do with the delays in communication, especially verbal competence, vocabulary and capacity to understand verbal instructions. Delays in learning to read are very real for many boys.

> **"Boys are three times more likely to struggle with reading and overall are worse readers throughout their school lives. This has long been a problem, and very recent research shows that it is not going away."**
>
> — Steve Biddulph, *Raising Boys in the 21st Century* (2018).

In fact, research from Perth's Telethon Institute for Child Health Research has demonstrated that boys with high levels of testosterone in their umbilical cord blood were between two and three times more likely to experience language delay.

Struggling with feeling misunderstood and being unable to connect with others, particularly their carers and teachers, needs to be considered when addressing poor behaviour in little boys.

As I've discussed, research suggests that generally boys' brain development lags behind that of girls. Surely, this is why sometimes little boys who spend hours in the sandpit making strange grunting and engine-like sounds are possibly doing exactly what they need to be doing — rather than being forced to sit for long periods of time on a mat practising phonics in isolation. This is the reality of many little boys' lives today.

This may also partially explain why boys' fine motor skills are also more delayed than girls. I now have granddaughters and have been fascinated with how long these little girls — currently under four years of age — can sit quietly and colour, glue and play with stickers, without needing any encouragement or supervision! Quite frankly, I never saw any of my sons do this at that age, despite my encouragement. Can you imagine how it feels for a little boy to watch a little girl colour in neatly within the lines and be able to write her name when it is well beyond him to do either of those things? He will notice that he is unable to do it and it will frustrate him.

I learnt not to ask for paintings when my lads were in kindergarten or preschool because they simply were not interested in painting. Indeed, their efforts were really quite hilarious – a few big, bold strokes and "ta dah", and that was it. This delay in development of fine motor skills is well-accepted and early childhood educators invest a lot of time and energy helping our little boys develop these skills that are generally more difficult for them.

A popular activity used in early childhood settings to enhance fine motor control is the activity of gluing legs onto a caterpillar – aka an egg carton. I encourage any mum who has a son, and who may help out in such a setting, to observe what happens with this activity. Now, just say this little boy glues three legs on that caterpillar and then runs outside to play. Should the little boy's mum notice that the little girl sitting nearby has completed the activity – mastering 34 legs with glitter and evenly spaced to boot – there could be a tendency for that little boy's mother to feel a bit disappointed. I need to give you a possible explanation for that little boy's behaviour. Firstly, boys and men tend to be quite pragmatic. For some little boys being able to master gluing three legs on to the caterpillar would mean there is no point gluing the other 31 legs, because he has already succeeded in the art of gluing. He possibly runs outside thinking he has done a seriously good job! The second explanation is that he may have noticed the little girl beside him – and that she was obviously very capable and competent – and that there was no way he could compete with her. Instead, he simply gave up and went outside to play because that was going to be more fun. As loving mums, we often want to help our boys succeed, however, we need to be cautious. If you 'help' by gluing one more leg on that caterpillar and your son comes in and notices that – he will think he is not good enough or that he needs your help.

> "We told our youngest (DB 5) he couldn't sleep at night without his night nappy till he had a dry one in the morning for three days in a row. Miraculously, he did within a week so we let him sleep with just his jocks on for the first time. After wetting himself three times through the night on the first and second nights, we gave up and switched him back to nappies. Confused on how he had managed it before, we discovered a week later that he had changed into clean nappies each morning and hidden the wet ones behind his bed. Argghh!!!"
>
> — Mum of Clever Monkey

A similar thing happens in high school when mums think that finishing their son's homework or helping with their assessments is actually helping them. In actual fact, it is doing the reverse. It is making them dependent on you rather than themselves and it can make boys quite lazy. It is also telling them, in an indirect and invisible way, that you think 'they're not capable', when quite possibly they are capable and they just need some encouragement to keep working harder. Such a small thing that seems to come from a place of love can have such a negative impact long-term.

> *So, please, no more gluing legs on the caterpillars and no more doing their homework.*

By all means you can help them organise themselves to do their homework, reminding them in gentle ways that they actually have homework, and ensuring you keep healthy boundaries around technology which may distract them from doing their homework. However, just don't do it for them.

Many early years' educators talk about the sad/angry boy syndrome, when a small boy who feels abandoned and anxious will quickly convert that into hitting or aggressive behaviour. I have found this to be the case both personally and professionally, and encourage parents to keep this in the back of their minds when choosing child care for their sons.

Smaller groups of children, like in family day care settings, seem to help boys with their separation from their parents. I have also seen similar behaviour in boys who have been sent away from home to boarding school – often they struggle with deep grief and a strong sense of being abandoned. This is not for all boys of course – and with some honest communication these transitions can be made easier. Gradual separations with flexibility also really help sensitive boys and girls adjust to change, and can save a lot of heartache in the long run.

> **"Boys do not have the same ability as girls to calm themselves down. This is because of the basal ganglia and the fact that they do not have as much oxytocin in their system. Nor do they have as much ability to process serotonin, which tends to make them fidgety."**
>
> – Ruth Hanford Morhard, *Wired to Move: Facts and Strategies for Nurturing Boys in an Early Childhood Setting* (2013).

Early years' educators have been telling me that they have noticed that little girls are tending to be meaner and are practising more relational aggression at a much earlier age than they have seen before. Girls can also tell lies much better than boys. These are just two more of the signs that show that our little boys are simply not tough emotionally and socially. When we invest heavily in nurturing them, helping them to understand big, ugly feelings and teaching them ways to make better choices warmly and compassionately, we can change the future lives of tomorrow's men. We must invest in these early years so that we can reduce many of the statistics at the front of this book. The first place we need to start is to stop shaming and hurting our boys.

TOP TIPS

- ✓ We need to challenge the stereotypical view that boys are tough.
- ✓ There is an emotional vulnerability to boys.
- ✓ Boys can struggle to communicate their emotional world.
- ✓ Boys often express themselves physically rather than verbally.
- ✓ Boys do feel deeply, however, can struggle to interpret these feelings.
- ✓ Boys are particularly vulnerable to poor attachment especially from mothers.
- ✓ Boys' mortality rates are higher pre-birth, at birth and in the first 12 months of life.
- ✓ Boys' fine motor skills take much longer than girls to develop.
- ✓ Boys often need much more movement in the early years.
- ✓ Boys often default to anger when feeling emotionally overwhelmed and vulnerable.
- ✓ When boys are feeling unloved and disconnected they can emotionally shut down.
- ✓ Often, boys' behaviour is their language.
- ✓ Boys often compare themselves to the more-capable girls in their homes and early childhood settings.
- ✓ We need to be mindful of not speaking negatively about little boys' later development in the first five years of life.
- ✓ Many boys are struggling with stress and distress with the challenges of early childhood education.

CHAPTER FOUR

TRANSITIONING little boys from **HOME** to care and then to **BIG SCHOOL**

> "My mum taught us to be courageous. That we are capable of achieving anything as long as we are willing to dream and work for it."
> – Men's Survey 2017

We are highly sociable beings and we quite naturally identify that some of our relationships have a higher priority than others – that is why I am so passionate that babies, toddlers and young children have strong attachments to their key caregivers. When children default to their safe grown-ups, they learn by interacting with and modelling from the adults they spend most time with. Invisibly, this is how children develop their own unique sense of self. If children are spending the majority of their lives with other children, rather than their key attachment adults, they can quite easily substitute their socialisation, growth and development away from adults, especially adults who are strongly invested in them, and to other children. Some researchers suggest this can make children more resistant to being parented or educated.

Given that little boys are developmentally between six to 12 – even sometimes 20 months – behind little girls we need to be cautious about making one-size-fits-all choices, especially around who spends most time with our little boys. We need to be careful that the people who are around our boys are aware of their fragility – emotionally and socially. Strong mothers can become fierce protectors and, to be honest, many little boys need us to do this for them, however, without overprotecting. We must keep them away from toxic people and especially people who are still driven by the old male code. Sadly, this may sometimes be a grandparent.

There seems to be some confusion about what works best in building young children's socialisation skills – or their ability to get on with other children.

There is a perception that if your child is not in child care, then they will not become 'socialised'. Child psychologist Dr Louise Porter believes that children are technically unable to master social skills until around three years of age. She recommends that young children play with tiny clusters of other children – including children a year or so older than them.

Dr Gordon Neufeld, a well-respected Canadian psychologist, is very concerned that we can cause problems when we force socialisation on young children:

> **"Premature socialization was always considered by developmentalists to be the greatest sin in raising children ... [w]hen you put children together prematurely before they can hold on to themselves, then they become like [the others] and it crushes their individuality rather than hones it."**
>
> – Dr Gordon Neufeld (quoted in Andrea Mrozek, 'Nurturing children: Why "early learning" doesn't help'. *Institute of Marriage and Family Canada*. 2012).

Finding care for your fragile boy

When making decisions about your little boys in the first three years of life, keep these things in mind. Little boys are biologically wired to need significant time with maternal attachment that is warm and consistent. Our more sensitive little boys – our 'lambs' – can struggle more than our bold 'rooster' boys with being separated from their mother or mother figure, especially in the first three years (I write more about mothering roosters and lambs in Chapter 7). This does not mean they should not be transitioned into child care – just that parents need to be mindful of why and how this transition happens. It may require more gradual steps than for a more emotionally capable girl of the same age.

Obviously the way our society works now, for many parents child care is a necessity. However, Neufeld's message for parents is that if you are placing your child into long-based child care so that they will be 'socialised', you may like to know that your child will benefit more from being around caring parents than peers. That way, they are developing a strong sense of self, which means that when they do eventually become immersed into environments with other children, they can mix, mingle and play without needing to defer to the needs and wants to others. Their inner sense of security will be strong and they will be more respectful of the adults and teachers who will be caring for them.

If you are unable to delay having your boy in long day care then try to choose an environment that values building relationships over educating your child. What works best is when a little boy can have one educator as his primary caregiver – someone who will be a substitute mother for him. For some, this may be family day care. Also, aim to minimise the time he is spending there when he's under three. If your son's secondary attachment needs are met and the educators are aware of the unique differences between girls and boys and they respect this, the chances are good that your little boy will be fine.

With boys' development being slower than girls in these early years, I meet many a mum who's concerned because her 3-and a-half-year-old daughter is running rings around her 5-year-old son. This same boy by around eight tends to catch up if he is not forced to do things that he's developmentally unable to do, nor has he had repeated struggling experiences. Repeated failure creates mindsets like, "I am dumb. I am stupid".

Psychologist and researcher Professor Carol Dweck researched mindsets with 4-year-olds and found that a significant number of them had already decided that they were smart or dumb, or good or bad! So, for a little boy who is developmentally not ready to perform some of the tasks being asked of him, he runs the risk of creating one of these negative mindsets. Not only that, but day after day his self-worth barometer is emptied. Repeated failure will trigger any little boy to display distress in the only language he knows – through his behaviour. I seriously think this is one of the main reasons why Australia has such a high rate of 4- to 6-year-olds – mainly boys – being suspended and expelled from school. These mindsets are very difficult to change once they are entrenched, and they can become self-fulfilling prophecies. This is where my concern about the push-down of formalised learning into the early years starts.

> "My mum is always there for me whenever I need her. Always." – Men's Survey 2017

Is school ready for your lad?

I strongly advocate that you seriously consider delaying the start of formal schooling an extra year if you have the slightest concern about your son's readiness. Often, boys can be cognitively ready and yet socially immature, or the reverse. Often boys still need to move their bodies a lot more than our formalised settings allow. Some boys struggle deeply with separation distress, and exhibit signs of anxiety that can manifest as aggression, silliness or sobbing. I have never met a parent who regrets giving this extra time to allow their boy to shine, however, I have met so many who wish they had.

In 2013, I wrote a submission to the Australian Federal Government, *Stop Stealing Childhood in the Name of Education*. In preparing this, I heard from so many parents, early childhood educators and allied health professionals about their deep and profound concerns regarding the push-down of formalised learning in Australian early childhood settings. Paediatricians complained about the numbers of perfectly healthy little boys who were being sent to be assessed for ADHD simply because our expectations of what they can do before they are developmentally able have changed so much.

The ridiculous pressure to make our kids smart before we ensure they are able to: get on with others; communicate and be understood; have hours of joy and delight as kids; learn to cope with disappointment and setbacks; and enjoy the freedom of being a magical child under seven is making our children sadder, sicker, fatter and more disconnected than any other generation before them. Professor Margot Sunderland in her book, *The Science of Parenting*, writes that the stress-regulating systems of children that are set up in the first five years will become their stress-regulating systems as adults. Every week in the media we are hearing of young people struggling with mental illness and stress-related illnesses. Indeed, our emergency departments are struggling to cope and our mental health services are at bursting point. Wouldn't it be wiser to prevent the pressures that we put on our young children rather than try and fix the damage it causes later in adolescence and adulthood? There is no evidence that says learning to read at five has any benefits over learning to read at seven and yet we seem to be hell-bent, particularly in Australia, to make this the new reality.

> "For Mother's Day this year my son (aged 8) wrote a persuasive text at school about why I'm the best mum. Loved reading that I'm a 'kind lady because she takes me to the dentist'." — Kind Mum

Children who are pushed too much, too soon, have a much higher chance of struggling with anxiety, depression, addictions, poor health and poor relationships throughout their lives because they become wired to be hypersensitive to stress.

Given that our boys tend to be developmentally behind our girls, we need to invest more heavily into nurturing and caring for our little boys instead of pushing and forcing them into environments that create more stress and anxiety.

Speech pathologist Amanda Styles wrote to me with her concerns for the children she has predominantly worked with over 20 years who have "developmental difficulties, ranging from speech and language difficulties, learning disorders, ADHD, Autism Spectrum Disorders and emotional and behavioural problems".

> **"Now, with the push for early formalised learning, these children are even more at risk for developing behavioural, learning, social and emotional difficulties. They will lag ever further behind their peers and, as we are already seeing, there will be significant increases in concurrent problems (e.g. behavioural issues within the classrooms). Instead of having the much needed time to further develop their oral language development, self-regulatory skills and social emotional maturity through the much needed play experiences that pre schooling has previously provided, their attention is pushed towards formal literacy and numeracy training. They do not have the verbal and social prerequisites to cope with this level of teaching. It is like asking a child with a physical disability to run a race they are not yet physically able to run. They cannot run that race. Similarly, these children with developmental difficulties are cognitively not ready to cope with the demands of formal learning."**
>
> – Amanda Styles, speech pathologist (personal correspondence)

It is not just in Australia that we are seeing statistics indicating boys are struggling. The Lost Boys Report 2016 in the UK found that more than 80,000 boys had fallen behind girls by the age of five. Also, UK boys were nearly twice as likely to be behind in early language and communication skills than girls at the very beginning of primary school.

Early years' educators can also help with parent decision-making. These are the key guidelines they use in Australia when determining whether a child will transition well into full-time, 5-year-old school:

- **Physical health and wellbeing** – especially fine motor skills, good health, well fed, well rested, sitting, listening skills, able to grip a pencil, turn pages in a book, build with blocks, able to toilet themselves, feed themselves, dress themselves, some degree of focus to task, blow nose, wipe bottom, wash hands

- **Social competence** – primary need is to be able to get along with other children, cope with the stress of new situations and new learning tasks, have healthy assertiveness, ability to play solo and with other children, have pro-social behaviour. I know some grown-ups who need some help here?
- **Emotional maturity** – some ability to self-manage their emotions, be able to cope with minimal adult contact in large groups, develop friendships, able to separate from parents ... even if gradually!
- **Language and cognitive skills** – basic counting, following basic instructions, basic thinking skills (N.B. *basic*)
- **Communication skills and general knowledge** – basic conversation skills, manners, ability to communicate needs, understanding of wider world – again this is a work in progress ...
- **Independence** – Toilet themselves and, for children with special needs, can they have additional support?

There are so many skills, behaviours and capabilities that our young children need to be competent in, other than just their capacity to count to 100 and know their alphabet. I have serious concerns about how our digital children will navigate their world socially and emotionally as these human competences are only formed through spending hours interacting through play with other children in the present moment.

The Longitudinal Study of Australian Children (LSAC) has shown that many boys do have a tendency to struggle a little more in the early years. Some studies have shown that boys express themselves less clearly than girls, have more difficulty writing their names, recognising numbers and letters, and tying their shoelaces. Similar results can be seen on the data from the Australian Early Development Census. This data also shows that boys and Indigenous children feature much more highly as children with developmental vulnerabilities when starting 5-year-old school.

If it is possible financially and otherwise, please seriously consider allowing your child the extra time they may need to grow, to mature and to bloom. **Every state** has flexibility around when your child can start full-time, 5-year-old formalised schooling. Rather than see it as delaying, see it as allowing. Remember, too, that you know your child best.

Whether it's your son or your daughter, really reconsider starting school if they are obviously socially immature, if they tire easily, have poor self-regulation, have a significant developmental delay or their ability to communicate is weak. There is no rush and no competition and you need to make decisions that suit the unique needs of your child at that time.

Here's an extract from an email I received from a mum after her son started kindy:

> "My son loved his first term; it was a stimulating, exciting new environment with all these new people to talk to. But second term, something changed. He started feeling the pressure and became aware that he was struggling and according to the speech therapist and the OT, he had deficits. When he walks into his kindy class each morning, he starts the day having to write his name and show proper pencil grip. At three he was expected to hold his pencil properly and form the letters of his name. He couldn't and he knew he couldn't. My happy, carefree, confident son started each day in tears, was clingy, experiencing night terrors, would have complete meltdowns over minor things, started exhibiting violent behaviour towards his little sister, was not making friends and did not want to go to school. It broke my heart. I felt like a failure. I'd obviously done the wrong thing in not sitting my child down and teaching him how to hold a pencil ... and be a student. My poor kid was so exhausted and he was still just three."

This is a fantastic illustration of the damaging effects that the push-down of formalised learning onto young children is having on our boys who need more novelty, more movement, more adventure and more people who understand and appreciate the unique differences between girls and boys.

There has been a lot of research around self-regulation and, for boys who are developmentally behind others in the class, their struggle to regulate can cause them to become stressed and exhausted.

Dr Stuart Shanker was the Thinker in Residence for the Commissioner for Children and Young People in Western Australia in 2012. Perhaps the world's leading researcher on self-regulation and author of the book *Self-Reg*, Shanker shared this message during a keynote address for the commissioner:

> **"The problem is that some children have to work much harder than others to perform the same tasks and it is this expenditure that so seriously depletes their capacity to meet subsequent challenges."**

Shanker would really like us to see much of the poor behaviour – especially disengagement, inattentiveness, restlessness and emotional outbursts – as being more about poor self-regulation than 'bad' children. I agree with him, especially when it comes to our boys.

I have worked with men in very senior positions who, at times, struggle with a form of 'imposter syndrome'. This means they are concerned that at any moment people will realise that they aren't very smart. When I explore where this idea comes from, it is often traced back to when other students laughed at them when they couldn't read or remember something in preschool or Year 1. Such is the power of painful memories and the way they shape our minds later in life.

Negative mindsets set them up for failure on so many levels. We simply need to accept that there are some things that boys tend to do differently from girls that do not support their transition into school. They think differently, they hear differently, they communicate differently, they are highly sensitive, and the list goes on.

The following is part of an email received from a mum that also beautifully captures some of my concerns around boys transitioning to school. I have had several similar emails explaining how boys were being sent for professional assessment because their teachers felt there was something wrong with them only to find they were within 'normal range'.

> "My boys were lucky enough to have gone through kindy a few years ago before the compulsory five full-day week went through. At that time, when the suggestion to increase the days was raised, I remember writing an email to the Minister while both my boys were bawling in the background absolutely exhausted from the day. They did NOT cope and I made the decision to brave criticism from the school by insisting they take the Wednesday off each week to ensure a rest day.
>
> Both boys (one of whom is now being extended and the other who was evaluated by the school psych and noted as being very bright and in need of extension) struggled in those early years as they were not developmentally ready to sit at a desk and give up playtime – it took a number of specialists' diagnoses to convince the school that there was nothing 'wrong' with them. Each specialist told us they were just very bright and we even got quizzed as to why we were "wasting specialists' time with what was clearly a 'normal' child". The reason was simple. The school needed kids to cope with the new expectations and our boys just weren't ready.
>
> Admittedly, some children did appear to cope in school, but those parents shared with us how their children melted down as soon as they got home. What are we doing to our kids? How does this sort of policy 'enhance' education or allow our children to thrive? Any education policy should seek to do these things before all others, and the new system fails at these key aspects immensely.

> As a parent and an educator myself, I cannot believe that given ALL the available research and worldwide case studies which show that these ideas are bad practice, that our policy makers are choosing to IGNORE the facts and do the exact opposite. It is our children who pay the price. If this doesn't count as child abuse, what does?"

This piece of correspondence is a perfect illustration of the mismatch between expectations placed on children, and their normal (and highly variable) developmental capabilities.

Rather than force our unready children into formalised learning earlier, surely we need to ensure that they are in environments where their biological needs are met, where play-based learning is valued and respected, where outside learning exists, and where little boys can be cared for with enthusiasm and warm discipline.

The more words that children hear in the first three years of life, whether in conversation or by being read to, the better that child transitions into formal schooling. We need to invest heavily in marinating our little boys with real language – not digitally delivered language – and we need to help build their self-regulation so they are able to cope with being in group environments. We need to value, respect and prioritise their need to move, rather than seeing something wrong when a boy or girl still needs movement to create the dopamine levels that ensure engagement and good concentration.

When boys continually fail, whether that be at colouring within the lines, writing their full name or undertaking a craft activity – they see themselves as a failure and it can set up a mindset that there is something wrong with them or that they are dumb or stupid. As I have mentioned, I have worked with many men over the years who have struggled to overcome this mindset, regardless of being successful in their own field of work.

> *We need to take the pressure off boys in the early years and invest heavily in building their emotional and social competence because later in life these count a lot.*

Also, we need to let parents know that it is not a sign of poor parenting if your son needs longer to bloom and flourish. Indeed, it is actually a sign of good parenting. Research still tends to suggest that repeating year levels once you have started primary school does not have the success rate we would have hoped for.

My four sons were slow to bloom in the first three years of their schooling lives. Indeed, one of them had the misfortune of sitting next to a girl who was reading *Charlotte's Web* on the first day of Year 1. He was still unable to write his full name. I was devastated and felt I had failed him, especially as I have taught many illiterate boys as a high school English teacher! Luckily for me (and him), things were less pressured back then and by Year 4 he had caught up with all the girls. Mind you, I did have to convince him at times that school was more about playtime and lunchtime and you just had to do all the other stuff so you could play with your friends – because, seriously, he was not enjoying the formal side of schooling. Indeed, this was common for each of my four sons all the way through their schooling journey, particularly in high school, but I'll come back to that later.

Men who have struggled in the early years due to boys' common developmental delay or because of harsh punishment, often lack motivation, healthy ambition, resilience and the capacity to form meaningful relationships. Indeed, the mindsets that boys create in the transition to school often come back into play in the transition to high school and then the transition to life at the other end. We must ensure that little boys can find some form of success while they are in our school environments because without this sense of capability they will struggle, and that struggle often transforms into aggression, driven by anger.

My top tips for little boys starting big school

- Don't 'oversell' school like it's going to be exciting, fabulous and "you are going to love it!"
- Don't tell them they will learn to read. Many boys express regret at the end of the first week when they haven't yet learnt how to read.
- Having a good friend or making some good ones ASAP is a critical factor in the success of his transition.
- Promote the value of recess and lunchtime and playing as a high-quality reason for going to school.
- Hope and pray (indeed, seek out) that the school has a fabulous nature play space or allows lots of free play – kids love to have freedom in their play.
- Know they are unlikely to poo at school, and avoid going anywhere after school that doesn't have quick access to a toilet.
- They will be starving the minute they see you at the end of the day – be prepared.
- Meltdowns in the car are one way of showing how much they have missed you.
- Be prepared for such meltdowns by having funny props to shift their emotional mood – wigs, false teeth, masks and a farting cushion are great tools for all parents to have handy.

- Don't interrogate him – "How was school? What did you learn? Who did you play with?" Your boy may not remember a thing until possibly bath time.
- Let him refill his energy cup before mentioning the 'H' word – homework.
- He needs 'wind-down' time. Allow some quiet TV time or playing with the dog or shooting hoops – whatever works for your son. Avoid putting pressure on him in this window – he is a warrior who feels like he has come home from the battlefront.
- Read fun and quirky stories, and joke and riddle books to him often to keep him keen to learn to read, especially as reading can be much more difficult for most boys.
- Share lots of moments of non-verbal love and connection.
- Don't harp on about school or how important it is and why he has to be good for the teacher.
- Talk about plans for the weekend as much as possible so he has something to look forward to beyond the school gate.
- Help him get his bag organised the night before.
- Don't have too many expectations on school mornings when he's little. Three things is a lot for a little boy to manage (or a 14-year-old!). Get up, eat, get dressed and remind him kindly about doing teeth. Leave the bed and mess of toys in his room – too much extra stress!
- Have all his school clothes and shoes, socks and jocks in one pile ready the night before.
- Have a step-by-step plan in his room (visual cues as he can't read yet) – and possibly on the fridge – of what to do in morning. Young boys can really forget, especially when they're tired and not that keen to go to school. He can go check his plan without asking you ... this reduces nagging too.
- Encourage, coax and be positive about school and especially his teacher. Never let him hear you be negative in any way about either.
- Have a good girlfriend/mate with whom you can regularly debrief the frustrations of the transition time, and remember coffee and chocolate.
- Always remember that most little boys would prefer to stay home with their mum and dad, rather than go to school. They gradually get better at this, however, forcing them, commanding and demanding makes the process harder rather than easier.

> *Remember boys can be as sensitive emotionally as girls and many of these hints may help your daughter in her transition as well.*

Separation distress

> "I have three boys. My 6-year-old started kindergarten this year. I asked him if he ever thinks of me during school and he goes, 'I painted your head in my brain so I always look at it'. Very cute and funny."
>
> — Keep-a-straight-face Mum

Separation distress or anxiety is quite common and Sunderland believes this distress can influence children even as old as eight. Little boys can struggle with this and, rather than be able to communicate it, they often act out by being silly, overly energetic and hyperactive, needy, or through anger and aggression.

Changes in environment, people, routines and the number of other children they are interacting with can all cause spikes in the hormone cortisol, which creates the stress symptoms that you may see in your son — crying, clinging, tummy aches, refusal to leave your side, poor appetite, restless sleep and even outbursts and tantrums.

Remember, this means the downstairs brain is registering threat and is acting accordingly. They key stressor for children is separation from the most significant grown-up who is their protector and, in the early years, boys find most comfort from a maternal figure, as we have already explored.

As a starting point, it is useful to explain to kids that new things, places and people often make even adults feel those same feelings of being a little unsettled or anxious.

Young children usually have strong imaginations and I have found that some small techniques that strengthen the connection to both Mum or Dad while they are away can help lots. Here are some suggestions to try with your boy:

- You could help him create an imaginary protector. Children can imagine having their huge protector with them while they are away from you! I have an audio track that can help with this, called 'Safe 'N Sound'. You can access it for free on my website.
- Fill an empty, clean, small container that has a lid with kisses from everyone your child is fond of, and tuck it in the bottom of his

backpack so it's there if he needs. This tends to only work for our lamb boys and not our roosters!

- As he leaves home, always place a kiss from Mummy in the same hand and one from Daddy in the other. It is magic and stays there all day.
- You can draw a small heart in the palm of your boy's hand and one in the palm of your hand. If you have an early childhood educator who he is fond of, they can also be a part of this connection ritual. When your son feels anxious, he can come and hold their hand and match the two hearts together.
- Practise sending him rainbows of love from your heart to his at recess and lunch, and ask him to send one to you when he misses you.
- Put a really small stuffed toy, maybe smelling of your perfume, Dad's aftershave or with a lipstick kiss, in the bottom of his backpack. Again, he won't feel so separate and alone.
- Draw funny pictures on his lunch bag or put funny notes in his lunchbox.
- Take a small bite out of his sandwich.
- Teach him how to take three big breaths and breathe out the butterflies hiding in his tummy, or show him how to gently rub his tummy, telling the butterflies they are safe.
- Teach him how to calm himself by singing 'Round and Round the Garden' while making circles in his hand, just as you would do. Music and touch trigger feel-good hormones.
- Put a laminated photograph of his parents in his bag so he can go and reconnect with you whenever he feels sad.

These are just a few things that may help your little boy transition from the safety of your home and you, and become braver in the real world. Our biggest challenge is not to resort to telling a little boy to toughen up to be like a man. He especially does not need to hear this from the men he loves in his life.

The initial transition from home lays deep foundations for future transitions in his life like going to high school, leaving for boarding school and leaving home when your son eventually heads out into the big, wide world. Some boys just take a little bit more time to take these giant leaps away from the safest people in the safest place they know. Take this transition as gently and as honestly as you can, reassuring your son it will get easier, he will get braver and you will love him no matter what.

"One of the best things my mum has done for me is to instil in me the curiosity to travel the world and to notice different cultures and ways of being. This has influenced me to be more open-minded in my work and in my life. There are always different ways of living and viewing the world." – Men's Survey 2017

Supporting boys to cope with school

In my counselling experience with boys suffering despair, depression or even ideas of suicide, I have found these lads often feel overwhelmed by their emotions. Emotions are unresolved, running rampant inside them. Many of these boys feel deeply flawed and like a failure; they believe that those closest to them do not love them. This deep sense of alienation and feeling separate came up so often when listening to these troubled lads. They were starving for deep, meaningful connection not only with their parents, but also with other significant adults in their life. They often felt completely misunderstood.

Many schools still use shaming, sarcasm and strong criticism when dealing with poor behaviour and many boys carry these scars right through life.

We must remove the old boy code that existed in the 20th century. Because they are socialised to hide their feelings, boys may be more vulnerable than girls in terms of their inner world and we must change how we discipline boys. An excellent way to help a boy explore an inappropriate way of behaving is to walk him around an oval or up the street as you have a dialogue with him about the incident. The movement will help him to feel safe and it is less confronting and more private than sitting still, face-to-face, so he will stay engaged with the communication.

Boys need to have significant adults who 'see them' and accept them. Sometimes it may be a family member, an aunty, uncle or grandfather. Sometimes it may be a school chaplain or a family friend who is trusted to keep confidentiality, or a sporting coach or teacher that a boy believes likes him. A boy needs a safe person in his school to act as an adult ally or mentor, someone who he can trust to help him when he needs. This is a profound need in today's schools to help boys better cope with our confusing school environments.

In my experience with boys in schools and, of course, with my own sons, I have discovered that boys need quiet spaces to help them sort out their thoughts. I am sure that many parents and teachers overwhelm their boys with too much talk and too many questions! It took me a while to realise that my boys settled better by playing by themselves outside, especially after a full school day.

> **"Silence is often an excellent way of letting our sons find their own solutions rather than us imposing our own."**
>
> — Ian Lillico, *Boys and Their Schooling* (2000).

Even though most boys are activity-based, they still need time to switch off and recharge their batteries. 'Chilling out' in front of TV or playing on computers are ways that boys do this, 'tuning out' to conversation is another, or day-dreaming. Time spent alone in their bedrooms also works well. Boys often need separation time to adjust from being at school to being in the home environment. School and home are two different battlefields, in a sense, and the armouring needs to change.

Boys value and appreciate quiet spaces to think, and yet they often are the ones making the noise! Just like girls, boys learn best when they feel safe and cared for and are in environments with adults who treat them with kindness and fairness.

> *I believe that boys who learn how to bring more silence and stillness into their lives manage the emotional rollercoaster of adolescence better than those who have no idea about how to become quiet and still.*

The constant activity and busy-ness of boys may also lead them to create stress-related illnesses in later adulthood. Heightened cortisone levels, from being in a go-go-go state, can create serious problems with anxiety and, later, fear-based mental health problems. Constant activity can also cause sleep deprivation as winding those bodies and busy heads down for sleep is not easy. The magic of silence and stillness for boys must be taught as well as modelled because it is not a normal activity for most boys. The earlier the better!

> "I arrived home from work one day, and my 3-year-old son said to me, 'Mum, I can see that you are missing something'. I turned around and said, 'Oh, am I? What is it?' My son Rhys replied 'a big cuddle' and he wrapped his arms around me so tight and gave me the best hug. Warmed my heart, made me smile." — Loved Mum

Please remember that the views of the old boy code – either that 'boys will be boys' or that we need to toughen up boys – need to stop immediately. Indeed, in all my research around boys from birth to adulthood, it is their vulnerability that worries me the most. One of the best books to read if you have sons is, *He'll Be OK* by researcher, social advocate and New Zealand's first female prison officer to work in a men's prison, the late Celia Lashlie. This is how she described her thoughts about boys in adolescence:

> **"There were moments when their vulnerability washed over me and I was wondering how we actually manage to get so many of them safely through to adulthood ... Their childlike naivety ... their dependence on their peers to define their behaviour, their desire to live in the moment and their associated unwillingness to plan, all combine at a time when male hormones are raging through their bodies and the blood appears to be going down rather than up."**
>
> – Celia Lashlie, *He'll Be OK* (2005).

As I wrote earlier, when my first son started school he was unable to write his full name and nobody seemed to mind. Nowadays he would have had so many assessments and most likely would have been labelled a delayed developer. He gradually settled into the school journey and, as with many boys, he didn't really 'have all his lights on' until around Year 4. In those days, there was no serious concern about the gradual settling in of boys in terms of their formal schooling. That lad now has two degrees and works as a very competent professional. I have concerns that we don't allow flexibility for boys who are having difficulty in transition. It seems that with the push-down of formal learning, taking a day off a week for a boy is no longer a possibility because he will miss out on something incredibly important. The fact that he will be struggling emotionally, socially and probably cognitively is obviously not anything that is considered worthy of attention. How sad.

If we can support our boys with their emotional and social development from an early age, they will learn how to cope with the mistakes, the failures and the many times that they will make poor choices. It's not just about succeeding at school. This will teach them how to be good warriors who will one day become good men. It is really important to validate boys' feelings for them when things go wrong because this is emotional coaching, which can help them right through life.

> *It is so much better for a boy to be able to identify the strong feelings he is experiencing, rather than having to default to anger because he is feeling vulnerable and confused.*

In our school system, too, we have feminised the curriculum in many ways, disadvantaging typical boys. By having cumulative assessment more than tests, many boys are not quite sure how well they are doing and external validation is important to them, remember. When a boy's school report says 'progressing' rather than pass or fail, how can he work out how much effort or not to put into his schoolwork?

Another change in our classrooms has been the shift towards cooperative learning, which means there is more group work. What often happens during group work is that our verbally strong girls tend to dominate group activities and do a lot of directing and organising, which really frustrates boys. Group work can be really effective and helpful with both genders if there are some careful guidelines put in place by the teacher.

When I was teaching, I introduced 'paired shared' conversations in my English classrooms. In these conversations each partner was given a number one or two, and first up, only the number ones could talk and only for a short time of about one-and-a-half minutes while the other partner had to be listening, and not interrupting. Then, they would swap. It was really interesting as the first few times we did the activity many boys were unable to keep talking for a full minute-and-a-half. However, after a few weeks they were well able to do it.

> *A boy came up to me one day and said he couldn't believe how good it felt to know that he was being heard and he wasn't going to be talked over, especially by a girl.*

This activity is also very good to teach roosters to be good listeners instead of the motor mouths that they often are – often dominating conversations if not complete classrooms! This exercise is also something that could be easily adapted for home life during family meetings, high-emotion conversations and conflict-resolution situations.

Your family could introduce a talking stick or talking teddy or whatever object feels good for you, which one family member holds while they speak. Only the person holding the talking object is allowed to speak and no one else can interrupt. I guarantee everyone in the family will benefit from this exercise, not just the boys!

TOP TIPS

- ✓ Be mindful of the 'when' and 'how' you transition your boy into out-of-home care.
- ✓ Boys can struggle with separation distress by acting aggressively.
- ✓ Many boys benefit with an extra year of maturing before starting formal schooling.
- ✓ Try to avoid comparing little girls and boys under seven.
- ✓ Developing a strong connection to one key caregiver or educator can helps boys transition better.
- ✓ Have realistic expectations of how stressful and exhausting being away from home can be for a little boy.
- ✓ Never tell little boys they need to toughen up.

CHAPTER FIVE

SOME more INTERESTING things about BOYS

> "My mum taught me to cook, clean (to some extent), and that it was OK to cry." – Men's Survey 2017

From my own years of experience and research into the literature around boys, I would add these following differences (warning, broad generalisations ahead!).

Boys:

1. **Prefer to do** – Think for a moment what tends to happen if the average man buys a flat pack from Ikea or Bunnings. He will generally start building it without reading the instructions. Not only that, when he finishes building his flat pack there are often bits that have not been used and the mammoth hunter just sweeps these aside because they "must be unimportant!" What has actually happened is that the hunter has been on an adventure, which he has then conquered through his own choices and autonomy. This gives him great fuel for his self-worth barometer. Often men will come looking for people to show off their latest project to. They are so proud!

   In a way, the same approach applies when we're out driving and become lost. Before GPS arrived, our beloved males dreaded stopping to ask for directions thinking instead that very soon their actions would lead to the desired result. They would much prefer to try and solve the problem without asking for directions. Let's be honest, most men do have superior spatial skills that have been developed as a cave man when hunting mammoths (think women and road maps?). Indeed, I notice if ever I am running an activity in a seminar involving using left or right, there is often a pause from most women as they double-check which one is their left and which one is their right hand. Men don't tend to have that difficulty and, possibly, that is why they can reverse-park trailers. Again, we need to remember this is not all men or all women as we now have many fantastic women truck drivers who can navigate precise manoeuvres just as well as men.

We need to keep this in mind as mothers and as teachers. When we want our sons to do something, we increase the chances of getting it done if they are allowed to have some autonomy in how to get it done.

I found in my high school classrooms that some boys worked better when they were sitting on the floor than when they were sitting at their desks. The fact they could choose where they did their work was deceptively important to them and a small sign of respect. Little things matter and having complete authority that is mandated – which is a very big thing in the traditional ways of raising boys – simply makes most boys defensive and resistant.

2. **Listening is a challenge** – One of the most common sources of conflict between mums and sons is that sons never listen or they seem to never hear what we say! Let me give you a possible explanation as to why it may seem like that.

   Let's pretend that your son is watching TV in the lounge room. You call out to him from the nearby kitchen, asking him to turn the TV off because dinner is ready. You notice he makes absolutely no sign of hearing you. So you use a slightly louder voice. Still no reaction. And then you shout at him very loudly. You may notice your son turn quickly with a slightly distressed look on his face wondering why on earth his mother – the woman he loves more than anyone on earth – is suddenly shouting at him! You see, in a way he was really busy – his single focus was completely consumed by the TV and he did not hear you the first two times. I suggest that rather than call out across the room, you walk over quietly and possibly tickle his back to get his attention, then give him five minutes to turn off the TV. Boys are not good at transitions, especially a move from an experience they are enjoying. Heck, none of us are good at that! Just before the five minutes is up, go over and again gently tickle his back, stroke his head or stand really close to him and, in a loving voice, ask him to turn the TV off because dinner is ready. So often I meet mums who genuinely think their son is deliberately ignoring them. Almost every time you will find they are completely consumed in a single-focus moment and genuinely do not hear you. Have you ever tried talking to your male partner when he is using his phone or his laptop?

3. **Boys generally hear less** – Maybe this is what is happening when I glaze over sometimes when a group of women are talking at the same time, resulting in three different conversations taking place in exactly the same location? It would seem that boys' capacity to hear, especially to take in long-winded explanations and directions, is significantly different to how girls hear. Have you ever noticed that girls can often listen to what you're saying while they are talking as well? I can certainly attest to this in my classrooms where I would often be giving a detailed description of what was required with an assessment task. Inevitably, two or three boys would put their hands up and ask what they needed to do. More recent research suggests that rather than boys hearing less, especially when women talk, this trend may have more to do with boys understanding less. Either way, this can be really frustrating for mums of sons.

4. **Boys get 'information overload'** – Boys tend to struggle with too many requests given at one time or when too many words are spoken. You may often see a glazed look on their faces because they can't remember any of the requests you have just given. This is often because of an information overload.

   Imagine your son and the look on his face if you asked him to put his dirty glass in the sink, go wash his hands and come to the table for dinner. Seriously, there is a look that suggests, "Uh oh, I am gonna get into trouble because I didn't hear what my mum said!" It's interesting because boys don't tend to remember the first part of the request or the last part – it simply causes a minor freeze in their brain and that's when you see the glazed expression.

   Give your boy a good chance to be a success in communication.

   Try to ask him to do one thing at a time and then, when that's done, ask him to do the next thing. Often single words with clear non-verbal messages like waving hands and arms, can get better results. For example, you may say, "David – shoes" (pause and point to shoes) "in your bag" (point to bag), "now, please" (big smile or wink). If you have his attention before you make your single request you really do give your son a much better chance of succeeding. Remember that he really wants to please you. If you can keep your requests to **around 10 words or less** you also increase the chances of him succeeding.

   The cycle of requesting and nagging and more nagging is a sign that your communication is not working with your son and not a sign that he is deliberately being disobedient, no matter how frustrating it can be. You can see how mornings become a disaster zone if you have a son who is still half asleep, who is poorly prepared for the day and who is hungry – and you're rattling off instructions to help him get ready. If you can get into the habit of connecting with your son in a gentle, tender way that does not require words before you make your request, you will be lowering stress levels for both your son and yourself. This habit will really help you when your son becomes an adolescent, when forgetfulness and disorganisation reach a whole new level due to the brain changes. Sometimes simply leaning on your son lovingly and pointing to his dirty plates still on the lounge and then to the dishwasher and then pointing to him, can communicate far more effectively than any amount of spoken words.

5. **Boys have shorter attention spans** – Boys' attention spans appear to be shorter if they perceive the activity they are doing no longer deserves their attention or they do not think it is worthwhile. Remember, the inner self-worth barometer that he is continually gauging himself against? He simply does not want to waste his energy on things that are not going to make him feel better about himself or that are not going to be fun. I believe this may be to do with boys processing dopamine differently from girls – as soon as the dopamine level drops, boys will start moving in order to build the level back up again. Boredom to boys is akin to failing or losing and that is why sometimes a young lad who is watching TV might also be jumping up and down on the couch. So many little boys in our early years' settings are still getting punished and disciplined for being unable to sit still on a mat for as long as the girls can. Indeed, I have also heard from a physiotherapist that crossing the arms or legs for any length of time for some boys can be painful due to the differences in the development of boys' and girls' muscles and tendons around the wrists and ankles. Punishing boys for not being able to do something that they are developmentally unable to do is not only ridiculous and unhelpful, it is cruel. Little boys are biologically wired to be physically active for longer periods of time than girls and at a later age than girls. If we continue to ignore this, we do so at the peril of more little boys who struggle in their transition to big school. Movement matters and I will explore that in more depth in the chapter on play.
6. **Boys need greater stimulation** – Boys need to be sure that the activity they are about to participate in is worthwhile, interesting and something they want to do. Girls tend to be much more amenable to starting things without necessarily having a high level

of interest. As an English teacher it took me quite some time to convince some of my boys that English was a worthwhile subject that could be helpful later in life. There is a question that is burning inside every boy, every day, and that is:

"What's in it for me?"

A mum recently shared a funny moment with her son after she had been to one of my seminars and had changed her communication style to better suit her boy. They were having a quiet cuddle when her little lad looked up at her and said, "I love you Mummy". She replied that she loved him too. They sat for a while longer and the mum thought she could use this moment to say more – so she told her son she was proud of the way he was playing with his sister, and how he was doing well at preschool and … and … when her son interrupted her by saying, "Mummy, ssshhhhhh – no talking!" She knew she had stepped into invading his quiet space, and yet it was so hard to resist!

I have had other mothers email me to tell me that after just a few days of them speaking less, nagging less and being more tender physically, their little sons were coming to them without any prompting telling them how much they loved them. These little boys were feeling so much safer in their world and, in that beautiful tender way that most boys have, they wanted to show what it meant to them.

7. **Memory issues** – Hopefully, following the exploration of the influence of biological drivers, the key hormones that influence behaviour and an understanding of boys remembering things that matter to them at a single point in time due to their single-focus characteristic, mums can now appreciate why boys forget stuff! If there's one issue that drives mothers to need more coffee and chocolate, it is how frustrating it is for our sons to remember things. What we do know is that memories are anchored when there are strong emotions present, which is possibly one of the reasons why we remember quite vividly very painful moments of childhood and tend to forget the more bland, normal moments. So boys will tend to remember their successes and their failures, and not most of the other stuff that we mums think matter.

"DB (4) recently asked me why I only have one child. I responded that it was so I don't have to share my love with anyone else and he gets it all. He pondered on this for a moment before asking me, 'Does this mean I get all your food too?'" — Constantly Laughing Mum

A few years ago when we were away on a family holiday, my two younger sons were having a conversation about snakes. One of them had been seriously spooked when he was having a sleep on the lawn one day, and woke up to find a tiger snake – a highly venomous snake – curled up next to his shoulder. Needless to say he has been the brunt of snake jokes ever since. They began sharing another snake story from their boyhood that I had never heard of and it sort of went like this:

DB (8.5) and DB (5) had been riding their bikes around a lake that was probably half a kilometre from home. This was a serious wetland and definitely a wonderful place for snakes to hide and breed. Apparently, the oldest son rode straight over a tiger snake that was across the path. He pulled his bike up quickly and warned his younger brother to stop. He told him he would ride around the track and come back the other way and pick him up. For some reason completely unbeknown to anyone with half a brain, my youngest son decided to try to outsmart the snake, by pretending to move one way and then the other! Then, very quickly he ran around the snake's tail, jumped on his brother's bike and they rode all the way back around the track to collect his bike. By the time they got home the experience was over and done with. The fact that they could smell spaghetti bolognese cooking on the stove could have also contributed to the focus being led away from near disaster to a well-loved dinner that was coming. Who knows? I never heard about this experience until around 22 years after it happened. There was no deliberate intention to deceive me ... they just forgot about it.

Little boys are notorious for accidentally weeing on the floor and they can also be known to have a quick poo – not at school, remember – and run out without wiping their bottom, flushing the toilet or washing their hands. Sometimes it's not so much about forgetting as being distracted by something else. If there is a game going on, playing trumps everything and boys will sometimes wet themselves because they cannot drag themselves away from a game. Sometimes at school, little boys will not eat their lunch if they can get an extra 10 minutes play in at lunchtime, and we know that a hungry boy is an angry boy so after lunch he is going to be difficult to teach because his concentration will be totally focused on his growling tummy that he forgot to feed!

Valuing your sons' privacy

As I've mentioned and as I will elaborate more on later in this book, we girls and women tend to process our feelings through verbal communication. Generally, women love to chat about their lives and feelings – we enjoy sharing our experiences and stories with our girlfriends. As mums, however, we need to be respectful of an innate need for a lot of boys for privacy. We need to always ask them before we share information – whether it's chatting to grandma on the phone, sharing on social media or chatting to their teacher. Please be ever mindful of this and always ask your son if it's OK before you share information, anecdotes or stories with others online or offline, no matter how proud you're feeling.

The art of gentle reminding

In the early years and primary school, a really useful practice for mums of sons is the art of gentle reminding. Sometimes I used a sticky note on their school bag to remind them to put their lunch box back in it, or I left a reminder note inside their lunchbox – especially if I needed them home straight after school. We just need to accept that little boys, and often our good men, can benefit from our exceptional memories. We just need to do it with compassion.

For those of you have a good man in your life, I guarantee there are nights he forgets to take the bin out. I know that sometimes, as a stressed woman, you may think he did it deliberately. He didn't. Your good man does not sit down and think, "Wow, I'm going to really annoy my good woman tonight by forgetting the bin!" No way. However, what possibly could have happened in his single-focus brain is that there is something difficult happening at work, or he may be concentrating on doing his footy tipping or he may have a nasty rash on his scrotum! Either way, he has been distracted by something else and he has innocently forgotten it's bin night. So can we please reframe male forgetfulness as having a deliberate intention and recognise that we can help our men succeed to be better men, partners and fathers by practising the art of gentle reminding. Again, this is not all men or all women, however, the explanation I have just shared has improved many mum-dad relationships over the years and I have been informed that some dads now ask mums to remind them of important things. So, next time your good man looks like he's forgotten the bin, try gently walking over to him, rubbing his shoulder or giving him a quick peck on the cheek and saying, "It's bin night babe". Seriously, let's work together to get things done. Send him a text to remind him that he had promised to come home early because his mum is coming over for a visit, or text him if you need him to pick up one of the children after sport. Everyone wins and no one loses, especially your son.

Boys are known to be a lot less organised than girls and this is another area where you can help your boy manage his life a bit better. Draw up lists, timetables and rosters for chores so that he can go and check them when he can't remember. This means he doesn't feel quite so silly and it saves him asking you.

I can remember observing something interesting when I was still teaching in the pre-digital world. Many of the upper school boys were carrying enormous bags full of books around every day of the week, whereas the girls were bringing only the books they needed. I spoke to a boy one day about why he didn't leave some of his heavy books at home on the days he didn't have those subjects. Seriously, he looked at me like I was possibly a little insane: "No, Miss, I could never do that. What I do know is that by carrying this heavy bag around I've got what I need every day".

So what seems like common sense to us, is sometimes just simply too difficult for our boys to be able to manage. The worst thing we can do as mums is complain, criticise or make fun of them as they struggle to remember the things that are important day to day.

Your sons will forget your birthday, Mother's Day and they will forget to call if you are sick because they get easily distracted by other things. Please do not take that personally – and be mindful to not express your disappointment to them! You can make a humorous attempt at reminding them. I would often mention that my birthday gift had not arrived and wonder if the delivery truck broke down? It became a light-hearted way for me to tell my boys they had forgotten. I text all my sons and their dad and step-dad to remind them of family birthdays – it just helps them to remember. Even though they forget, they still absolutely love you!

"My mum sat with me through long nights of asthma before puffers were available." – Men's Survey 2017

Growth spurts

There are times when your son's behaviour is really going to confuse you. Out of the blue he will become oppositional, grumpy, uncoordinated and so hungry! This could mean that a growth spurt is about to happen. Human biology has determined that boys and men have a higher percentage of muscle than girls and women. So when a growth spurt is going to happen, a boy's body needs to stock up some energy in order for it to grow because it has to grow muscle whereas we women tend to grow fat. Some of these growth spurts happen particularly around the ages of four, eight, 10, 14 and then randomly into the early 20s.

If you have not yet lived with an adolescent boy, you have a surprise coming. To watch a young lad who has just eaten a full dinner with a good balance of protein and carbs go straight to the toaster and eat eight pieces of toast, is a sight to behold. Not only that, when they are hungry they can eat a kilogram of yoghurt in one sitting. Cereal can become a lifesaver and you almost need to keep a few boxes hidden in the laundry cupboard in case two of your sons have a growth spurt at the same time. One thing that is really important is to ensure that the food your son is consuming at a high rate is good quality and that it contains good-quality fats and protein. I found toasted ham, cheese and tomato sandwiches a godsend when my boys were having growth spurts. Growth spurts can also be a really confusing time for your son because the body is focused on growth — not on concentrating in class, managing moods or being happy or cooperative. Please cut him some slack.

One of my lads, DB (14), came into the kitchen one morning in the midst of a growth spurt that had been going on for weeks. I noticed white horizontal streaks down one side of his back from his shoulder blade to his buttock. Initially (because I am a mother of sons only) I thought maybe one of his brothers had attacked him — playfully of course. On closer inspection, I noticed they were stretch marks that had quite simply appeared overnight. My son was oblivious to them because they were on his back and he merely gave me a grunt when I explained my discovery. I tried to lighten the moment by saying that I hoped the other half of his back might grow soon or he would end up being stooped over to the right. He did not think that was very funny at all. It took another four days of eating and being pretty grumpy before I noticed the stretch marks up the other side of his back. Within a couple of months he had grown 15cm. So, mums, please be mindful and supportive of the growth spurts your son is going to have — over and over again. Once the growth spurt is over your son magically returns to being who he was before ... just like magic!

Favourites

If you asked your son to go and get dressed because it was his Nanna's 60th birthday and you were going out for a special celebration, it would not be uncommon for him to appear dressed in some seriously old clothes. The seams on the stained T-shirt may have come apart, the jeans may only just fit and the shoes that he's chosen may certainly have seen better days. What your son has done is choose his favourite clothes to celebrate his Nanna's birthday. Again, I think this shows there is a sensitivity inside our boys that we can sometimes trample without realising.

Boys can have favourites with their picture books as well. Sometimes these picture books might seem really boring to us especially when they are about a digger or a truck. After reading them 1000 times we really wish they would move on. Please don't because these are the things that make him feel safe, secure and loved. When your son eventually leaves home, please check with him before you throw anything out because many boys would still like you to keep (somewhere in the back of the garage) a few of his absolute favourites from his boyhood.

The same goes for teddy bears and special blankets that he obviously has no need for as he grows into being a teen or even a man. These symbols are still really important and I have had men share with me how absolutely crushed they were when they requested a favourite teddy bear that they thought their parents had kept, only to find it had been thrown out. There are many men who have a favourite football jersey or jumper hiding somewhere in their wardrobe. It may not fit any more, however, it represents something really important to these men and we need to respect that. As a funeral celebrant, I know how often these symbols appear at the farewell ceremony for a man.

I once stayed with one of my DBs (26) and, when I hung his washing out, the elastic band around his favourite boxers separated from the main part of the shorts. When I took them inside and told him that he would probably have to throw them out, he looked at me in all seriousness and asked if I could sew it back on because I have a sewing machine. It took everything in my power not to laugh. I am sure he had had those favourite boxers for maybe 10 years. Such is the invisible sensitivity that many of our boys and men have around items that are special to them.

When I moved from Western Australia over to the East Coast, my DB (20) was helping me pack. I asked if he would help me pack the Duplo more tightly so it would fit into a smaller box. As I was busy stacking the blocks, I noticed that my son had found the Duplo petrol pump and was quietly turning the handle listening to the clicking sound. That Duplo is now being used by his daughter and his son. I am so glad I kept it and that the petrol pump still works!

Temperature

Another thing that can be really annoying for we mums is when our precious sons refuse to wear a jumper when it is freezing cold. Indeed, they tend to head off to school in the middle of winter with shorts and short-sleeved shirts. Equally as confusing for me was when I would sometimes find my sons wearing jumpers in summer. Apparently the high muscle mass in boys and men means they don't feel the cold the same as many girls and women. My suggestion is to put a jumper in their school bag and stop nagging them. There will be times he will come home complaining bitterly of how cold he is and you will think, "Yes, at last he will start wearing a jumper". But by the time the following week comes around he has completely forgotten he has been cold and will again neglect to take a jumper. We need to let our boys work some things out for themselves and this is certainly one of them. Save your breath for a much more important challenge in the mothering of your son.

The penis

Let's start with an obvious statement here: Mums do not have penises. It can be quite amusing when your son suddenly realises that you don't have a penis and, indeed, I have heard some very funny stories about little boys being really worried because their mummy has lost her penis. Women do not have prominent external genitalia so how can we really know what it feels like to have a scrotum and a penis that is completely outside the body. We have no idea that it can feel really good for a boy to hold those special parts of his body in his warm hands and to stroke them and play with them.

A boy's penis is really important to him and, in a way, knowing that it is still there brings a boy great comfort, which is partly why boys and many men seem to need to regularly check that it hasn't fallen off. Boys often find holding their penis and scrotum calming and soothing and, heck, it's theirs – it does belong to them. Maybe it's because they value their penis so much that they like to play with it so much. I need to reassure all mums out there that the penis will not break when it is being used as an air guitar or being pulled into strange shapes or being made to disappear completely. In a way, when he is little, a penis is a boy's friend rather than a part of his sexual identity. For some little boys it can act as a comforter like a soft toy – and when he feels stressed he may seek this special friend to help soothe him.

By the way, when you are talking with your son, please use the word penis rather than doodle, willy, John Thomas or dick – having different names can confuse boys later and it's also recommended by body safety and child protection experts.

> "I walked in to check on DB (8) who was having a bath. He very happily and proudly told me, 'Wow Mum!! When I tickle my penis, it just jumps right up!! I don't even know how that happens!' A mind of its own." — Aussie Mum

Many boys prefer to be naked because they enjoy their bodies. Many boys dislike wearing undies because they prefer their genitals to be free. I jokingly called some days of the week 'no undy Mundy' or 'no undy Sundy', because the boys preferred to go without undies. It can take many conversations to help them understand why wearing undies may matter on some occasions. Sadly, in today's pornified world we can no longer trust that little boys will continue to play quite innocently with their penises in the company of other boys. There has been a significant increase in incidences of inappropriate sexual play among children under five. We need to start young when talking to our children, especially our boys, about appropriate safe touch, consent and sexual body awareness. Little boys are also being groomed online by sexual predators and quite often their naiveté and desperate need to be liked by anyone, particularly a male father figure, means they can be a target for sick individuals. I strongly suggest you start speaking to your boys around the age of four about public and private parts of the body and who has permission to touch your body and when. I have a list of books and other resources on my website that can help with this. Just go to maggiedent.com and under the Parent Help section find the topic: 'Body Safety/Talking Sex'.

One of my lads, DB (3), suddenly decided that he did not want to have any more baths or showers. I tried all sorts of approaches to encourage him, but he even refused chocolate as a bribe. So, after giving it a lot of thought, I tried a much more creative approach. My conversation went like this:

"Babe, Mummy does not have a penis, however, if I did have a penis and a foreskin and I didn't wash it and clean it I think it would go mouldy and it might fall off. Guess it's lucky Mummy doesn't have a penis."

He was back having showers and baths frequently after that conversation. It worked because I appealed to something that really mattered to him – his penis – and the thought of losing it was just too big a risk. He took the appropriate action to ensure that it would not fall off.

It really does not help our little boys or our adolescent boys, both of whom can have very badly behaving penises, if mum exhibits any sign of disgust or that there is something gross happening when he gets an erection. Seriously, boys have very little control over their developing little penises and it must be quite a curious experience for them so we need to be careful not to shame them in the face of that curiosity.

Farts

I have been known to say on national television that I think mums need to learn to fart more if they have sons. A well-timed fart can lighten the mood, defuse a conflict and be a wonderful bonding connection with a son.

I have used farting as a behaviour management technique when travelling in a car. I warned the boys to behave better and to be less noisy and, when that did not work, I threatened to fart. They thought it was hilarious and so I did fart and then I locked the windows on the car. Seriously, they were much more cautious after that. My deadly fart works so much better than me shouting or being crabby.

In adolescence, we mums to have to step back a little and I found a little fart every now and then kept me connected. We do have to talk about where it is not appropriate to fart with our boys out in the public world and especially not in a lift! I once met the CEO of a large organisation after a seminar and he told me a story about how one morning he was in the lift at work with one of his young male employees. On the way up, his employee dropped a large fart and commented that he thought it was 'a beauty'. He did not realise who he was sharing the lift with. It wasn't until later that afternoon at a large meeting that this young man realised who his lift companion had been. It's so important to teach your son to save his farts for around home or around his mates in the wide-open spaces of Mother Nature. Teach him to be able to apologise for an accidental fart that can sometimes happen in the classroom or in a workplace environment.

For my birthday this year, I received a card from one of my sons featuring all different kinds of farts and, I have to admit, we all laughed until we had tears rolling down our faces and I was left hoping that I would never have a Trojan horse fart!

I still stand beside my declaration that I think mums of sons need to be able to fart more. There may be more about farting later in the book.

> "After hearing my DB (4) sniffing repeatedly, I asked him to go and get a tissue. He replied, 'Don't need one mum, I'm just putting my boogies on this spoon I found instead' #resourceful" — Mum of Boys

Touching

> **"Boys learn by touching and doing — and often do not see the risk until after the event ... boys are more impulsive, non-cautious, eager and liable to take risks. Girls on the other hand are more controlled, logical and analytical."**
>
> – Neil Farmer, *Getting it Right for Boys* (2012).

A significant number of boys are visual-kinaesthetic learners and this means they learn by seeing, touching, doing and moving. I have sometimes watched frantic mothers in department stores trying to stop little boys from picking things up and touching things as they walk past. This is in their biology. If we really want to help our sons, especially our little boys, we need to avoid taking them to places where touching things could end up in things being broken or lost. There is one place that you can take boys where they can touch things and that is hardware stores – a good wander through Bunnings will seldom end up in a major disaster.

This is why I have often suggested to delay taking boys to coffee shops because they will want to play with the sugar, the salt and pepper shakers and anything they can get their hands on. They are also most likely to only be able to sit still for up to five minutes and then they will be standing up on the seat or running around between the tables because this is what they are biologically wired to do.

My boys' paternal grandmother had a lovely home with lots of beautiful china and crystal, and after one visit with just two of them we agreed it would be much better for everyone if we met in a nearby park in future. Toddlers and little boys love pushing things, jumping on things, tipping things over and climbing on things. Again, they are biologically wired to do so. Can you create an environment that allows them to do this in your home? In their playroom? In your garage? How about, better still, outside in Mother Nature. One of the reasons why I'm especially fond of the nature warriors who are taking our boys back into nature, is that they are creating an environment where they can do all these things often in an adventuresome way. I especially celebrate the Perth folks at Educated by Nature because their philosophy is to simply be mentors and guardians of our children in a natural environment. They encourage them to build, explore and use tools and equipment and (oh my goodness!) fire in responsible ways. I seriously hope we see organisations like this popping up everywhere to support families to get their children back into nature – the best place they can learn while they are children.

> "My mother has raised me to be respectful, curious (ask questions), and to be patient. She has always put me first and continued to have unconditional love when things are tough." – Men Survey's 2017

I'm hoping that I have been able to tease out a few more things that may help you improve your understanding of the world through your boy's eyes, and improve your communication with your son. If we just don't sweat the small things we can lower our stress levels and have the energy to hold a strong place for the big stuff. When we simply change the lens with which we see things, the choices we make and the way that we parent shifts gently and easily. We are all doing the best we can and sometimes new knowledge is all we need to improve the capacity to love and care for our kids.

TOP TIPS

- ✓ Communication differences can create conflict between mums and sons.
- ✓ Respecting a boy's preferred communication style can make him feel safer and more loved.
- ✓ Boys have favourites (clothes, toys, stuff).
- ✓ Growth spurts really make a difference for up to two weeks.
- ✓ Boys have a serious affection for their penis.
- ✓ Boys often don't seem to notice the cold.
- ✓ Boys often learn by touching things.
- ✓ Boys' need for movement can make it difficult for them to sit for long periods of time – five minutes can seem like forever for some boys.

CHAPTER 6

Helping **OUR BOYS** to **BECOME** good **FRIENDS**

> "My mum introduced me to many new experiences as a child, especially encouraging me to get outside and be active as much as possible. I think it helped me develop a lifelong love of being outdoors, gardening and exercising." – Men's Survey 2017

In my life and my own childhood, through to my teaching career, my counselling experiences and to my parenting journey raising four sons to adulthood, I have learnt a thing or two about boy friendships. Thankfully, there are many men who have strong friendships with other men – some from childhood – and some from more recent times. However, many men do not have a significant friend in their life – just acquaintances. Some of the research into the high suicide rates of men aged 40-44 years of age is suggesting that profound loneliness is a contributing factor. This suggests some men struggle making, maintaining and nurturing friendships and, in particular, with other men.

Many boys have told me how they struggle to understand the nuances of being a good friend. Indeed, many have told me they find it confusing and often their attempts to show affection or desire for connection – with male or female friends – result in public embarrassment. Having a girl mate who is not your girlfriend is a huge asset in a boy's life especially through the tumultuous teen years. For boys in the early years, making friends with others can be challenging, and mums can help them to do this.

The research is significant in acknowledging that girls develop their capacity for effective communication well before boys. The ability to form friends and to keep friends can be a challenge for young boys right from the start.

For healthy human relationships to begin, there must be a way for two individuals to connect. I am still astounded by the ability of most little girls to have real conversations that explore their common interests, help them play games and negotiate, and to experience moments where they squeal with delight and enjoy mutual bonding. They also tend to have a better grasp on the non-visual cues of building rapport such as smiling, waving and hugging. They often express their love and affection for each other well before they're three and, yes, they can nag their parents endlessly in a bid to spend more time with their special friend.

Interestingly, there has been a lot of research on the origins and nature of same-sex friendships, but the most renowned study was in 2009 by the National Institute of Mental Health (NIMH) and Georgia State University with the use of fMRIs (Functional Magnetic Resonance Imaging). This was the first time scientists had looked at what actually happens inside the brains of children aged eight to 17 in response to potential friendship opportunities. The results showed a significant difference in the way boys and girls respond to the anticipation of making a friend. Various areas of girls' brains (areas associated with reward, hormone secretion, social learning, and subjective feelings) lit up with the prospect of a new friendship, while the boys' brains showed almost no activity and even, in some cases, decreased activity. There are many ways to interpret this information, and scientists are reluctant to pinpoint causation, but it's safe to say that there's a lot going on for girls in the face of friendships. It may also begin to explain why many boys struggle in the friendship world. It also suggests that we need to support young boys on this journey as best we can and not just assume that it will happen in a similar way to girl friendships. I think that creating the feel-good neurotransmitters in the brain happens more easily for girls, even before they connect with friends and siblings (when they are not fighting with them).

I believe that many angry boys in our early childhood settings are feeling really sad because they do not have a special friend, and when this anger is misinterpreted a young boy can feel hurt even more than he already is. My heart almost breaks when I am in an early childhood setting and I see a little boy being sanctioned for crying. I have heard a 4-year-old boy in a long day care environment told to "use his words" to explain his distress. This is something very few 4-year-old boys are developmentally able to do, and when he was not able to do this he was told to go outside because he was a sook!

Angry boys who have been unable to express vulnerable feelings can become very angry men also unable to express vulnerable feelings. Who wants to be friends with an angry little boy?

Dr William Pollack, author of *Real Boys: Rescuing Our Sons from the Myths of Boyhood* and one of the leading boy experts in the world, believes that while girls communicate more in seeking attachment, boys tend to develop attachment indirectly through activities or play. So, for boys to develop the same sense of bonding, they need to spend significant amounts of time playing with other boys. While 'play dates' are a reasonably recent happening, in days gone by there was more of an acceptance of children playing for hours either in each other's backyards or at sporting events that occurred frequently. I can remember the boys playing in our backyard with possibly a few other boy friends with rarely any conversation occurring. There was, however, a lot of strange noises that they seemed to all understand, and they would be having fabulous fun. Another reason why some of our boys are struggling with social anxiety is that these lengthy play times have disappeared, and recess and lunchtimes are much shorter than they used to be. Also, many boys are infatuated with technology and this diminishes the amount of time they are spending connecting to other boys in 'real' time.

As well as helping most boys discharge excess energy, the importance of play has another enormous value. It helps create feel-good neurochemicals which come from having unstructured fun with other boys who also prefer to follow the unspoken randomness of boy play. Often, boys engage in very vigorous play because they do tend to have more energy and physical strength. In the past, this play frequently included adventures, hunts and target practice. In contemporary Australia, as houses get bigger and backyards get smaller (as do play spaces in many early childhood settings), there is simply not the space for our boys to run freely or to indulge in adventuresome play. I have written a chapter about play where I explore much more about this.

In the chapter on ***"Boys are not tough"***, I shared the story of a little boy who at the end of the day at kindergarten – when he realised his best mate was leaving – ran up to him and punched him in the head. In no way did this boy mean to hurt his friend, however, at that moment his actions – which looked confusing to everybody else – were an attempt to express how much he liked his friend and how much he was going to miss him. Many boy experts write about 'aggression nurturance' and many of you who have more than one boy in your home will know there is an awful lot of wrestling, jumping on top of each other and throwing things at each other. Given that boys struggle with words to express their hunger to connect and have fun, these actions are often designed as ways of showing their love of play and, in a seemingly warped way, the affection they feel for each other. Of course, with siblings this can be quite short-lived! These forms of physical connections can sometimes lead to painful exchanges that we can interpret as being intentional, when often that was not the intention at all.

Coaching our boys about the difference between intentional and accidental hurting of others is another important part of helping them develop a healthy play code.

Boys who are lousy losers make lousy friends. Learning to lose well is another skill that many boys can struggle with, especially our feisty 'rooster' boys (but more on them in the next chapter). Playing many games with other children and grown-ups is an excellent way to build this emotional competence. Noughts and crosses, best-of-five shooting basketball hoops, card games and many other quick games such as these expose boys to losing. To identify what disappointment is and what it feels like is incredibly helpful for all children to learn. Again, I write more about this in my chapter on ***"Movement and play for little warriors"***.

Learning to lose well is especially important for our boys because it impacts their self-worth barometer so deeply. It helps when parents and educators can make mistakes and express disappointment in healthy ways, as this modelling is how many children learn how to make better choices in emotionally challenging situations.

One of the ways I have found that boys cope with failing, losing or being unsure of what is expected of them in any moment is to be silly or to try to be funny. Humour is a very powerful way that boys defuse big, ugly feelings rather than using anger or being aggressive. Yes, this also means they have a passion for cheeky conversations around bums, poo and farts – which can be quite annoying at times, especially for their mothers. Young boys can also often enjoy playing naked in quite an innocent fashion and can often laugh endlessly as they have a farting competition.

Sadly, with the combination of the screen-driven world and the easy accessibility of pornography, we can no longer trust that this innocent play will stay innocent. So, another coaching that our boys need is around body awareness and protective behaviour. They need to know that touching another individual's private parts is unacceptable – even with consent – when they are children. There are many excellent picture books you can access to teach this vital information to your boys and, while most little boys have never seen pornography, those who have can act out what they have seen without realising that it is not normal early sexual questioning and exploration. Dr Joe Tucci of the Australian Childhood Foundation has reported a massive increase in enquiries about inappropriate sexual play with children under five, especially of a penetrative nature. As I mentioned earlier, take a look at the 'Body Safety/Talking Sex' section on my website under 'Parenting Help' to find some resources, to help with this.

So often, a little boy's behaviour is their language. Sometimes it can be really annoying as they poke, prod and lean on their siblings and friends – especially in the back seat of the car. Sometimes this is merely a way of saying, "Come on, let's play," or "I would really like to connect". It can be helpful if mums can teach their sons how to ask for these things using a few words. This is one of the reasons why I suggest if you have mainly boys in your house that you have lots of cushions. They really do like throwing things and hitting targets, especially their siblings. Cushions are a lot less painful than wooden trucks. Common sense really?

We need to help our boys learn welcoming and farewelling strategies that avoid punching, kicking or simply jumping on top of someone. I suggest teaching them that a high five can be a welcoming strategy or possibly a secret handshake between mates. Other things that you may teach them are to smile and call out "hello" using the other child's name. It can be helpful if you role-play this lots because boys take a while to anchor new messages in their memory. Given the amount of time that boys now spend isolated with a screen, you will appreciate my concern that we actually need to do this more than ever in the real world so they can develop some social cues and confidence to be able to play well with other children. This is particularly crucial for our more non-verbal boys.

Many years ago, families were much bigger and so boys would be exposed to social interactions in their own home and nearby. Families are much smaller now and children are a lot less likely to be playing together in their neighbourhoods. It is a bit sad because these were great opportunities for all children to learn the social and emotional competencies that come from playing with other children in real time in the real world – without the looming presence of parents. Proximity to other children and the frequency of interaction with others are two things that helped our little boys come to understand the confusing social world that exists out there.

A great idea that I have seen happening with some groups of mums in Perth is to meet once a week in a park for an extended play after school. This is incredibly helpful for our boys as it gives them a sense of predictability and teaches them how to pick up some useful play strategies that enhance social and emotional connections with other children they know. It works really well when there are multi-ages present as well. This also helps you to develop stronger connections with a circle of parents or your tribe who all know your children – the good the bad and the ugly – and it creates a web of support. So often when boys behave badly without intention, they are punished or dealt with harshly without the time being taken to coach them into how to make better choices. A safe tribe helps boys develop feelings of trust and affection, and in such a safe place that is familiar, the play can become the essential teacher that it is meant to be.

> "I absolutely freaked out and questioned my parenting skills when my DB (3) challenged his DB brother (15mo) to a pirate sword fight, only instead of their pretend foam pirate swords, they attempted to use our steak knives. Fortunately I was able to intervene before the duel began and, needless to say, steak knives now live in high kitchen cupboards." — Freaked-out Mum

Mums have a huge part to play in helping boys develop caring bonds with their brothers. Some research suggests that siblings who play a lot together tend to stay positively connected as adults and I have found that to be true. Deliberately setting aside time and energy to encourage playing together — as messy, noisy and unpredictable as necessary — as often as possible, will definitely help your sons become mates and not just brothers. If they are able to share a common interest in an autonomous way, frequently the bonds of friendship tend to develop naturally. This means that sometimes you may need to let your sons sleep in a teepee in their bedroom or in a tent on the back lawn just for the fun of it. When you set up frequent family rituals that everyone enjoys together, such as movie nights, bush BBQs, long bike rides, building cubbies or going camping, you are setting up lots of possibilities for building genuine, caring bondedness between brothers. There will always be teasing and ribbing each other all the way through their lives and this is a little bit like the aggression nurturance I mentioned — a male way of showing they care. We still need to guide them about when they are going too far and to be kind. Even though your sons may argue and squabble at home, they tend to step in and protect their brothers if they are threatened outside the home. Genuine loyalty can only be formed after hours of having fun with their brothers.

Boys who struggle to find someone to play with at long day care or school can become angry and aggressive as a way to express their sadness and pain at feeling excluded. Even underneath the strongest rooster boy is an incredible sensitivity to being excluded and, in the early years, there is a window of enormous potential to teach and guide our young boys in how to create friends. I created an audio visualisation track to help children who struggle to make friends or for those who are too bossy. 'I Am a Good Friend' explores welcome and farewell strategies, while guiding children in how to be kind and caring to others.

We all want our children to transition well into school and having a friend, or more than one friend, who will be attending the same school will really help. Knowing no one, and being in an unfamiliar environment, will trigger his survival instincts and his behaviour and capacity to make new friends may become a source of conflict. The same can happen when transitioning to high school. Boys who have friends at the same school tend to transition better than those who do not. Indeed, boys who are transitioning into high school who have friends sharing the journey at the same school general definitely transition better. One of the main reasons why this is so is that having a friend and belonging lowers a boy's stress level, and he will have more energy to manage all the other things he needs to do. Again, self-regulation needs to be seen as a part of the friendship map of a boy's wellbeing.

Helping your son find someone else with a similar interest is one of the best ways to help him make a new friend in a new environment.

Again, many boys transitioning to high school find enormous comfort in gaming from the safety of their bedroom. Adolescence can be a lonely, bumpy ride without any friends in the real world, and it may be helpful if you need to, to talk to the school's student services team to see if they can help in some way with your son's transition.

It is the policy of many primary schools to try not to separate friends unless they feel they have become disruptive in class. However, some schools make mistakes when making these decisions. Many boys have told me of their heartbreak at being separated from a special boy mate at school. Many times these boys felt powerless to express how painful this was. Often, these boys became very angry and aggressive at home and it took quite some time for their parents to realise how destructive this choice had become. Indeed, one of my own sons had this experience and refused to return to that school. When questioned why he was separated from his two best mates, the school said they thought he had lots of friends.

Boys very rarely have a lot of friends because they are unable to sustain many friendships at once.

Please have conversations as soon as possible with your school regarding where they are placing your son if you have concerns.

"Bullies are not born, they are made." We've heard that before. Some feisty rooster children, our strong characters, have a tendency to be dominating and bossy, plus an insatiable hunger to win or be first or best! Some rooster children can also lack empathy. Children who become bullies have learnt how to be a bully from someone. I firmly believe the first five years of life are where we have to invest time, energy and compassion into helping all children develop empathy and an understanding of how to be fair and kind. There are many excellent picture books nowadays that can help parents to do this (you can find a list on my website if you search 'empathy'). Parents need to become proactive if they have an alpha boy who is over-exerting his power and, to be honest, this coaching is best done at home away from peers and teachers. I also recommend the resources from Best Programs 4 Kids, which demonstrate strategies and techniques that parents can teach their children at home to empower them to make helpful choices in social situations that are difficult and challenging. We cannot expect our schools to be able to resolve all difficult social interactions, especially bullying, because it is difficult to resolve human conflict in any large space. Sometimes, the issue might be childhood nastiness rather than bullying. In normal childhood friendships, there will be moments where children will be spontaneously mean or nasty — heck, this happens with siblings a lot — and we need to help our children know how to bounce back from these 'ouch' moments.

> "My mum has always been there for me to talk to whenever I have been down or low about where my life is at that point. She is the one I go to with the most important questions I'm not sure about."
> — Men's Survey 2017

I need to mention something that came up often in my counselling rooms as a reason why boy friendships disintegrated. We must stop this homophobic teasing of boy friendships that goes on. This can come from men as well as other boys and it needs to stop. Calling boys who are close friends 'gay' or worse has contaminated many boy friendships — and again it may have seemed an attempt at being funny without a planned intention to hurt — and yet it has.

> "My mother passed away last year and we had a fantastic relationship. She was married for 30 years to my dad but came out as a gay woman at age 60. She taught me that the path to true happiness was to be brave, choose love and live your truth." — Men's Survey 2017

My youngest son met his best mate at preschool. All the way through primary school they tended to spend alternate weekends at each other's houses and were rarely apart. These two boys are now 28 years of age and, even though they are both engaged to be married, this friendship is as strong as ever. They do remember having an argument once when they were nine and, for this reason, when they headed off to university they chose not to share a house in case they had another argument. This friendship has weathered some of life's toughest challenges — death, divorce, family adversity, health crises and lost grand finals. I wish all young boys could find a lifelong friend like this when they turned up to kindergarten.

As a mum, you can do many things to support your son to develop friendships.

- Prioritise having his boy friends spend significant amounts of time in your home especially in the early years from two to eight – preferably the same boys so they can develop authentic bonds of affection. Keep screens out of bounds at these times.
- Do everything you can to support their common interests – whether that be building go-karts, racing motorbikes, dancing, having a band, playing a sport or surfing.
- Know that food can be a bonding experience for boys – ensure many loaves of bread are always available.
- Have gentle conversations with your son about how to be a 'good' friend.
- Teach your son to say, "I'm sorry I hurt you" – even when he didn't mean to cause hurt.
- Help him to remember his friend's birthday and help him to know how to support his friend if an adverse event occurs in his friend's life.
- Ask warmly about his friends from time to time – don't interrogate, just ask.
- Express your affection for his friends.
- Always tell his friends they are welcome at your home and your door will always be open to them.
- Reassure your son that you will always love him no matter what happens in life.

As my four wonderful sons are now men, I am deeply grateful for all of their friends (and cousins) including their girl mates who have cared for and loved my boys over the years. My heart is filled with love when I meet their friends as adults and, even more so, when I meet their babies and children. It has not all been easy. They have been to the funerals of friends and family, and they have had friends endure accidents and suffer illnesses. To see how supportive they are as grown men to the friends they value – through thick and thin – makes me a very proud mum. To be honest, I call all of their boy mates 'my boys' and we do laugh about many of the imperfect 'bugger-up' moments that occurred as they went from boyhood to manhood. There are many, and probably many more that I don't know about. Mums have an enormous part to play in developing the capacity for their sons to make friends and keep friends.

Please help all little boys learn how to be good friends – don't leave it to chance. It is too important.

TOP TIPS

- ✓ Girls tend to find forming friendships much easier than boys.
- ✓ Boys need to spend a lot of time playing with the same boy to form a friendship.
- ✓ 'Aggression nurturance' can be misunderstood.
- ✓ Boys need space and time to play vigorously.
- ✓ Being excluded or being without a friend can trigger the primitive brain.
- ✓ Teach boys ways to be kind, fair and to have empathy.
- ✓ Mums need to teach boys ways of connecting with other children.
- ✓ Teach your son to say, "I'm sorry, I hurt you" – even when he never meant to cause hurt.
- ✓ Talk to your son about how to be a good friend.

CHAPTER SEVEN

Mothering **ROOSTER** sons and **LAMB** sons

"My mum instilled in me a belief of being humble and to take different paths from my peers." – Men's Survey 2017

One of the 'basics' of parenting wisdom that seems to have been lost in our information-rich world is that babies are born wired to be a certain temperament. I have termed the temperament spectrum, "the rooster and lamb continuum". Even though our children will be influenced by their biological temperament, which has come through on their DNA, their sense of needing to be loved, valued and also feel that they belong is exactly the same.

It can be helpful to see temperament on a spectrum that is not fixed, with our feisty roosters at one end and our gentle lambs at the other. Our job in our children's early years is to help them gravitate to somewhere in the middle of these two polar opposite positions. We want all our children to be able to access courage and assertiveness, without being dominant and narcissistic. We also want our roosters to be able to access empathy and compassion. So let's explore temperament and how we mums can help our boys grow in understanding and awareness of how to make better choices in their lives – eventually!

My best girlfriend had a son the year before I had my first son. He was a classic lamb as a baby – gentle, easy to soothe and, as a toddler, he even took himself off for a nap sometimes! Needless to say, I thought I was going to get a baby like that. I didn't. I got a rooster who, from the moment he landed on our planet, has had a very loud voice, a very strong sense of his own importance, has been fiercely competitive and very driven and, in many ways, has co-parented our family.

Roosters

You will know if you have a rooster boy firstly because he'll be a strong-willed, high-energy child from quite early in life. If most nights you collapse on your couch from exhaustion because of his high energy levels, you most likely have a rooster. I had two. My third son was a classic rooster who hated sleeping and who had unbelievable energy and attitude. It seemed from the minute he was born he was trying to chase his two older brothers and, if possible, outdo them at anything he could. Around the age of four, I realised the war I had with him about going to sleep was causing anxiety and conflict in the family. I knew it was time to negotiate a new deal. The new deal meant that provided he was quiet and did not use the toaster or any adult equipment that could cause harm, he could turn the lights off and go to bed when he was ready. Essentially, we had no more fights and he did turn the lights off in our house from that time on. He simply needed less sleep than his mum, dad or brothers. He loves the night hours and, unsurprisingly, now works in a finance investment company where he often does night trading from 9pm until 5am. When he was little, I knew he was managing our lights-out arrangement because he still bounced out of bed at six o'clock every morning with the same amount of energy as he had done before the new deal. He also liked being given the responsibility and freedom to take himself to bed. Some roosters benefit from having special 'deals' that show appreciation for their confidence and ability. When they encourage responsibility, such deals can have long-lasting, positive benefits.

Some characteristics of roosters are:

- They yearn for independence.
- They prefer to do things for themselves, often before you think they are capable (Gee, that makes them angry if you don't let them have a go).
- They yell louder.
- They are often very stubborn.
- They have so much energy and drive – they often exhaust you by 9am.
- They need less sleep – they often wake up very early, and are last to get to sleep.
- They question you and argue (even before they can speak!) over almost anything – food, clothes, toys, your parenting style – so many things!
- They want their own way and make their own choices.

- They can be manipulative and selfish.
- They think they are more important than anyone else.
- They always want to go first.
- They dislike having to share their things.
- They are impatient and impulsive.
- They learn fast and like to learn by making their own mistakes, not by what you tell them!
- They get frustrated and angry often.
- They ask a lot of questions.
- They can be entertainers — or 'party animals'.
- They sometimes explode and run away when they get angry — especially boys.
- They sometimes disappear at large public events because they like to explore on their own.
- They throw the most spectacular tantrums in the supermarket — they prefer a public audience.
- They will embarrass you in front of grandma, in-laws, teachers and doctors.
- They are very sensitive about what other people think and yet cover it behind a mask of "I don't care!"
- They will question almost every decision you make — Oh, I already said that — just wanted to make sure you know this is normal for a rooster!
- They quite enjoy change, challenge and adventure.
- They prefer spending time with older children and grown-ups.
- They will often make you feel you are the worst parent ever!

Roosters have a strong sense of their own importance, a powerful character, and that is possibly because they are meant to find a pathway in life where they can lead, change or drive others to a better way of being.

Parents who have a son with rooster tendencies need to invest time and energy to build the 'caring' traits of emotional awareness, empathy and understanding before age five or their children will tend to be dominant, bossy or even a bully. If a rooster child is unable to build those emotional competences, they can also become narcissistic and overly self-focused. This can manifest in a self-absorbed, overly important "I am all that matters" approach to life that often causes problems when building friendships. Boy roosters need to have power at any cost, which then becomes a hungry drive – this is not always a bad thing. If they begin a project or set themselves a target, they are often incredibly persistent and prepared to commit enormous amounts of energy to achieve that goal. Both my rooster sons have needed very little encouragement or support to strive to do their best, however, they have needed significant mum guidance around not being too confident, arrogant and insensitive. Roosters have a PhD in 'pester power', especially in the shopping centre. Seriously, taking rooster boys to shopping centres at any time of the day or night is asking for trouble and for everyone's wellbeing and sanity it is better if you can leave them with someone else while you go shopping. They have a really strong "I want" and "I need" drive that can emotionally cripple the strongest parent, and exhausted mums can cave in more easily than dads.

Rooster boys often love challenge, change and adventure.

They can get excited when new opportunities for adventure or challenge occur and they can get very frustrated if they have a lamb sibling who struggles with the very same opportunities. Often, rooster boys will turn a perfectly safe environment into one that has danger and risk and, to be honest, the occasional natural consequence of a wound or even a broken arm can be helpful for that alpha boy to realise that he is not invincible, and sometimes he will make poor choices and hurt himself.

Another annoying trait of roosters is they tend to question your parenting – often. "But why?" is a very common plea from a rooster's mouth. If you can, bear in mind that this questioning is not happening because your child wants to annoy you, but rather because they are seeking clarification about the choice you are making on their behalf. This can cause parents angst, especially if parents have expectations that their children are meant to do as they are told or are meant to be seen and not heard.

If you were raised with parents in the more traditional fashion, then you may struggle with a rooster boy who questions you a lot. It is helpful if you do not take this personally and you learn ways to stay calm because, ironically, if we want our children to grow up to value themselves and their choices, and to encourage self-assertiveness, then we need to value and respect their needs and wishes by *really* hearing them. That only happens when we *really* listen. Being heard – and I mean really being heard – is incredibly important for the rooster boy because it helps him feel connected, accepted and respected.

> **"The parenting task isn't to crush self-assertion, but to foster it so the child becomes a full-fledged person who knows their own mind and is unafraid to express their voice regardless of the fact it may rattle our ego and run contrary to our movie."**
>
> – Dr Shefali Tsabary, *Out of Control* (2014).

In my counselling rooms, I found there was an incredible emotional fragility underneath the rooster boy. No one likes failing, and rooster boys are particularly terrified of it because when they have been unable to activate their emotional self-worth barometer to the level they were hoping for, the pain cuts incredibly deeply. If they have multiple experiences that occur in a cluster, they can begin to question themselves, their ability and the capacity for people to love them. So, please, do not be fooled that your rooster does not feel because he does. His feelings are just not always released until a few days after the event, and he will most likely display some anger as a mask to cover up his vulnerable emotions.

One day, when I was working in rural suicide prevention programs, a very wise man said to me that the drive to be a warrior, or mammoth hunter as I have already explored, is especially strong in the alpha male. So when these types of male personalities have major experiences that can be perceived as failures, it can be easier for the warrior to die rather than to lose publicly. This is one of the reasons why mums need to work closely and compassionately with their rooster sons, especially before they are five when their temperamental tendencies may be less fixed.

Top tips for mothering rooster boys:

- Focus on building positive attachment and a strong heart connection.
- Avoid shouting, shaming or criticising roosters, as they will learn how to do this to others.
- As they often get into trouble by pushing boundaries, ensure you deeply reassure them that you love them when you have moments of connection, such as at bedtime.

"Don't sweat the small stuff" is a good motto for parents of roosters. Make sure you hold firm boundaries for the big stuff – safety near roads, aggression towards siblings and other children, and healthy participation in chores like everyone else.

- Play card games and memory games that build their capacity to wait, to take turns and to learn to lose without being too dramatic.
- Really listen to your rooster when he wants to tell you how he thinks things could be – being heard is incredibly important to roosters.
- Be mindful of avoiding conflict with your rooster when either of you are angry, tired or exhausted. Allow cooling-off time before negotiating restorative justice or discipline after a conflict.
- Work out what thing – either an activity, toy or special privilege – when removed, will show your rooster that you are the parent and they are the child, and that there are unpleasant consequences for really inappropriate behaviour. Tough love can be hard – however without a sign of a significant consequence, our roosters will see that as a power grab and they will know they can beat you! Think this through carefully because you only want to do it rarely and remember, make sure he can still feel loved while the tough love is happening.
- Give him small opportunities to develop autonomy or independence that make him feel important. Let him be the only child who collects the eggs, the mail, gets himself a snack or maybe uses the camera, Dad's telescope or a technological gadget that no one else in the family can use. One family I know encouraged their rooster to breed ducks and hens – it engaged him for hours – and the interaction between him and his feathered friends helped him foster plenty of patience and consideration for others.
- Rooster boys of school age can benefit from team games and some individual sports like swimming, BMX, pony club and cross-country running. This helps build a more healthy understanding of competitiveness and also helps discharge excessive levels of energy.
- The arts are another powerful way of expelling energy and keeping rooster boys positively occupied – dance, drama, music, visual arts and craft are all excellent. This also showcases activities where competition with others is not the main purpose.
- Make time to help your rooster build his emotional intelligence, especially patience, calmness and empathy.
- Avoid your rooster sons becoming dependent on (or addicted to) competitive online games – they miss the necessary social learning that is gained when playing with others.

- Nature can be a powerful source of sustenance and calmness for roosters – bike riding, cubby building, skateboarding, gardening, sailing and fishing have all been used by parents to keep their high-energy children active and interacting with others and their world.
- Roosters benefit from having other significant adult relationships where they can spend time and give their parents a much-needed rest! Grandparents, aunties, uncles and non-family people like neighbours or the parents of their friends can all offer respite.
- Be careful not to drown boy roosters with too many instructions and explanations as this often makes them very frustrated and annoyed.
- Please avoid repeating yourself as this also frustrates the rooster boy.
- If you have a really exhausting and full-on rooster lad who often completely overwhelms you, it is really important to cultivate another significant adult ally relationship so you can have regular respite from their intensity.
- Get a puppy, kitten or guinea pig for your rooster boy so he can learn how to be kind and gentle.
- Encourage him to be your 'special' helper sometimes.

Many boy roosters have low empathy, or I am sure some of you will think none at all. Read them stories that encourage building an understanding of empathy and kindness from an early age – birth is probably the best age to start. Again, I have some great lists of books on my website ... just search 'empathy' and 'kindness'.

Boys tend to learn best from experience. Many of you who have attended my seminars will know I recommend getting a guinea pig when your child is between two and four. If they have never held anything quite so small and gentle, many rooster children can try to squeeze the guts out of the guinea pig. That is a natural response for a small child who has never held something so small before. This is an opportunity for us to guide them and show them how to be gentle, how to pat very gently and how to take care of that little creature. The neuroplasticity of the brain means you would need to keep an eye on that little guinea pig and your toddler until he has really come to understand what 'gentle' means. And seriously, with a rooster boy, I would still keep a close eye on him and the guinea pig because there is a curious part of him that does want to know if you can squeeze its guts out!

When my number three son arrived, he did so in a hurry. Originally unplanned, he eventually made his appearance on our earth on 31 October, which is Halloween. With two older brothers, he very quickly became a force to be reckoned with and he was very keen to show his eldest brother, also a rooster, that he was just as good as he was!

He took quite some time to learn compassion, gentleness and humility, however, he has all those things in bucketloads today as an incredibly loving and patient father and husband. Some days I shake my head wondering if my memory could possibly be correct – especially my memories of my boys and their pet guinea pigs. One afternoon recently, while sitting with my grown-up number three son and watching him be the most gentle and loving daddy imaginable, I had a conversation about those guinea pigs. I suggested to him that it was lucky we had four guinea pigs, as it was the fourth guinea pig that really created the magic which helped shape him and allowed him to grow into such a gentle, loving dad. He looked at me with his one-eyebrow-raised expression – a mannerism he used on me many times in his childhood. Essentially it means WTH? I went on to explain that he never cried when the first guinea pig died. He never cried when the second guinea pig died. He never cried when the third guinea pig died. But when the fourth guinea pig died, he was really upset and he cried for ages in his bedroom. So, hang in there with your rooster boy and know that as a mum you are the main person who can guide him into the gentler part of his nature – the part of his being that is hiding under that great 'warrior' mask. And, yes, there is hope that your strong, often fearless, rooster son can grow up to be a tender, loving man.

Meg Meeker, in her book *Strong Mothers, Strong Sons: Lessons mothers need to raise extraordinary men*, argues that mums of sons need to be strong. And they almost need to be the strongest for their rooster sons. She writes:

"Strong-willed boys need stronger-willed mothers."

Holding strong boundaries and investing time and energy into building a moral code and emotional competence needs a strong, committed mother. Ironically boys feel safer when they know there are boundaries and consequences. Boys will need these to be constantly reaffirmed in their lives, however, when mothers do it with warm discipline, rather than punitive shame-based discipline, their rooster sons can truly grow into caring, good men.

Often, it is the boy roosters who benefit the most from the quiet chats in the bath, or the pillow talks in the dark because, in some ways, it is like they are able to take that tough rooster mask off for a few moments.

"My mum gave me space and freedom as a kid." – Men's Survey 2017

Winning at all costs

Some of the rooster boys I have worked with have told me that the drive to win has sometimes been so great, it has also driven them to cheat. So, you may encounter moments in your son's childhood when he will cheat to win. These could be great opportunities for you to help your son develop empathy and to reassure him that while winning is important, you simply can't always be the winner. Being able to teach your son how to be a good loser is incredibly important as well. Role-play with him and show him how to approach the other person who has won and shake their hand and congratulate them. Fortunately, there are many wonderful videos on YouTube that show grown men doing this in highly competitive situations. What is really important when you catch your son cheating is that you don't shame him, hurt him or make fun of him. That is, indeed, the fastest way to create a mother wound that will last for life.

Sometimes, it takes a lot for a rooster lad to accept that he can fail. There was once a DB (10) who came home and announced to his mum that he was going to win the high jump at the school sports day. His mum tried to gently prepare him for the reality that his chances of winning the high jump were not very good given that he hadn't practised, and that he was 30cm shorter than his friend who was also competing. His mum tried again by reminding him that all the athletic men on both sides of his family had not been high-jumpers – they had been swimmers, footballers and basketballers. He was still not convinced. On the day of the sports carnival, he remained certain that he was going to win the high jump. He was actually knocked out in the first round because of all the reasons his mother had already explained. Absolutely devastated, he ran to the family car and hid in the back where he sobbed his heart out. His mother had a strong urge to go and comfort him but fortunately, from somewhere deep and wise within her heart, she realised that her rooster son – her overly confident, sometimes arrogant rooster son – was in the process of learning humility. So, rather than leap into the car and soothe him, she gave him some time to really feel the emotions that came with being beaten so easily. After 15 minutes, she knocked on the car window and made a gesture to check if it was OK for her to come inside. By then her son had expressed many of his big, ugly feelings, and he welcomed her comforting arms and the fact that she sat with him without saying a word. There is one other part to this story that explains why this DB was particularly shattered – one of the boys who was competing in the event only had one leg because he had been born that way. This lad came from a family of serious athletes, and today is a proud Paralympian who competes for Australia. What are the chances that the universe lined up this experience for this rooster boy so he could learn some humility and grace that could temper his burning desire to always be the winner?

So, mums, if your rooster son has a major experience of failure, especially in the public domain, firstly move him somewhere private as quickly as possible and then simply allow him to sit with the experience, and to feel it for as long as he needs. If you comfort too soon he will cry even more and that will make him feel even more of a failure. If you try and rationalise the loss you will make him very angry. Just let him be and make sure that no one else intrudes on this private time, while letting him know you're there. In time, he will move himself through the big, ugly feelings he is experiencing.

> *Big emotions create energy in the body and they create an intensity that is quite uncomfortable, especially for our confused boys.*

His self-worth barometer has been shattered and it does take him time to rebuild it and, despite your loving intentions, he needs to be the one to rebuild his own sense of self-worth. Yes, I know that does sound counterintuitive to a loving mum, however, you need to trust me on this one. In the chapter on ***"When boys muck up"***, I will explore other ways to help your boys rebuild their sense of self.

Please remember that temperament does not have to be destiny – it is a tendency. In families there will be a tendency to have a mix of roosters and lambs and, statistically, firstborns have a much higher chance of being roosters. Many roosters who are firstborn can struggle with a mum who is a micromanager and who wants to govern and direct everything about her son's life. Having a lack of freedom and autonomy can create enormous moments of anger and rage in little boys. However, by improving your communication with him, and the way that you see how he views the world, things can improve quite quickly with just a few changes.

> "My mum did things for me instead of letting me decide for myself, and succeed or fail on my own." – Men's Survey 2017

There was once a rooster DB (12) whose relationship with his mum had started to become difficult because he was communicating with negative words and a negative attitude. As the two had a good relationship, the mum found some quiet time, after a really good dinner, when she questioned him gently about why they weren't getting along as well as they had before. Her son replied that he was becoming annoyed because she was trying to manipulate him. In a wise move, this mum asked her son to give her a couple of very specific examples of what he meant. To her surprise he was correct. She had been trying to manipulate her rooster son to do things that she wanted him to do rather than allowing him to make his own decisions. With humility, she agreed with him and asked how she could fix it. He said quite simply, "I need you to let me make my own decisions". The mum reminded him he was only 12. He said he still felt he was capable. The mum then went on to explain that when you make decisions there are always consequences – sometimes they are good and sometimes they aren't. She asked him if he was prepared to accept the consequences of his choices and he agreed. He also told his mum that if he needed her help or advice, he would ask for it, and he would prefer if she didn't offer it unless he asked for it. She agreed. That young lad has made every decision in his life from that moment on and their relationship returned to the same respectful and warm place it had been before. And, yes, there were times he came and asked for her advice. He has seldom made a poor decision and, indeed, he has made some exceptional decisions that required him to display great maturity for his age.

> "For Mother's Day this year I went to have my relaxation bath with lavender bath bombs my DB (3) son made me at daycare ... turned on some relaxation music, poured a glass of wine ... and then he hijacks my bath, pees on me and makes me play dinosaurs. Raaaarrr. What better way to end Mother's Day!" — Pee-and-lavender-bath-anyone? Mum

If you have two adolescent rooster boys in a family, things can get very interesting and even more challenging. There will be massive surges of testosterone which almost intensifies the warriors within our sons, particularly our rooster sons. Indeed, when this was at its most intense in my household when the eldest DB was 16 and the youngest rooster was 13, I would encourage one of them to go and stay at a friend's house most weekends. This helped reduce the opportunities available for the roosters to compulsively try to outdo each other. I also found that when both roosters had a friend stay over at our place on the weekends, it helped diminish the simmering conflict between them.

When the boys were older they actually lived together for five years while attending university and they then lived together for a further couple of years when they moved to Sydney. Adolescence is a volatile time and your boys will need support to manage their intense emotions and the unique stressors of this time of life. Mums have a huge role to play in protecting rooster boys from themselves. Yes, you will have to practise tough love with your rooster sons at times and you will find it difficult, however, teaching them that there are boundaries that are not negotiable is essential in preparing them for life later. Remember kindness can work on roosters too.

When I look back over my parenting years when the boys were home, I notice that I never had to be mean to my lamb sons. They never pushed the boundaries or deliberately did things to test their power. My now adult rooster sons take great delight in telling me about my 'mean' moments – one complained at my 50th birthday that I was a tough mum at times. His worst punishment was he wasn't allowed dessert for two weeks for a repeated misdemeanour – and given that he was such a dessert lover they must've been the longest two weeks of his life! There will be times that we have to practise tough love for our rooster sons, and we can do that without crushing their incredible spirits and breaking the hearts.

Our rooster boys need a lot of help to develop the emotional and social competences to be caring human beings. Helping them learn to lose and be more emotionally buoyant are really important strengths that must be taught as a priority before they are five. If you invest heavily in this window, then your boisterous, highly energetic, often totally insensitive little rooster boy will also thrive and grow up to be a loving, patient man who will enjoy his relationships immeasurably better.

"My mum misunderstood my boyhood sense of wonder and adventure as being difficult and misbehaviour." – Men's Survey 2017

Lambs

Lambs are typically quieter, more patient, more accommodating and generally more content with life. As babies and toddlers, lambs are delightful and they make you look like a fabulous parent. It is so easy to fall in love with a boy lamb because he seldom causes you any angst or stress.

Some characteristics of lambs are:

- They love sleeping.
- They often dislike noise and too much stimulation.
- They are even more sensitive to being sanctioned or growled at.
- They get distressed easily when shouted at.
- They may keep a comforter like a blanket or teddy well into childhood.
- They quite like solo time.

- They are very patient and can happily wait while roosters go first!
- They get distressed easily by strange people, places and things.
- They prefer routines and predictability.
- They prefer small numbers of children to play with.
- They tend to take longer to adjust to change.
- They can take longer to warm up in social settings, even ones they are familiar with like playgroup.
- They withdraw when they feel frightened.
- They often hide in their bed or a cupboard when scared.
- They can easily be bullied or bossed around by roosters.
- They can struggle with social dislocation more than roosters, e.g. new teachers, schools or change of home or relationship.
- They can lack assertiveness and can be slow at making decisions.
- They can struggle with large social situations and often will avoid them!
- They can struggle with shyness.

Lambs can have a tendency to be 'slow to warm' in social situations. This means that even with people they know, they can take a while to be comfortable interacting. I have a very special great-nephew who is a gentle lad. When he was a much younger boy, I observed that whenever I visited, even if I stayed overnight, that on first seeing me he would often hide behind his mum or move away to hide behind a couch. When I smiled at him or winked and said, "Hello", I allowed him to make the moves of connection. Once he had warmed up, he was very happy to play with me and would allow me to hold him.

Forcing children, especially boys, to connect or interact before they have 'warmed up' can be quite stressful for them and it can often make them even more fearful in the future. The same goes for all shy children – slowly building their confidence by respecting their sensitive nature is the best way to go.

There was once a DB (3) who was with his family on an Easter holiday. At the conclusion of the Easter egg hunt, this gentle lamb came up to his mum and said: "I have three eggs and I only needed one". Awww. Needless to say, his rooster brother soon sorted that problem out by taking them off him!

Another example of the sensitivity of our boy lambs comes from a Year One teacher. She had taken a lesson about things in the world that may be a cause for concern because she wanted to widen the students' perceptions of the world and being part of a global community. Most of the students wrote down just one issue, like, 'We need to save the whales!' She said that one of her beautiful boy lambs DB (6) had written quite a comprehensive list that included: saving the whales, stopping the bushfires, helping the starving children, stopping people getting cancer, helping the koalas not get sick, giving more money to the poor and stopping people who hit children. This is the thoughtful capacity of a little lamb boy and one of the reasons why we need to protect them from watching the news, because they can absorb the world's disasters and feel incredibly powerless to help.

As lambs often lack personal courage and confidence, it is important for parents to help build these emotional competences while they are under five, if possible. Encouraging them to take risks in their play and learning, and ensuring that you build their capacity to be more assertive and capable socially, can really help our lambs become stronger and more resilient. Never force a lamb to do something they are reluctant to do. This can scar them for life.

> "I wish my mum hadn't made me do competitive sports as a child, because I hated it." – Men's Survey 2017

Even though the role of temperament has a big influence on parenting choices, it is helpful to think of the continuum as a guide to what competences or qualities children need to develop in order to be a blend of both rooster and lamb traits. In families, roosters and lambs can help each other – the roosters can assist to toughen up the sensitive lambs, and the lambs help to build sensitivity and gentleness in the roosters.

> *Sibling rivalry is Mother Nature's way of softening roosters and strengthening lambs.*

Do not be fooled that lambs are by nature weak just because they are sensitive. I have found that, with positive parenting and opportunities to develop mastery, lambs can be very determined and capable as they grow older. Also, not all roosters are selfish and insensitive – they can become very thoughtful.

One mum of three sons – two roosters and a lamb – told me the biggest difference she had noticed was that if her rooster sons had been given a certificate or award at school, they quite simply wanted to tell the world. They would ring aunties, uncles and grandparents to tell them the good news. Actually, they would tell the checkout lady in the supermarket as well about how great they had done. She said there were times when she was cleaning out her lamb son's school bag at the end of term and she would find a crumpled certificate that her son had forgotten to tell her about. Lamb sons do not need to do the same chest banging that rooster sons do. However, they are quietly proud of their achievements and their self-worth barometer does get the same pick-me-up when they do well.

> "I wish my mum had not ignored my feelings." – Men's Survey 2017

Lamb sons can still be courageous and brave in certain situations that find the rooster son being suddenly more cautious. I have seen this a number of times in my own family and also on school camps. Whether it be rock climbing, jumping off a height into the water or surfing, there were so many times when the quieter lamb boy would tackle a risky situation more quickly and more successfully.

Even today, as grown men, my number two lamb still surfs bigger waves than his rooster brothers. So, don't be fooled into thinking your gentle son will grow up to be a wimp.

Mums of boys need to be careful they don't favour their lamb sons, because it is very easy to do. You will seldom have loud conversations or arguments with your lamb. He automatically helps around home and, at a much earlier age, is able to take washing off the line without the pegs still attached! He will be the son who notices when you seem a little stressed and he will make you a cup of tea without being asked. Seriously, it is really hard to let your lamb son leave home because he brings so much joy and comfort to you and so little angst. Holding on too hard and too long with your lamb son can make him struggle to walk over the bridge to becoming a man.

Top tips for mothering lamb sons:

- Focus on building positive attachment and practise gentle love.
- Avoid shouting, shaming or criticising lambs as they can be crushed easily.
- Avoid comparing them to other rooster children, whether siblings or friends.
- Ensure you spend extra time building comforting patterns when they are babies and toddlers – soothing lullabies, night lights, teddy bears, blankets, calming music, massage and bedtime rituals.
- Create opportunities to develop mastery at small things to gradually build their self-confidence.

- Keep their world predictable with regular routines.
- Affirm and encourage the caring side of their nature while teaching them to be careful not to be used by others.
- Explain that assertiveness is different to aggression.
- Affirm that lambs are worthy and deserving of love, affection and acceptance just the same as roosters.
- Gradually expose them to social functions in small doses, however, when they have had enough, respect their needs and take them home to safety.
- Avoid large groups of similarly aged children until they are four or five and feeling braver.
- Reassure them often that you are beside them and that when you leave them for a time that you ARE coming back.
- Nurture close friendships with a small group of same-age children and have them over to play at your house until your lamb builds the courage to play at other people's houses.
- Avoid sleepovers until they feel ready – for some it can be around eight or 10 before they are ready.
- Avoid forcing them to do things when they hesitate – encourage and be enthusiastic, and tell them, "You will be able to do this when you are ready".
- Connect deeply to nature – many lambs are serious lovers of animals and nature.
- Allow them their own space, when they want. Many lambs have a secret, quiet place they love to visit when things get tough, tiring or confusing.
- Teach them how to take deep breaths when they feel anxious.
- Encourage them to have conversations with you – even if it is when you are in the toilet – as they often find it hard to be heard when there are roosters around.
- As they have less energy than roosters, encourage them to have rest times or quiet space to themselves before going out to social situations. This helps them build their energy reserves.
- Ensure lambs get plenty of sleep.
- Teach them relaxation strategies to help them when they feel anxious and stressed.

Often children who are born with a lamb temperament have a deep-seated desire to help others, whether animals or people. They have a natural degree of empathy from an early age and can sometimes become worried when things happen, even on the other side of the world. Lambs can often have an irrational fear about the safety of their parents or people they love. It is important to be mindful of the TV programs that lambs are exposed to. They are easily scared and sometimes these moments of terror can be etched into their mind forever. I worked with an 8-year-old lamb boy many years ago who, while on a sleepover, saw the scary movie *Terminator*. It took many months of counselling before he was able to sleep at night without night terrors or nightmares. Even though a 5-year-old child may want to watch a *Harry Potter* movie with Dad, there is a chance that even rooster children, particularly boys, can experience a damaging moment of intense fear. Even some PG films have scary scenes – think of the sharks in *Finding Nemo* – and it can help to simply offer your children a blanket at the beginning of every film. If they feel scared, suggest they close their eyes or hide under the blanket. Often these scary scenes are a tiny part of an entertaining child's film. Whenever we watched movies together as a family, my two lamb sons and I always had a blanket close at hand to hide under when things got scary.

I am really concerned that many of our lamb boys are seeing things that are distressing them online. Not only is that unexpected pornography, it is senseless violence or one of their own favourite TV programs that has been altered by some sick person somewhere in the world to make it incredibly threatening and scary to our precious children. Many little lamb boys find solace in their childhood by being outside in Mother Nature and, nowadays, fewer and fewer of our children have that opportunity. While watching other children play Minecraft on YouTube is not in any way going to cause your lamb boy concern, he is just one click away from accidentally seeing something that can steal his innocence for life, so do your best to monitor what's happening and tell him he should talk to you if he does see something the freaks him out.

If you have a very sensitive lamb aged between four and 10, there are two free audio downloads on my website that have been a great help to many children. 'Safe 'N Sound' and 'Sleepytime' both use the metaphor of an enormous protective character to help children feel safe in our world.

It does not matter what temperament your child has, the ability to have a calm, harmonious home environment is determined by the loving connection that children feel from their parents and the communication that occurs between everyone.

> *This is a salient reminder that the relationship you have with your children is the greatest protector you can give them in our crazy world.*

We need to work hard to avoid the digital abandonment phenomena that is happening, which is where children know their parents are in the house not far away, however, they are not present because they are distracted by their smartphones or other devices.

Temperament definitely influences our relationships with our precious boys. I found that because I was a rooster, I was able to understand my rooster boys, especially when they were being driven towards a goal or striving for something. I could support them possibly better than I could my lamb boys when they were resisting 'having a go'. So, mums, keep in mind that your temperament can also influence the relationship you have with your sons. Some rooster mums and rooster sons have an amazing war going on that can make it really difficult to build the heart bridges that make your son feel loved. So, before we finish this chapter, it may be helpful to explore how we can communicate compassionately with our children regardless of the temperaments that are present in our homes.

> "My boys perfectly illustrated the difference between roosters and lambs for me recently. They each had a password I had to guess before they would let me pass. My rooster DB (3)'s was 'I am the best!' and my lamb DB (6)'s was 'Namaste'. Love them to bits!" — One Lucky Mum

Caring communication between mums and sons

Communication seems such a simple thing to do, however poor communication is one of the key factors underlying conflict in our families. We simply misunderstand each other. For young children, this happens a lot because of their inability to respond verbally. I remember getting quite a shock when I asked my 10-month-old firstborn to take his towel into the bathroom instead of letting Mummy do it. He was walking by this stage. Sometime later when I went into the bathroom, I was staggered to find his towel there. So, even though our young children are unable to communicate verbally for quite some time, we need to remember that babies and toddlers are constantly downloading the cues and nuances of communication, probably before birth — especially our boys. What you demonstrate and model will become their template for communicating with each other later.

It is our job as mums to create safe boundaries for our boys so that we can protect them. However, in our fear-driven world, many mums are fearful of almost anything that could possibly cause pain and sometimes, in their desire to keep their sons safe, they may actually be encouraging them to do the opposite.

Our brain is wired to zone out things that we hear often and that's one of the reasons why nagging is quite unsuccessful, especially with boys.

This means that often well-meaning mums are telling their boys "don't" a lot. We spend so much time telling our young children what they can't do, rather than investing our time and energy in showing them what they can do safely. I was once visiting a family when the 3-year-old son began to climb on the back of the couch. I was intrigued with his mum's response:

"John stop that immediately or you will fall over the back of the couch and you will land on the tiles and your head will split open and your brains will come out – now get off!"

Needless to say the boy just kept climbing – I am sure he has heard those words many times before. Also, as a curious 3-year-old, he has no comprehension of danger and could be quite fascinated with the idea of seeing his own brains!

We also need to keep in mind that being physically active by climbing, jumping, pushing, and skidding on the floor are all biologically important movements for children, especially young boys. Yes, they may accidentally break your large-screen TV by hitting it with the toy hammer because they're simply practising hitting and have no intention to cause any damage. With boy toddlers, it's important to remain mindful, remembering to see the world through their eyes and putting things as far out of their reach as possible until this developmental stage is over. Punishing a little boy for jumping up and down on your beautiful couch when his mind and his body needs him to be jumping is unhelpful for your son. If he is in his jumping stage, you need to find somewhere he can do that often and frequently until that developmental stage has passed. And it will pass.

If you are struggling with a certain form of negative behaviour from your son, take some time to consider what that behaviour might mean for your child and then ask what would be the polar, positive opposite of that behaviour. Then, in a calm and encouraging voice, ask your son to consider doing something different and give him some suggestions.

Let's explore something that has come up a number of times for mothers of sons.

A DB (3) is playing in a sandpit with a number of other toddlers. He is playing with a truck and he is really enjoying playing with that truck. A little girl comes over and sits on his truck so he is unable to play with it and, out of frustration, he bites her. Now, no one wants their child, boy or girl, to become a people-eater! Also, biting is quite common in toddlers for lots of different reasons. From where the little boy is sitting when he bit the girl, she did get off his truck and so his needs were met. So often I see little boys in particular punished for such behaviour, and they are often separated from their peers by being sent to a naughty chair or given 'time-out' by themselves. Given what we now know about the sensitive emotional self-worth barometer, that young boy will be feeling confused and, in time, may feel sad or angry. In the heat of the moment he can be confused about why he is being punished because the little girl definitely got off his truck when he bit her.

Little boys are incapable of working out a better choice as an alternative course of action should the same situation arise again. This early window of child development is where mums of sons can make a huge difference. This is the sort of situation when the mum needs to be the voice for her son and help him decode the experience, and explain why biting is not acceptable without shaming or hurting him. Her next important job is to give him some suggestions on what to do and how to cope next time. She may teach him to put his hands up and say "no" – she could even add "off". She will practise that a few times with him and the next time he is in the same situation, before he gets out of the car or leaves his mum's side, she will remind him again about how to say "no" using his voice and his hands. Again, you do not need to hurt little boys to improve the choices that they make.

> "My adolescence coincided with the hardest years of my mother's life and, for a time, she became, through stress and fear, sharp-tongued and overly critical. The unfair criticism didn't end until I was nearly out of college, and I confronted her about it. It stopped immediately, and forever, with one conversation." – Men's Survey 2017

As I said earlier, boys hear "don't" an enormous number of times in our homes and early childhood settings! What happens when I ask you, "Don't think of a blue elephant"? This is a simple example to show you that when we use 'not' or 'don't', which are non-literal words, they simply don't register in a child's mind.

Ensuring that we use language that is 'specific' really helps our children understand our expectations around their behaviour. Rooster boys are constantly seeking power and position, and they will challenge any unreasonable requests that you make that threaten this for them. Susan Stiffelman, in her excellent book, *Parenting Without Power Struggles*, suggests that parents need to be the "captains of the ship". This means that they are in charge as a parent, which is not the same as being in control. This differentiation can be really helpful when mothering strong sons and I encourage you to read Susan's book, as it can be such a useful support to learn different strategies about how to parent without over-controlling.

Another helpful method I found for when boys are little and we are trying to correct their behaviour and the choices they are making — quite impulsively — is to practice the art of showing rather than telling. In a way, that is what I just described with the boy in the sandpit — his mum showed him a different way to behave in that moment. If you are in a coffee shop and your son has run out of dopamine and so now is standing on his chair instead of sitting, rather than repeating yourself endlessly about putting his bottom back on the seat, I encourage you to try this innovative technique instead. Stand quietly and walk behind your son and gently uncurl his legs and place his bottom back on the seat, then gently lean over and kiss him on the forehead or stroke his back. You have shown him what you want him to do. Remember, young boys don't respond to verbal dialogue the same way that girls do, especially when we repeat ourselves. In the heat of the moment, that can sound something like this:

"David that is the third time I've asked you to put your bottom back on the seat! Now do as you are told. If you don't do what I have told you to do I will put you in the car and lock the doors. I will never bring you to the coffee shop ever again. Now stop it and put your bottom on the seat. David, do it now. Don't stand up on the seat. David I need you to put your bottom on the seat now or we're going home right away before you get your milkshake ... blah blah blah ..."

David is not listening because he can see better when he stands on the chair and it is more fun standing on the chair than sitting on the chair so his single focus is certainly not on what's coming out of his mum's mouth. How quickly do we resort to threats and often bribes in the heat of the moment with our boys? Don't worry, I have been there, I have that T-shirt!

Take another example. Your son is playing with his food at the table while your family is having dinner. I would suggest to him twice that he might stop playing with his food and then I would quietly reach across the dining table and remove his plate, place it down next to you, and then return to eating without saying a word. You will have your son's attention. He may even ask you why you did that. Calmly and quietly you are able to ask him if he is ready to eat his dinner properly, in which case you will return his plate with his food to him.

So, remember that sometimes showing alternative behaviour choices through your calm and grounded actions, can help your son learn how to make better choices without being shouted at or shamed.

Being heard

Just because our boys have a tendency to talk less as well as an inability to understand too many words that are spoken at once, does not mean they don't have the same fundamental need to be heard. If you are a mum of a son you will know that quite often he will run in and have a chat with you while you are on the toilet having a poo or while you are in the bath. Maybe he intuitively knows that you are fully present and that the chances of him being heard are much higher when you are in either of those places.

Here are some phrases you might use to let your son know you are really hearing him:

- Let me put this down so I can give you my full attention.
- Wait a second while I turn off the TV/radio/computer, so I can really hear you.
- Let's have some time together now.
- What shall we do when we have our time together tomorrow afternoon?
- So, what you mean is ...
- Tell me more about this.
- Awwww ... really?
- Wow that's interesting ...
- Let me see if I understand you so far ...
- That must have been ... for you ...
- Are you open to some feedback from me?
- And all sorts of encouraging sounds that are not words – oh, ah, duh ...

To communicate that you are really listening to your son, use your body language: kneel in front of him as he speaks, lean in closer, put your head in your hands or sit really close to him.

Remember to keep your mouth closed and ears, eyes and heart open – being fully present – and bring in your sense of humour. Boys have a tendency to give you a tiny bit of information to start with, just to test the waters of whether you really will listen. My sons would often chat to me while I was having a bath, especially before they became adolescents. My lamb sons continued to see that time as a great chance to have a good 'mum chat' during adolescence and beyond. On a family holiday a couple of years ago my DB (26) came in while I was soaking in the bath, sat on the edge of the tub and started talking. It was one of those slow and lingering chats about a whole range of things and it was really a very special catch-up. When he left the bathroom, the only person who felt remotely uncomfortable was me and that was mainly because I didn't have a flannel. He saw our exchange as a perfectly normal, comfortable opportunity to have some time with his mum without anybody else around – just like he had done as a little boy.

So, mums, make sure you are catchable.

Learn to read the non-verbal cues indicating that your son wants to have a chat with you without anyone else around. Sometimes they kind of hang around the kitchen while you are cooking or they come in and out while you're doing some work on the computer. Learn to be catchable and learn how to listen deeply because so often it is not just what your son says, but what he doesn't say that is also equally important.

Another way to help boys communicate is to do something physical with them like walk the dog, shoot some hoops, go for a ride on a bike or cook together. When boys are busy doing, it seems to make it easier for them to talk.

An interesting thing I have observed with boys is that they prefer not to enjoy face-to-face communication, but seem to feel more comfortable when they're at a 45° or 90° angle to you, and this is one of the reasons why chats in the car can be really worthwhile. Women love face-to-face, eyeball-to-eyeball and so often you can threaten your son by trying to do the same thing, especially around a topic he is finding difficult to discuss. Now is a good time to appreciate why pillow chats in the dark can be such a fabulous way to talk about topics he may feel uncomfortable with, embarrassed about, or really sad about. The darkness gives him somewhere to hide so he can dive deeper into his emotional world without being seen and yet while still being heard.

Often when I was working as a full-time counsellor, mums would tell me they had booked their son in to see me and he had told them that he wouldn't say a word. Funny, because with a considered effort at building rapport, I found boys could be very forthcoming at sharing things with me. There were times when a boy, on leaving my office, would ask if he could book another appointment and his mother's mouth would drop open in surprise.

We can find it difficult as mums to let our boys open up to us because we are so dependent on long, intense conversations and they are our preference, but not necessarily our boys' preferred mode of sharing. We must remember that these conversations are quite rare with our boys and men, and yet they are possible.

Asking for help

In counselling there were times when very troubled adolescent boys who had attempted suicide – teens who had reached their tipping point – would come to my office so relieved because they had finally found someone who would listen without judgement.

It is especially important for us to do this because we must encourage 'help-seeking behaviour' so that as our boys grow into adolescents and men, they will ask for help. Men now often recognise when they need help, or that something is wrong, but unfortunately, help-seeking behaviour has been conditioned out of them. Asking for help is something they need to feel OK to do – and that can start with their mum.

Meg Meeker – the author of *Strong Mothers, Strong Sons* who I mentioned earlier – believes our sons want three things when they talk to someone.

- They want someone who isn't shocked by what they hear.
- They want someone who won't ignore them.
- They want someone who won't feel sorry for them.

They also really want their mothers to do all of those three things and still accept them and love them.

When I asked some of the struggling teens in my counselling room why they were unable to tell their parents that they were at that dangerous place, so many of them responded, "I just didn't want to disappoint them again and see that look of disappointment in their eyes". This is so incredibly sad. Little boys notice when their mums roll their eyes, say "tsk, tsk, tsk" and turn their backs because they are wired to understand non-verbal communication much better than verbal. Every time you do that, it hurts your son and, in a way, it is telling him that you do not love him in that moment. When boys are repeatedly experiencing these moments of emotional rejection, it can create the mother wound deep inside their soul. Over and over again they feel that their mum does not, and cannot, love them. This belief then feeds straight into their emotional barometer and convinces them that they are unable to love themselves. This is why we need to look very seriously at how we interact with our boys when they make the endless mistakes that they make in early childhood. Discipline is more about teaching and guiding than punishing and that's why I have devoted a whole chapter to helping our boys when they muck up.

Mums, I want you to keep reassuring your little boys and your bigger boys that you love them as you help them to understand that making poor choices is a part of life's learnings and it's a part of being a little boy, not a sign that there something wrong with them. Please resist the ineffective habits of nagging and lecturing because boys learn very early to zone out when this happens. Try singing your requests or whispering – the novelty often captures their attention!

> "Recently my son DB (5) comes to me and in a very matter-of-fact manner asks, 'Mum, can we say fuck?' I was a bit taken back as our children have had it drummed into them not to use bad language. I replied with, 'No mate, you can't say that word.' He quickly turned to his brother, Master 4, and said, 'See, I told you we can't say fuck'. He then proceeded to the living room to tell his sister that she can't say fuck either. It was a 'hide the laughing and provide discipline' moment."
> — Amused Mum

Our little boys desperately want our acceptance, love and approval and they know the best chance of getting that is by doing things that please us. Seriously, they try really hard to please us, it just might not look that way at times. From an early age we need to reassure them that our love is unconditional. Unconditional love means that I may not like your behaviour for a little while when you have hurt your sister, broken a window or thrown a tantrum, however I will never stop loving you.

My DB (8) rooster came to me when he was about eight years of age and said:

"Mum, did you know that you call me a pain in the neck quite a lot lately. I am a bit worried that if you keep calling me that it might damage my self-esteem."

Ouch! Needless to say he was absolutely correct and I upgraded my language immediately. I heard what he was saying and it mattered.

Compassionate communication requires us to be present in a calm and grounded way during the communication. Being over-tired, exhausted or distracted by technology are certainly not the best states to be in when communicating with anyone, especially our children.

Here are some questions and suggestions that encourage conversations with our dear little boys that respect both children and parents:

- **"Does that feel fair to you?"**
- "Tell me what you were hoping to do."
- "How can we make this better?"

- **“What do you think needs to happen now?”**
- “Sounds like you/we have a problem.”
- “Whose problem is this?”
- **“Does that feel kind to you?”**
- “There is a problem here. How can I help you to sort it out?”
- “Check it out inside. Does it feel right?”
- **“What were you trying to do here?”**
- “Do you need my help right now to sort out what is happening?”
- “I know you can handle it!”
- “What would you like to do now?”
- **“What would a good friend do now?”**
- “I noticed that ...”
- “Now that’s interesting!”
- “Having a go is important – we can’t all win!”

The power of sorry

There is no question that there are no perfect human beings on our planet. Of course, there will be times that we yell, misinterpret our children, misunderstand what they want and generally bugger up. One of the most powerful things we can teach our boys is that when we make mistakes, we own up to that mistake and we apologise. This shows them that this is the right thing to do. Part of the old male code seemed to teach boys that apologising was a sign of weakness. Seriously, I have seen this time and time again with the men in my personal life and professional life. We need to teach our boys that saying sorry when we really mean it is a sign of courage and strength, not a sign of weakness. It is also about taking responsibility for your actions, which is important for boys to learn. I think mums have a wonderful opportunity to teach this to their sons because sometimes we can become quite shouty and unreasonable when our emotions get the better of us. Being able to come back when we have calmed down and apologise is not only the right thing to do, it is teaching our sons that even grown-ups have moments when they can make poor choices with the people they love.

> “[I wish my mum had not had an] ... inability to say sorry when it would be very healing.”– Men’s Survey 2017

If we keep in mind that boys tend to be highly visual and kinaesthetic, then modelling healthy, authentic communication from as early as possible in their life is the key to helping them manage their emotional and social lives much more effectively. Just because mums and sons have different preferred styles of communication, like speaking English and French, we can strive to meet in the middle ground. One of the hardest things, again, for mums of sons is to be able to hold in what they need to say until a boy has a chance to process the big, ugly feelings that he may be experiencing. Sometimes this can take up to 24 hours and sometimes even more. Learning to trust that this will improve the outcome of the conversation is one of the biggest challenges mums of sons have to overcome. I know I became much better at this with more practise in my home, my counselling room and my classrooms.

Boys are hungry for meaningful communication and yearn to be heard just like every other human being. Nothing bonds us together closer or builds more authentic intimacy in our most important relationships than being heard and understood because this builds the three big things that matter to boys – acceptance, respect and love.

> **"Children who are listened to without interruption learn to process and move through even their most difficult emotions more swiftly; emerging refreshed and renewed. Our listening becomes the model for their self-acceptance, the basis for their resilience and a cornerstone for their emotional intelligence."**
>
> – Robin Grille, *Heart to Heart Parenting* (2008).

Getting boys to listen

1. Build rapport first – with gentle touch or calling-out using a term of endearment.
2. Keep verbal instructions short.
3. Make a connection and ensure he is listening to you. They can listen without eye contact and while doing something provided you make the initial connection.
4. Use non-verbal communication especially encouragement – thumbs-up.
5. Use gestures to help them connect to what-where-when.
6. Give time warnings/suggestions around transitions.
7. Try the whisper ...
8. Give choices and request politely rather than demand or command.
9. Don't sweat the small stuff.

I have been concerned that hiding under some of the male abuse in intimate relationships, is a wound that comes from childhood when a boy never felt heard by his mother. Another part of this wound is that many boys learn that it is quite often better to be silent because often what they tried to communicate was misunderstood, laughed at or ridiculed. This can happen for both our rooster and lamb boys, and mums can really help their boys become good communicators with patience and endeavour. We know that for relationships to be healthy there needs to be opportunity for emotional honesty and, while this tends to come easily for girls, it can be much more difficult for boys – and most difficult for our rooster boys.

TOP TIPS

- ✓ Rooster boys have a strong sense of their own importance.
- ✓ Rooster boys have high energy and a hunger to win at all costs.
- ✓ Mums need to help roosters develop empathy, compassion and a sense of fairness.
- ✓ Rooster boys need firm boundaries and consequences.
- ✓ Strong rooster boys need strong mums.
- ✓ Rooster boys can become alpha males.
- ✓ Lamb sons can be sensitive and easy to dominate.
- ✓ Lambs need to develop assertiveness and courage.
- ✓ Lamb boys are often quietly strong and capable.
- ✓ Caring communication for both temperaments is important.
- ✓ Improving communication with boys can make them feel more accepted, heard and loved.
- ✓ Helping all boys develop a healthy sense of emotional honesty will help them all through life.

CHAPTER 8

MUMMY, do you **LOVE** me?

"My mum made me really emotionally repressed." – Men's Survey 2017

"Emotions are how we handle the world. When little boys see or hear something terrible, which despite our best efforts, they sometimes will, they will need our support to feel. To sob, to weep, to shake and have us stay close and be okay with that.

Grief is a part of getting used to living in a world which is both beautiful and terrible in equal parts. Some boys never have this chance and their hearts harden in terrible ways.

If we can support them and let them know that feelings are okay, then they grow with a very different kind of strength – to stay in the world with an open heart."

– Steve Biddulph, Facebook Post, 23 March 2014.

It is really easy to break a little boy's heart and, without a doubt, having your heart broken by the first woman you have ever loved — your mum — can be the worst wound our little warriors can ever experience in this life. We need to avoid this at all costs. Indeed, I have found a strong link between men who struggle with addictions, abuse and aggression in their lives, and those who have a 'heart' disconnect from their mothers. I explore the 'mother wound' in an upcoming chapter and so this chapter explores how a boy feels loved by his mum or his mother figure.

I have worked with many boys and men who were completely disconnected from their biological mother and yet had strong loving bonds with another maternal figure. Research into attachment shows that strong, loving bondedness can be formed by non-biological caring adults, and those lucky boys who have strong attachments to more than one maternal figure will tend to feel incredibly secure about being loved and also capable of giving love. I mentioned in a previous chapter Celia Lashlie, the well-respected and passionate boy champion from New Zealand who certainly believed this, and she linked the probability of going to prison very strongly with the absence of a strong maternal figure in the Maori culture. Historically, this has also been this case in the First Nations people of Australia, and in many communities the voice of the grandmother still holds great strength.

Firstly, remember that every child and every boy is unique. What works for one boy may not work for another. Secondly, the metaphor of a 'love cup' is really helpful to remember; if your son's love cup is full, he feels loved. If his love cup is not full, he may feel disconnected, unloved and un-special. Boys tend to understand this metaphor sometimes even better than girls. I remember a mum telling me how she had introduced this to her highly volatile 6-year-old son who was also on the Autism spectrum. She said it worked really well. One afternoon, after a particularly challenging day at school, her son came home and said that his love cup was not empty, it was full of poo!

"My mum has given me unconditional love." – Men's Survey 2017

More than 20 years ago, I conducted a funeral for a mum of two sons who were aged 16 and 18. Their beautiful, beloved mum had died after a long struggle with cancer. When I visited their home to prepare the ceremony to farewell their cherished mum, there was a haunting look in their eyes of enormous grief and also incredible fear. To have removed from your life your greatest ally, your safe base and your first love is possibly the most difficult thing for any boy to experience. To suddenly have to imagine your whole life in front of you, and know that it was now going to happen without your precious mum to guide you, encourage you and celebrate you, must have been terrifying and sad beyond belief. I can still see that look in those sons' eyes.

As a mother of four sons, I returned home from that visit with a whole new understanding of just how precious a loving relationship with a mum can be. Indeed, after most funerals that I have either officiated or worked at, I would go home and hug every one of my boys, telling them how grateful we need to be for the gift of life and how lucky I was to have four gorgeous boys in my world. Yes, there were times they rolled their eyes at me, however, I needed to remind them of the power of love and family.

It is quite obvious that strong bondedness and feeling loved and valued is the best way to keep all children feeling happy, secure and safe. Given the emotional fragility that I have already explored, and the inability of many little boys to understand the nuances of communication, especially in the heat of the moment, I need to explore how boys interpret feeling loved by their mums rather than how mums interpret that their boys feel loved.

A boy can feel unloved by a mum who really loves him a lot! This is an interesting phenomenon that I noticed again and again over my years as a counsellor. The mum thinks it is obvious how much she loves her child because of all the things she does for him and because she knows how she feels about her child. Children can feel gratitude for what is done for them but still feel unloved. The messages that I have noticed from the men's survey I conducted clearly show how many men struggled to feel their mum's love, even though she cared for them.

The ones who have the warmest and most connected relationships were quite simply the ones who had felt more loved and loved unconditionally, no matter how many mistakes or 'bugger-up' moments the men had had as young lads.

One of the things I can assure you of is that most boys do not often see that the endless tasks you do as a mother – cooking, cleaning and being a mum taxi – are necessarily signs of how much you love them. Our lamb sons (whom I discussed in the last chapter) often do appreciate the things we do and many will write sweet notes for Mother's Day about the things they value and appreciate. Conversely, most little boys feel deeply unloved when we shout, roll our eyes, turn away from them, "tsk tsk tsk" them, and definitely when we freeze them out. Indeed, many think we have simply stopped loving them. Interestingly, many men often come to understand and appreciate what their mums do once their prefrontal lobe finishes growing in their late 20s and beyond.

"My mum gave up everything to care for two of my sick siblings. She spent years travelling weekly or more to Perth (four hours) to and from hospital. She did this with five children to look after. She showed me that health and happiness are what really matters!" – Men's Survey 2017

Mums need to be particularly careful never to freeze their sons out. This is a female technique to express our displeasure at something. I once worked with a 14-year-old boy who had planned to end his life because his mother had frozen him out for a week because she had been unhappy with his school report. As he sobbed into my arms in my office he said, "I thought she had stopped loving me forever. I didn't want to live without my mum's love". Sad but true. Jokingly, I have suggested that you can freeze out your daughter because she knows exactly what you are doing. Indeed, she may be freezing you out right now. However, I have to say freezing any child out is not an example of warm discipline.

Little boys do not understand when mums and other women close their hearts to them. They feel it, they know it and it triggers an incredible fear that the 'freezing out' may be permanent. I have met some boys who have had a very difficult relationship with their mum in adolescence. Much of the wound was formed in early childhood because – in their eyes – "everything I did was wrong". In a way this internal perception can change into, "I am wrong" and then it becomes the voice of shame.

As we've explored, toddler boys and young boys are often highly impulsive, energetic and wired to move, touch and throw. Sometimes, in trying to contain these developmentally normal behaviours, frustrated mums can resort to shouting, shaming and hitting, especially if that was a part of their own childhood experience. For some boys in this situation, they simply give up trying to improve their choices and the 'I am bad' mindset becomes deeply entrenched. Sadly, their behaviour then follows. They often feel their mum cannot love a bad boy.

How often do we say those words to our sons: "I love you?" We say them lots because most girls and women like to hear the words that affirm a person loves us. That reminds me of the old joke about the couple who have been married for a very long time. The wife is complaining that her husband has not told her that he still loves her. The husband replies that he told her the day he married her, that nothing has changed, and he'll update her if it does.

Loving words are incredibly helpful for many of us women and, of course, they are important for our boys, but not as important as us *showing* them we love them, rather than just telling them. Also, if we repeat these words in the same way every time, then they can simply be lost from Mum's mouth to a son's ear, much like what happens when we ask them to use a plate when they have toast or to put their plate in the sink. Things heard frequently are often zoned out – yes, even the good stuff!

How easy is it to use terms of endearment around our boys when they're little? I tended to call the boys when they were babies 'bub'. I was once on a bus with my four sons and the youngest was six years of age. I called out to him and used the word 'bub' and I noticed an elderly woman smiling quietly close by. When we stood up to leave the bus, she leaned towards me and said, "I still have a bub and he's 54 years of age!"

Terms of endearment and special nicknames that express our affection can really help boys feel their mother's love. No matter what yours may be – please try to keep using it – especially when you need to have difficult conversations with your sons because they have mucked up. I tend to preface most of my text messages, emails and requests to my sons if they are in my house with 'babe'. I only noticed the other day that when I call any of my sons, I often start with "Hi darl ..." and I will do that until the day I die. When a boy has mucked up or made a poor choice, he will know that you still love him if you keep calling him by his special name. It may seem small, however, it really matters.

There is no question that the more time you spend with your sons, the more loved they feel and the same goes for our girls. They actually want to spend time with us and that is why I reiterate my deep concern that many of today's children are struggling with some degree of digital abandonment. Their parents are often at home, however, they are distracted by their smartphone and so, technically, they are not present. Boys are actually very good at noticing when we are not present and how often, as busy mums, are we doing five things at once in the kitchen (remember, we excel at multi-tasking) when our son wanders in hoping to have a connection with us? He can just take one look and realise that what he is yearning for is impossible right now. This is why I have already mentioned that we need to be more 'catchable'.

> "My DB (3) noticed my tummy was bigger so I confessed that there was a baby in there. Immediately he fired off: 'How did it get there? Did you eat it? What are we going to call it? Can I watch it come out? Can we call it Dominic?' — his name. The questions came so fast I only had to answer the last one — 'Having two Dominics would be very confusing'. He flung his arms out and exuberantly announced: 'If we had TEN Dominics, they'd be EVERYWHERE!' (And I'd be in a nice, padded cell somewhere!)." — Overwhelmed Mum

This mamma message above reminded me of one of my DBs (3.5) when I was pregnant with my fourth son. He came in thoughtfully and asked why I was getting fatter. I lovingly explained that I was growing a baby in my tummy. He said, "Yes, but what's happening in your bum 'cos that is getting fatter too?" Yikes - gotta love that honesty!

Many families struggle to find large amounts of quality time and it is not a sign that you are a lousy parent, it is the reality of life today. I have some great news for you because I have found that building more micro-connections into your family life is a powerful way of keeping your children feeling the love.

We can do micro-connections much more often and what they do is build a bridge between our hearts. I call these 'love bridges'. To be honest many of the suggestions in my micro-connections work far more powerfully for boys than girls because they notice and respond to non-verbal communication so much better. Some boys use humour and fun as a connection and this can always help them feel safer and more loved.

So, let's get started on lots of fabulous ideas that can ensure your son feels deeply loved by his mum, at least most of the time.

Family rituals

Given that we know boys' memories are not great, family rituals that are repeated over and over, throughout a number of years, can have a significant impact on improving your boy's perception of feeling loved and valued. Rituals are positive things we do in our families, which are unique to us and have a secret capacity to bond and strengthen loving connections within a family.

For example, does your family have a welcoming and farewelling ritual especially when your children are young?

> *In the chaos and confusion of mornings and afternoons we often forget to reconnect with our children, especially our boys, because we mums have got so many things on our to-do list that we can be distracted.*

The most simple rituals are the best and you need to work out what works for your son. Our sons need to perceive from us that we are glad they are home and that we have missed them. Simply kneel or bend down to eye level and say something like, "Hey you ... missed you". Better still, give him a really big grin and a wink. Smiling and winking at your son is a really powerful way of strengthening the love bridge to his heart – no, really it is!

You can also try some form of safe, soothing touch – it may be a gentle punch on the arm, or a ruffle of his hair, a secret handshake or maybe you could gently stroke his tickle spot. The tickle spot is high up on the back and apparently this spot is like an accelerator point for making the neurochemical serotonin. Many of us stand under the shower with the water landing on the same spot because it feels really good. This is possibly one of the best things to remember in terms of connecting with our boys, especially when we do it without any words. Not only is it soothing, it can also distract a boy quite quickly if he is struggling with low dopamine levels and starting to behave in impulsive and unpredictable ways. It works beautifully in long queues and shopping centres. If you stand behind your son and gently draw numbers on his tickle spot and ask him to guess them, he can suddenly become calmer and more focused. Every boy will have a slightly different preference for the physical touch that they prefer. Two of my sons really love to have their head massaged, especially while watching TV, and all of them love to have their feet rubbed with lovely, pleasant-smelling cream. The patterns of physical connection that you set up with your son when he is little will build a beautiful bridge that will connect you with him when he becomes a grumpy, moody and unpredictable teen.

One mum mentioned to me after a seminar how grateful she was that I had taught her about the tickle spot many years before her son became a teenager. She said there are times that she will quietly stand behind him and slip her hand under his T-shirt at the back and gently draw circles on his tickle spot without saying a word. She said she can always see his shoulders drop a little and he often leans back towards her. We need to build these bridges when our boys are little, and we need to do them over and over and over again, so they become anchored deeply in their brains.

Bedtime is a special time for most boys and, if it isn't, we need to make sure that it becomes special. Remember, routines and habits create patterns of predictability and having a good bedtime routine that includes a story or two, with bodies close together, is a fabulous way to start. I'm also a huge fan of bedtime rituals especially for our less talkative boys. This is a serious love cup filler or love bridge builder. I am a firm advocate of 'good-enough, imperfect parenting', so don't try too hard to accomplish a bedtime ritual every night if you are a little-bit-out-of-sorts Mum. We don't tend to build love bridges when our voice has that edge to it – enjoy your routine as many nights as you can and, on those other nights, it might be just hugs and kisses.

Boys, just like most men, tend to be spatially really competent and relate particularly well to numbers, sizes, locations and volumes. This is partly why the following bedtime words are a ritual that I recommend to really help young boys feel loved deeply.

I love you more than every star in the night sky. I love you more than every grain of sand on every beach in the whole wide world. And I love you more than all the hairs on all the bears.

I once had a lady come to speak to me after one of my seminars. She said she had a 4-year-old son and she paused and looked a little uncomfortable and then said, "It's not that I don't like him, we just are not close. Do you have any suggestions that may help me?"

I suggested that she try this bedtime ritual and I am sure she left thinking it would not be very helpful. One week later, I was surprised to see the same mum at another seminar and she again came to speak to me.

She said she wanted to tell me a story so that I could tell other parents what happened when she began the bedtime ritual. Apparently, the first night of the ritual, her son looked at her suspiciously, probably wondering where the heck she pulled this new thing from. On the second night, her son looked again as if to say, "Oh, she is doing it again!" However, this mum said that the following morning, after just two nights with the new bedtime ritual, her son came to her while she was washing the dishes. He wrapped his arms around her thigh — something he had never done before — and put his head against her leg and said, "Mummy I have got one more for us. You love me more than all the fluff on all the fabric in the whole world". As she told me this, her eyes teared up and she said, "It took just two nights for my son and I to fall in love. I can't thank you enough". Needless to say, the love cup was full and the love bridge had been built.

Over the years, I have heard so many stories about how boys have created examples of how much their mums love them — more than all the Hot Wheels in the world; more than all the hairs on Daddy's back; more than all the scales on all the bums on all the fish in all the seas; more than all the bears, the stars, the fish and smelly feet in all the world. When the concept of love is given a quantity or dimension, it makes much more sense for our precious little boys. We need to keep this deeply embedded ritual alive in small ways as they get older. You may sprinkle a few stars on the pillow some nights to reinforce it — because I'm pretty sure they wouldn't appreciate a pile of sand on their pillow. I can tell you that when these rituals are deeply embedded, they are never forgotten and they do play an enormous part in helping our boys feel loved.

There are many other family rituals that you can use and, again, the simpler the better. For example, our family accidentally created an end-of-term ritual when I took the four lads for a hot chocolate sundae after a busy school term during the year that I was a solo mum. I was relieved that we had survived — they had pretty good reports and no detentions (or, worse, suspensions), so I felt a celebration was in order. It was such a success that we did it every last day of term from then on.

I found that the last weeks of term were no longer a battle — the boys were counting down to the end-of-term treat. Interestingly, when the eldest was at uni, he called to make sure we didn't have the ritual until he arrived home. Such is the power of a good family ritual.

"For my mum, the list of good things she did is too long. She is an inspirational person. So caring and loving — always." — Men's Survey 2017

Physical connectors

Little boys love high fives — I mean they seriously love them. They also love something that we call knuckles (or you might know them as fist pumps), which is where a grown-up puts the knuckles of their fist next to the boy's knuckles and when they touch, we pretend they explode in the air! Boys really love it when mums form secret handshakes or even secret messages across the room by using hand signals. See if you can work out a secret way to tell your son across a crowded room that you love him. Nothing beats a big grin or a smiley face and winking — these are brilliant ways to fill low love cups! They are so simple, and yet so powerful, for boys.

Other ways might be to take a little bite out of their toast or the sandwich in their lunchbox. You can pretend that there is a love rat in your kitchen that does it but, secretly, they know it's mum. This was a habit I found hard to break when my boys became men and maybe, in some ways, it reminded them of something from their childhood that their crazy mum used to do. I have started to do this to my grandkids' toast too. We all need a love rat in the kitchen!

> "DB (6) pointing to a spot on my arm: 'Did you get bitten by a mozzie Mum?' Me: 'Yes I think I did'. DB: 'I didn't, I'm too fast for him!'" — Winging-it Mum

Boys may tend to forget verbal expressions of love, however, they seldom dispute it when these words are written down. Putting little notes into their lunchboxes, even if it's only a smiley face, or "Have a fun day!' or "Love you champ!" ... these messages can certainly put a smile on a boy's face. I can tell you that if you put a note that says, "It's your turn to do the dishes tonight," you won't get the same response.

The power of a written message from a loving parent to a boy should not be underestimated. Make an effort to find funny cards, use sticky notes and write messages on mirrors affirming often how much you love your son. Texting can also work in today's smartphone world, however, you need to be mindful of the timing and the frequency, and we will explore more of that later in the book.

> *Tickle attacks and rough-and-tumble play are ways that boys definitely feel more connected and more loved. There are so many times that boys need a physical connection to show that our emotional connection is real and valid.*

Sometimes just sitting on his lap spontaneously or leaning on him when he is standing, or even treading on his feet with a big grin on your face, will remind your son you see him and you love him. A well-timed fart can also enhance a moment of connection with your son, especially in the years when they're aged 14 to 16, when triggering a smirk might be all that is needed to reinforce your message of love.

Your rooster son can sometimes have days when he seems to have made an awful lot of poor choices – been in trouble with the teacher, used inappropriate language on the school bus, been a bit mean to his sister and didn't eat broccoli for his dinner – and this might mean that he's not feeling too good as he heads off to bed. It can be difficult to manage a warm and loving bedtime ritual when your son seems to have had such a bad day and you are shaking your head about how you can help. Hopefully, your son has received some discipline at school and for his behaviour on the bus because we need our sons to be made accountable for their poor choices.

So, in this scenario, my suggestion is to try the 'surprise bedroom attack'. It works like this: around five minutes after the lights have gone out in your son's room, you run in and launch yourself on top of him. (A small warning about the surprise bedroom attack – avoid the joint two-parent attack without careful planning. I do know a couple who ended up with mild concussion when they executed their simultaneous surprise attack for their full-on 'rooster' son after he had had a very difficult day. Although, apparently when their heads collided, their son thought it was hilarious and cheered up enormously.) This 'surprise attack' is followed by tickles, blowing raspberries on their back and possibly sticking your tongue in their ear in an attempt to trigger the endorphins of laughter. After a minute or so, you run out of the room and close the door. What's left behind with your son are endorphins of love and laughter, and yet he is still 'busted'! I seriously recommend you do not do this with your lamb sons because you could possibly traumatise them for life and create a permanent anxiety disorder. I also want to offer a word of caution: if you have an enthusiastic daddy who loves this idea, please take it gently. We have heard of well-meaning dads who have accidentally broken beds, cracked the plaster on the wall and dislocated their shoulders. It is only a small leap, not a spectacular dive from a 10-metre board with a triple pike – just a little leap.

> "I got a warm, fuzzy feeling when my toddler son came up to me and gave me a big hug without my prompting or asking him. As I was praising and thanking him for his cuddle, I quickly realised he'd only hugged me to wipe his itchy, snotty nose on my jacket." — Cuddly Mum

The gift of presence

Our kids love it when we sometimes stop and join their world and pretend we are a part of the game. The number of times that I enjoyed crawling into the cave that my sons had built in the bedroom, listening to see if there was a bear coming, were fewer than I'd have liked. I also regret that I didn't make myself a red cape when I made all the boys red capes in the days when they pretended to be superheroes. I also wish I'd played more hide-and-seek games with my sons or gone outside to shoot more hoops, and left the washing to wait a bit longer.

Regularly scheduling a mum date or a dad date with just one child is a really powerful way of ensuring that our children, especially our boys, can really know that we love and value them. Please try to avoid breaking promises too because that has the reverse effect and is really painful for them. Every single time you are present and having fun with your son, you are filling up his love cup, and you are ensuring that he knows he is loved and that your heart is open to him. This also means you will read his favourite picture book for the 798th time with the same new enthusiasm as when you first read it to him.

So keep in mind that quality time is fabulous if you can find it and micro-moments add up and they constantly remind your son he is loved. We especially need to add more micro-moments when they are getting tired at school towards the end of term, when it is a sibling's birthday or when they have major things happening at school that are causing them stress. To know that mum has your back, even when you are being a pain and annoying, is pure gold to our boys. They do find it difficult to come to us and ask for help when they are feeling overwhelmed and anxious, and especially when they feel frightened. We need to practise the art of observing their faces and observe what their behaviour is telling us because boys tend to communicate this way. Mums need to trust their gut instincts and then become a little bit like a detective trying to work out what is happening in a son's life that is causing him distress. Please avoid this phrase, "What's the matter with you?" or worse, "What's wrong with you?" These are incredibly hurtful phrases that communicate to our son that there is something wrong with him. If he knew what it was and he had the ability to communicate it using words, I am sure he would. A gentle tickle on the tickle spot and a quiet, sad look on your face is another way of asking "Are you OK?" or an abbreviated question can be "K?" – with an eyebrow raised in curiosity.

> "My mum has always been incredibly kind and invested unbelievable amounts of time to make me the person I am." – Men's Survey 2017

How does your son feel love?

Every child and every boy can have slightly different ways in which they perceive whether they are loved. An excellent book that explains how to fill your child's love cup is *The 5 Love Languages of Children* (2012) by Gary Chapman and Ross Campbell. Chapman and Campbell believe there are five ways that we fill our children's love cups.

- **Physical touch** – Physical touch works for many but not everyone. Given that many boys are visual/kinaesthetic you can see why some of the techniques I have suggested, especially the high five, fist pump and tickle spot can work really well. This is also why they like to sit on you sometimes.
- **Words of affirmation** – Hearing words of love, encouragement, guidance and appreciation works for some boys. They are sensitive to tone and criticism, often very sensitive. We can express these words in written notes or text messages as well.
- **Quality time** – If this is the primary way your son feels loved, he may sometimes drive you nuts with wanting your full attention. Kids who value quality time value real eye contact, one-on-one time, real conversations, sharing feelings and bedtime rituals.
- **Gifts** – These lads are very attached to the gifts you have bought them over the years and rather than be concerned with cost, size or shape, they are more tuned into the thought you put into purchasing the gift. Be very careful about buying meaningful gifts and of bribery and manipulation as your son will know the difference!
- **Acts of service** – These boys tend to respond to things you do for them. They notice and mention when you cook their favourite meal, come to watch them play sport or make their school lunch in good time. The main motivation behind your act though must be love, not manipulation or to get something. Also, be mindful of making requests and not commands.

I recommend that you read *The 5 Love Languages of Children* and explore with your child their preferred love language; to see how you can build on their feelings of being loved.

To help explain these differences, let me share a story. I once needed to fly to Sydney for a suicide prevention conference. When I returned home, each of my sons responded in a different way. My quality-time son wanted to know absolutely everything that had happened from the moment I left, including who sat next to me on the plane, where I stayed and what I ate. He was almost in my face as he was needing to fill up his special cup. My boy whose love language is physical touch was almost hanging off my leg from the moment I came home, not wanting to let go. My son whose love language is acts of service/words of appreciation quietly said that he had taken the bin out while I had been away. My last son who appreciates gifts quietly sidled up to me and said, "Did you bring me anything?"

Give some thought as to what are your two main languages of love because quite unconsciously, we often try to fill the love cups of those we love using the same ones that work for us and this can leave a child feeling powerless.

Small gestures of random kindness are also another way boys can feel loved by their mums – the best is when it is unexpected. Sometimes, just put a chocolate frog or a few of their favourite lollies on their pillows unexpectedly. They will want to know what it is for and sometimes you can say: "I just wanted you to know I love you". Other times you can tell them it is to acknowledge something that you have noticed them do that is positive and helpful: "I saw you go and feed the dog when it was not your turn," or, "I noticed how hard you worked on your homework last night". Small, frequent gestures keep topping those love cups up.

Given that our boys are usually highly visual, having lots and lots of large photos of happy family moments, especially with their siblings, can really help them realise that they are loved and they belong. I especially think your whole toilet wall should be full of these photos because boys and men tend to spend a fair bit of time in there, and the photos will trigger loving memories and positive neurochemicals. Also, again using their visual attributes, I suggest having lots of posters or framed prints with messages that affirm the importance of love. We had a huge, framed print of two polar bears hugging and no matter where we lived this positive, affirming print was in our lounge room. I found it really hard to let it go when we moved interstate after all the boys had left home. Inspirational posters and funny, inspiring quotes can subconsciously influence the mindset of our boys. There is research I read that explained that we are silently conditioned by the external environment because our unconditional mind scans things like this every time we go by, while the conscious mind may seem to not notice them.

> "My mum always encouraged and gave love no matter what, just being there." – Men's Survey 2017

The last suggestion that can improve your son's connection to you is to find an interest that you can share deeply and passionately – besides food. I was lucky that my love of basketball gave me that common interest with my lads – one that saw Mum and her four sons watch an NBA game together in Sacramento, America in 2013. I am not sure who was more excited, me or the boys, but it was certainly a memory I will never forget. Strive hard to find this common interest and know that each son may have a different way that he would like to connect with you around a common interest. Music is a fabulous pathway for many mums and sons, as is cooking and a love of nature. I know of some mums who watch funny cat and dog videos with their sons as a form of connection – bodies close with lots of laughter – gold!

Random cards with loving messages are always a winner. You need to accept that your son may not mention it, or want to talk about it, but just know that he will have felt it.

When did you last consciously focus on strengthening the love bridge to your son?

Hopefully, you will now have some great ideas on how to ensure you have a strong connection to your son's heart, and he to yours. There is definitely a fragility around boys' hearts and how loved they feel by their mums in particular. The bridge between your hearts needs to be built as strongly as possible when he is a young boy because it will weather some rough storms on that journey to manhood. I believe bridges can be rebuilt, however, it is much easier to ensure they stay strong and sturdy by using many of these ideas and strategies, rather than trying to repair a bridge that has been destroyed by making choices that are not respectful or loving.

"My mum showed her love through actions more than words."
– Men's Survey 2017

TOP TIPS

- ✓ Strong attachment is essential for wellbeing on all levels for all children.
- ✓ Having strong maternal attachments is really important for little boys.
- ✓ Boys often perceive feeling loved differently to mums.
- ✓ Frequent micro-connections of affection can help boys feel more loved.
- ✓ Family rituals also help boys feel more valued and loved.
- ✓ Actions can mean more than words to many boys.
- ✓ Kindness means love to boys.
- ✓ Write them love messages and notes.
- ✓ Show, rather than tell, them you love them.
- ✓ Reassure them you love them after they muck up.
- ✓ Explore your son's language of love.
- ✓ Use the 'love cup' metaphor.

CHAPTER 9

MOVEMENT and **PLAY** for our little **WARRIORS**

> **"If we love our children and want them to thrive, we must allow them more time and opportunity to play, not less. Yet policymakers and powerful philanthropists are continuing to push us in the opposite direction — toward more schooling, more testing, more adult direction of children, and less opportunity for free play."**
>
> – Dr Peter Gray, *The Play Deficit*, Aeon (18 September 2013).

I firmly believe that this shift away from play in the current social norms, especially in the early years and primary school, has unintentionally negatively impacted all young boys. Modern society is becoming almost phobic about allowing children the freedom to move vigorously and energetically, especially in their natural world – outside. It is an interesting irony that the modern world is hell-bent on creating gadgets and equipment to improve our lives, yet which end up making it hard for our children to do what they are biologically wired to do – to move in deeply encoded ways that ensure they gradually grow in all their competencies.

Movement is essential for all children, however, it is particularly important for our little boys. Some of the things that can occur if our children lack movement in the first two years of life are:

- delayed motor development
- poor co-ordination/balance
- tendency to be easily distracted, lack concentration
- language problems

- emotional immaturity
- motion sickness
- reading problems.

Given that boys already feature more highly in all our schools with low literacy and numeracy, poor behaviour and more disengagement, surely we don't need to compound these problems, or add to them, by refusing to let them move their bodies as much as their biology requires? Children seldom ride their bikes or walk to school, yet in previous generations this was one of the primary ways boys got to school. It also meant they discharged excess energy and had a high level of dopamine when they walked into the classroom. There are some schools in Australia (often driven by fear of litigation) who make children sit down outside the classroom before class starts, just in case they hurt themselves when they are playing. Years ago we trusted children to be able to play before class, without needing adult supervision. Each of these withdrawals of common sense that has disabled children's capacity to move their bodies is going to have a negative flow-on effect in other areas of their lives, especially for boys. We must address this dilemma in every school environment so that we can improve boys' ability to become engaged learners who can interact with other children in positive ways.

> *While play may seem like the fun, easy part of being a child, it is also vitally important for building connectedness and brain integration.*

These vital processes assist with literacy and numeracy, enhance emotional and social awareness, and inspire competence. Play can also build mental wellbeing and provide the building blocks for growing into loving, caring human beings who are capable of creating intimate relationships later in life. Just because we are unable to directly measure the benefits of play does not mean they don't exist. It's strange that we tend to be diminishing such an incredibly important part of child development simply because we cannot quantify it and, therefore, we cannot be accountable for it.

Anecdotally, many schools that have introduced nature play spaces back into their environment have noticed the increase in students' concentration in class and, more importantly, less truancy, less bullying and less reluctance to attend school. The children are happier and healthier, and are able to communicate more with the children they see every day. I am a massive advocate of nature play, especially when it allows autonomy and freedom and embraces risk and adventure. If you would like to see some of the wonderful, exciting nature play spaces that I have visited make sure you visit the nature play gallery on my website at maggiedent.com/nature-play.

Play is a much underrated but incredibly vital part of children's development. Put simply: "Play grows the brain." As Hara Estroff Marano highlighted in her book, *A Nation of Wimps*, play helps to grow the parts of our brains that control how we retain information, regulate our emotions and manage our behaviour. She writes of the cleverness of nature in giving us something that is not goal-directed (play) to "create the mental machinery for being goal-directed".

> **"Having sufficient time to play is important — big blocks of time without being disturbed and made to hurry is important for children and adults. We need time to chill out, relax, to let our ideas flow, have conversations with real or imaginary friends, to test our ideas and theories and replay, retest and rethink them."**
>
> — Neville Dwyer, *Being Adventurous* (2013).

From around two years of age, toddlers are capable of learning social skills that will strengthen their life-coping skills. They are starting to develop their sense of 'self' and need for autonomy and personal independence. The stronger a person's sense of identity and independence, and the life skills that support these attributes, the better their resilience. Movement and play facilitates this beautifully.

Much of the play equipment that was in the playgrounds when many of us grew up has now been removed because it is believed to be unsafe. These include the tall monkey bars, wooden seesaws, the big metal slides and the metal maypoles — equipment that had to be treated with deep respect because you could seriously hurt yourself. Did you ever get thumped in the chin when someone jumped on the other end of the seesaw? Has your bum been thumped when someone suddenly jumped off the seesaw? Well, it only needed to happen once or twice before you treated the equipment with the respect it deserved. It seems that today's largely safe playgrounds are the product of our risk-averse society, where things are built to prevent children getting hurt. Indeed, I think that if we returned the old-fashioned wooden seesaws to all community playgrounds we would have a lot of boys doing some serious learning about the choices that they make. Rooster boys, particularly, need to experience pain to learn to pay attention to the choices they are making — the hidden gift of a 'natural consequence'. Seriously, it can often take three or four smacks in the chin by the seesaw before a boy realises that he may be making a poor choice, regardless of whether he has warrior energy on board. Natural consequences that were considered a normal and healthy part of boyhood are, sadly, no more in many places.

Remember, for boys pain is not all bad and Michael Gurian writes that it can help boys mature, especially when self-inflicted or as a consequence of their own choices. Indeed, he writes:

> **"This male love of ordeal and 'pain' is a part of nature — it involves male biochemistry, brain structure and pain tolerance. There is a significant gender difference in pain response and in pain tolerance. This is part of why males on the average not only feel less pain than females, but actually go out and seek more pain than females. Not only are males more prone to go out and seek pain they are more prone to put up with more pain as a tool of maturation."**
>
> — Michael Gurian, *Saving Our Sons* (2017).

Tim Gill, in his book, *No Fear: Growing Up in a Risk Averse Society*, explores the long-lasting effects in the UK of removing risk from childhood.

> **"Activities and experiences that previous generations enjoyed without a second thought have been labelled as troubling or dangerous, while adults who still permit them are branded as irresponsible ... society appears to have become unable to cope with any adverse outcomes whatsoever, no matter how trivial or improbable."**
>
> — Tim Gill, *No Fear: Growing up in a Risk Averse Society* (2007).

Hugh Cunningham is Emeritus Professor of Social History at the University of Kent. His book, *The Invention of Childhood* shows that he, too, shares Gill's concerns. Cunningham believes that society in general has become so fixated on ensuring children are happy that we downplay their abilities and their resilience. Taking up the debate about our collective responsibility for shaping childhood, he is now an activist and lobbyist in the UK who works to ensure that children's opportunities to play and have free time without adult supervision are not forever lost.

Gill says today's parents spend much more time than previous generations in looking after their children. Parents are also constantly in touch with their children via their mobile phones. The long-term effects of such strong structuring, supervision and control of the children on their capacity to develop resilience is a key element of Gill's work. Children, especially our young boys, learn best by being able to manage their own worlds – including the risks they encounter – which facilitate large developmental benefits. Some experts claim that a child can build on his or her character and personality through facing up to adverse circumstances, especially where there is a known possibility of injury or loss. At the same time, the child learns about the qualities of being adventuresome and innovative. Overcoming challenging situations is a key aspect of resilience and there is only one way to learn about it, and that is through experience. Boys have a fundamental need for freedom and adventure – their innate biological drives mean they are 'mammoth hunters' and 'warriors', and these primitive qualities quietly influence their development almost until their mid-20s. So many boys in the 21st century are not experiencing the physical activity, the adventuresome play, and the bumps and bruises of a healthy boyhood because they are immersed in a virtual world on a screen. This worries me a lot.

The risk of no risk

One very nervous mum and her good bloke came up to me after a seminar to ask my opinion on something. Their 8-year-old rooster son who was large for his age had been begging to be allowed to walk the 400 metres from their front gate to a corner shop – on the same side of the road – to buy the milk and bread just like his dad had been allowed to do when he was the same age. We chatted about how to prepare the boy for this very dangerous outing and even suggested they put a really loud whistle around their son's neck just for their own sense of security. A couple of days later I got a beautiful email from these two loving parents. When they had first set their son off with the $10 to buy the milk and bread, they stood in the front yard watching him. He turned around and gestured to them and then yelled at them to go inside. For them it was the longest 10 minutes of their lives, however, when the front door swung open, an ecstatic and triumphant son ran down the hallway to them. He was holding the milk and the bread aloft saying, "I did it!" I know in a few weeks' time they will possibly have the conversation about why they were so worried? If you are not familiar with Lenore Skenazy please check out her website (freerangekids.com) as she and I share a very similar advocacy around allowing children to become braver when they are ready.

All children need opportunities for creative, exploratory play in stress-free environments with time and freedom. We hear of schools banning the game of tag or kids doing cartwheels because of the risk of injury. Heck, British bulldog was banned so many years ago now I can hardly remember how to play it. Thankfully though, many schools and communities are now embracing a less risk-averse approach to children's play. More and more research is showing that the modern, supposedly safe, playgrounds are diminishing our children's capacity to assess and manage risk. There are enormous benefits to allowing children to experience the bumps and bruises that can occur while at play. Instead of hovering over our children, we must challenge the perception of 'good-enough parenting' and allow our children to make choices, and experience the occasional setback and disappointment.

> *Even though over-protection comes from a place of love — especially a mother for her son — it is diminishing and disrespecting our boys' capacity to learn how to deal with life when it lets us down or we feel disappointed or unhappy.*

Allowing loss and disappointment

We need to allow children to experience disappointment before they start school and boys particularly need to learn how to overcome disappointment and failure because they tend to attack themselves and that further diminishes their self-worth barometer. A great way to start would be to change the rules of 'pass the parcel' back to its original game plan. I recently heard of a game of pass the parcel for a group of 4-year-olds. Apparently the parcel was so big (because it contained a prize for every child) that they needed an adult to sit between some of the children to pass the parcel. Quite obviously this shows how ludicrous this desire to avoid our children experiencing disappointment has become. As a resilience educator, I believe we need to encourage these experiences rather than discourage them. There is supposed to be only one winner so that we are able to coach and encourage our children to deal with losing or not getting what we want. We need to possibly consider having three games of pass the parcel with only one winner so that we are really letting our children experience the discomfort of not getting what they want, and of losing. We need to validate to them that losing 'sucks' and it doesn't feel very good. Emotional buoyancy can only be developed when you have experienced how to recover from a setback or a disappointment.

I encourage mums of all boys to spend hours playing games in the real world that let boys get used to learning to lose. Connect Four and simple card games like snap or Uno are great games that let our boys experience winning and losing. In the pre-digital world playing noughts and crosses, and hangman were really common in our homes and classrooms. Boys get used to losing often and every time it gets a little bit easier. Remember how losing can impact their self-worth barometer? Today, boys tend to do their winning and losing in an artificial world with a screen that does not have any emotions and where they can quickly, with the touch of a finger, begin a new game and distract themselves from the fact they lost the last one (even if they 'died' in it). In a way, this is teaching boys to shut down their emotions and to ignore them, and we know that is not a healthy pathway for positive development and growth as they mature into adulthood later in life.

There is no question that the screen world has also stolen many valuable hours from our boys' lives in terms of movement and play. It is almost ironic that the parental perception that your boys will be safer inside your house rather than roaming free in the neighbourhood has been shown to be incorrect. Many boys have been deeply scarred by what they have witnessed online and every hour that they are playing in a virtual world, they are not playing in a real world, and so their social and emotional learning will never be optimal. I encourage parents to use screens as little as possible in the formative years of your son's lives. Those precious hours that you give him, helping him to learn the emotional world around winning and losing, will ensure that he develops emotionally and socially before he steps into big school. I firmly believe that the increase in disruptive and inappropriate behaviour from little boys has a lot to do with them not playing with other children, and being immersed in the artificial world. Again, Stuart Shanker believes that poor quality food, lack of good sleep, too much stress, and too much TV and screen time are all contributing to the poorer development of self-regulation in all children. And as boys tend to develop this later than girls, this may be another reason why they are struggling with the transition to formalised learning, and staying engaged.

I noticed in my counselling work with teenage boys that some of the strongest rage towards their mothers had its core and beginning in being over-mothered and overprotected when they were little. We need to celebrate the 'ouchies' and the wounds, and teach our boys how to put their own Band-Aids on. I can still remember how powerful a kiss was when my boys were very little. I did have one very awkward experience when my DB (4) came running up to me in a public playground asking me to kiss his penis because he had hurt it on a swing. Luckily for me, I was a quick thinker in those days so I kissed my fingers and then transferred the kiss onto his trousers. Phew! I have to admit, I do miss the days when a mummy kiss could fix things!

A key driver for the over-concern of those who care for children is the threat of litigation. This is one of the unfortunate side effects of the modern world and this threat has shaped so many of the harm-minimisation ideas that have impacted children's playgrounds and school activities. It seems that accidents no longer happen where a child, or indeed an adult, injures him or herself because they were inattentive, careless or simply distracted. Instead, someone or something must be to blame.

Teaching accountability

This message is one that can be very debilitating for a boy to develop in his childhood and I will explore this in more depth in the chapter on ***"When boys muck up"***. Becoming someone who blames others and who refuses to accept responsibility for his actions is setting your boy up to be an irresponsible man who has a weak character. The need to blame external sources is surely delaying the development of emotional competence, of accepting responsibility for one's own actions, both of which could have serious repercussions later in life. As a former teacher, I can still remember how refreshing it was to have a student own up to being a source of conflict or inappropriate behaviour. Ironically, I usually let them go to recess or lunch early to honour the importance of being honest and able to accept personal responsibility.

Gill writes of how children in times gone by learnt to take personal care and manage risks because they knew that playgrounds were potentially dangerous. Today, children believe that playgrounds are safe and so they take little care and do not learn healthy risk assessment or management. This is commonly known as 'risk compensation'. Thankfully, there has been a shift of the pendulum and we are now starting to see playgrounds that are more adventuresome and allow children to stretch and grow. I especially celebrate my former home state of Western Australia because the nature play movement has returned to our schools and our communities and is embracing fabulous, engaging spaces for children to play. Dealing with a splinter, falling off out of a tree and getting very wet are all now acceptable experiences in the school grounds.

An Australian health professional validated this perspective for me when he told me that the number of children who suffer broken wrists nowadays is more than the number who broke their arms on monkey bars. The monkey bars were an excellent way of strengthening children's wrists and forearms. This is a beautiful example of how children learnt to manage the bumps and bruises of life, because they had opportunities to do so. They were not mollycoddled and wrapped in cotton wool.

Boys and competition

Accidents used to be seen as a part of a healthy childhood, and not a sign of poor parenting. Resilience is built from experiences of managing the things that can hurt physically, emotionally and psychologically.

If this is the reality, then why are we preventing our boys from experiencing the amazing learning opportunities that can come from the freedom to play, as well as embracing the lessons that organised sport can bring? In many team sports for under 14-year-olds in Australia, it is now mandated that no scores are kept so that we don't have children experiencing being upset when they know the team has lost. Sorry, but am I the only one who thinks this is a dubious decision especially for our young boys? Not only do they need to experience winning to build that inner sense of how it feels to have self-worth as little warriors, they need to develop competencies and skills to deal with failing and losing. By the way, every boy knows the score even if it's not written down.

> *Organised sport can help build boys' skills and motivation to work as a team instead of an individual, and this is really important — and healthy — for our growing warriors. So, who are we protecting when we don't keep score?*

I have already explored the wisdom of Michael Gurian, author of *The Wonder of Boys* and other books, who writes about the brain differences, male biochemistry, epigenetics and other factors that make our boys more wired for competition, territoriality and persistence. The ancient biological drivers also suggest that deep inside the DNA of our boys is a hunter yearning to do what he is biologically wired to do for the greater good of the community he lives in. Boys seem more wired to like risky behaviour and 'warrior' behaviour – often of an impulsive nature. Seriously, would humanity have survived if women made the decisions regarding the what, the when, and the how to kill the mammoth while at a lengthy meeting with other women, all needing to talk about how they were feeling? The mammoth would have killed them before they made the decision. The biggest challenge we have in parenting boys is to work with these tendencies so they can learn how to channel them in healthy and positive ways.

> "Whilst on the climbing rope on our jungle gym one day, my DB (6) asked, 'Can you please swing me on the rope so I can be like a Tasmanian?' His favourite movie was Tarzan." — Also Winging-it Mum

In a way, boys are unconsciously seeking worthwhile games to play that allow them to stretch and grow, and develop the inner capacity to be braver, stronger and wiser. There is no finer way to develop these capacities than for young boys to play freely in nature without adult supervision – complete autonomy around time and space. It seems all children are biologically wired to stretch and grow – to climb a little higher, to swing a little higher and to jump a little higher each time they come back to the same experience. One of the concerns we have had with the removal of long monkey bars has been that when children have reached the level that is comfortable for them and they are unable to stretch further to test themselves, they often use the equipment in a completely inappropriate and unsafe way. Children are wired to stretch to the edge of their fear, gradually taking it a little bit further every time. Our boys especially need opportunities like this in their world.

There was once a DB (10) who frequently played in the nearby bush or woodlands close to where he lived. He came home one afternoon and announced that he was going to dig his way to China. His wise mother managed to hold back her laughter and said, "Well, let me know how that goes". Every afternoon after school this little boy would disappear and return a few hours later completely exhausted and filthy. It took him a week to decide that he may not be able to realise his dream. When he informed his mother that it was impossible to dig his way to China, she gave him a really big hug and said, "Well done – it was still worth a go, eh?" Mums, please be careful not to shatter your boy's dreams or fantastic plans with your words. He is on an adventure and his actions really matter to him. When he is left to realise for himself that something is not going to work, despite his enormous effort, he is receiving a wonderful learning experience that every boy would benefit from.

In traditional communities, a boy was able to roam, to explore, to conquer and to challenge himself without having his parents, particularly his mum, at his side. Now, however, the ability of our instant 24/7 global news cycle to bring rare moments of catastrophic disaster into our lounge rooms has justifiably frightened parents, especially the mums of boys.

> *These endless hours where boys play with freedom and autonomy are also building the capacity to be able to read the invisible cues of friend versus foe.*

Dr Stuart Brown has written extensively about the importance of children developing a 'play code', which can only be refined after hours of play with other children. This play code sets up an intuitive awareness that can be carried through into adulthood and can help grown-ups sense when they are in an unsafe place or with unsafe people. Indeed, boys can pick up the invisible micro-expressions on the faces of others who may have evil intentions only if they have spent hours playing with other children, particularly other boys. I often wonder if the violence on our streets is a sign of a diminished 'play code' in grown young men – especially those who have been senselessly violent – aka the coward punch. Food for thought? There are some excellent videos on YouTube that show a ferocious, hungry polar bear coming in from the tundra and encountering a husky. Now, that husky should have been instant dinner. The footage shows the husky dropping into a play pose, wagging his tail and with his face close to the ground. The polar bear reads this message as an invitation to play and, disregarding his hunger, he plays with this husky rather than eating it. The play is quite extended and, in one of the videos, the polar bear comes back to play with the husky over a number of days. This shows the power of having a play code.

> **"Without a play code we can badly misread social situations and interpret a threat incorrectly and without the ability to defuse the situation."**
>
> – Stuart Brown, *Play: How it Shapes the Brain, Opens the Imagination, and Invigorates the Soul* (2009).

This play code that Brown describes reminds me of the need for boys of all ages to play in the company of both girls and boys. How else does a boy learn the differences between communication styles of most boys and girls? I was incredibly grateful that my sister and my brother brought gorgeous girl cousins close into my son's lives. They spent many hours together – often wildly exploring the family farm, building cubbies, blocking up streams, having mud fights and generally getting up to mischief. These experiences were pure gold for my sons as they combined quality and quantity.

I have worked with a number of DBs (18-19) who have spent much of their recreation time gaming in their bedrooms. When they emerged into the real world, they not only struggled to engage with girls, they also often struggled to engage in the unique banter of the bloke world. Many of these lads misread the teasing and the making fun of each other. Some took that banter personally and were wounded by it.

> *We need to ensure that our boys are having both quality time and quantity time playing in the real world, face-to-face, smelly body to smelly body, to ensure they develop this capacity to be able to engage with others.*

Starting conversations, knowing where a conversation is going, and picking up the cues that the conversation is about to end all take hours and hours of human interaction. This is also why I encourage families to limit the use of the screens, especially when they go out to dinner with other family members. Ensure that children spend at least the first half of the meal before dessert with no devices on the table and preferably all devices on 'silent' or ' do not disturb'.

Human linkages and human connectedness can only be built through human communication. How can nanna find out how your basketball game went last week when you are plugged into your phone? How can you hear your grandad's terrible jokes if you are also plugged into your phone? Please mums of sons, help them to be present in the real world by gradually building up their capacity to be able to interact meaningfully with others.

> "My mum literally dedicated her life to investing her time (and money) in me (and my sister) until we were 18, with a clear and stated purpose to set us up for success. She taught me numerous life lessons and personal skills in that period, which remain with me today. I would not be me without her." – Men's Survey 2017

Boys as 'warriors'

The instinctual/programmed drive of boys to be competitive has been a part of boyhood since time began. Evolutionary psychologists argue that we are wired to continue the primary patterns of our ancestors. So, imagine that your little boy who wants to play very competitively, often roughly and very physically, is practising to become a mammoth hunter or a deer hunter as his ancient ancestors would have done. This is why boys need a boyhood, not just a childhood, because those experiences I have just outlined are also ways that help boys become good warriors rather than jerks. Remember that some of our boys are lambs and their inclination to be as warrior-like as their rooster brothers or friends is not the same. However, I will argue that our lambs will often find other ways to test themselves privately, often well away from anybody else.

Before I go any further, I want to clarify that when I write about a 'good warrior' in today's context, I am not suggesting that we need to nurture in our boys a single-minded, beast-hunting thug.

> *To me, a mature warrior man treats himself and others with respect, strives to become a better person, and is not frightened to show love and other emotions.*

He is a man who owns life's vulnerable moments with courage, who laughs often – sometimes until he cries – and who accepts everyone he meets equally and with integrity. A true warrior is not someone equated with violence, but rather strength; this includes strength of spirit, mind and heart, not fist. However, this process of maturation naturally takes time, and nurturing. Mums can help affirm what a good man looks like and behaves like often throughout her son's boyhood.

It seems that a boy's natural impulsiveness could be rooted in his biology. Boys tend to have lower levels of serotonin, the calming neurotransmitter, and thus their heightened state could mean it is more difficult for them to manage impulses. Combine this with the possible influence of hormones and the observed brain differences mentioned before and we can appreciate the tendency for our boys to be incredibly physically active, competitive, risk-taking and seeking experiences to define their emerging manhood.

Boys definitely benefit from structure with clear rules and boundaries, but not too many. With consistency, predictability and strong emotional support and bonding, boys can grow into men who are able to manage the uniquely special qualities of being a man.

> "DB (4) and I went to a public toilet, DB looking me up and down as I go to the toilet. Very loudly, he asks: 'Mummy where has your penis gone? I can't see it!!' I could hear the giggles from the other cubicles!! Once I explained I have a vagina, I now get told every day: 'Mummies have ginas and boys have penis'." — Blessed Mum

Gun and sword play

As a mother of sons, I planned to keep my boys away from toy guns and swords thinking that would prevent them from becoming aggressive and violent. But, they were not very old when they began making guns out of sticks, Lego, bananas ... anything really. I realised that all of my friends' sons were doing the same. This then gave us an opportunity to help them learn safe ways of playing this way. It did not take me long to realise that the soft plastic swords I could buy were probably safer than the sticks they were using. Being adventuresome with a passion for exploration with freedom was something I came to understand and appreciate quite early in my parenting journey. Remember to check with your son before you throw out that stick you found under his bed because that may be one of his best weapons or one that has seen him through many endeavours. In other words, it may be one of his most favourite things.

We need to accept this warrior play as valuable and not shame boys' passion for guns, sticks and weapons. They may still need some guidance on how to play these games without causing pain to others, however, banning these games altogether is unhelpful. A word of caution here around the term 'boys will be boys': while they do often have a passion for playing games that are vigorous and may involve hunting, our little 'mammoth hunters' still need to recognise that their game must be respectful of others. If they are frightening some nearby children or they have been too rough, they need to be cautioned and given some words of advice around making better choices.

Remember, boy behaviour that is hurtful to others is not acceptable. Vigorous boys' play is considered normal, however, teaching our boys in their early years that they need to be mindful of others is really important. Again, we don't need to hurt or shame our boys as we teach them these valuable lessons in life.

Discharging energy

As I have mentioned, having complete freedom away from adults is not only good for boys mentally, it seems to build them spiritually as well. It also gives weary mums a great opportunity to have a quiet cuppa on the couch while the kids play outside. The longer boys sit still, even if they are engaged in an activity with a screen, the more excess energy they are building up that will need to be discharged. Sometimes, this excess energy can suddenly pour out as irrational, aggressive play, often towards their siblings. Shanker describes that as an issue of self-regulation and it happens when arousal states are flooded. It can occur for children when they have too much energy or they have run out of energy.

One of the best pieces of advice I can give you as a parent of sons is to find physical activities and pursuits that they really enjoy and keep them doing these as often as possible. One of my rooster lads took up competitive swimming when he was about eight and from the very first week he began training for two hours a day, five days a week. He used competitive swimming to develop his warrior skills – and I noticed that our whole home was a calmer place to be.

> "My mum always had time for me. She played countless games of backyard cricket with me when I was a teenager." – Men's Survey 2017

Rooster boys will have a stronger warrior drive than lamb boys when they are younger. However, with increasing confidence, lamb boys can often end up being much braver than their rooster brothers. It is really important to ensure that your boys get plenty of warrior play in the real world rather than just on screens. Even though they can learn strategy playing simulated games, they will not pick up the emotional and social cues that are crucial to help them on their journey to manhood.

Playing team sports can be an excellent opportunity for young boys to be warriors in the real world. Learning how to be a team player can also be an especially important life skill for boys who have a tendency to want to be the best at any cost. This will curb any selfish and narcissistic tendencies that can happen with boys who are roosters in their temperament. Even though team sports can be really positive, parents need to be really mindful of our boys not being exposed to coaches who come from the old school and who think that shouting and shaming is a good strategy. Steve Biddulph cautions parents to be mindful of the unintended negative side effects around certain sporting codes because sports leaders are like elders of the tribe and so a misogynistic, racist and homophobic coach can really be a powerful negative influence on your son.

Even though I encourage boys to participate in team sports, you can start too early and I have known lamb boys who have been enthusiastic about joining the soccer team and then by the third week they are over it. It just requires too much energy every week that they are unable to find. So, I suggest that if possible, you don't pay the fees until about week three if you can because by then your lamb boy may have decided that it's not for him. He may be ready to tackle it again in a year's time. You may also have a highly energetic rooster boy who is capable of playing two games of soccer every Saturday and who may throw a tantrum when you tell him he can't play the third game. Such is respecting the individual differences of our little warriors on a week-by-week basis.

Some of our young lads never take to team sports and that's OK. They are not 'less of a boy', they are simply a different sort of boy, and I've often found they have music in their soul, or a hunger for nature and animals or they are an artist of some kind.

> "My mum used to bike ride and do lots of active things with me like going over BMX jumps and canoeing." – Men's Survey 2017

More about growing good warriors

In today's world much of the early warrior development that traditionally occurred in boyhood – and which was guided by appropriately timed rites of passage – is now taking place in adolescence when our boys have bigger bodies, higher levels of testosterone, a malfunctioning brain, and much bigger and more potentially lethal risky play. In some early years' centres in Australia, hero play has been banned. This means that young kids are not allowed to pretend to be superheroes rescuing people from baddies – because they might jump off something too high and hurt themselves. In making this seemingly harmless rule, we negate a developmentally important part of the early warrior mindset – how to be a 'good' warrior who helps to conquer evil. The same goes for early gun and sword play with young boys – we fear it might turn them into psychopaths, but it may just help them one day find the strength to stand up and speak for someone who is defenceless against a bully. Warrior play may actually be more about respecting the warrior archetype – a deep, spiritual place of learning about protecting those more vulnerable and doing the right thing in times of conflict. I would love to see more girls encouraged in warrior play, as many girls can of course grow to be strong and fearless too. The recent Wonder Woman movie has provided a new sense of female physical power and endeavour. So, being a warrior who fights for the greater good is more about temperament and character than gender, as there are lots of boys who prefer to pursue gentler passions.

Essentially, our task as mums is to help our warrior children be warriors with heart who are mindful of how their actions impact others.

Rosalind Wiseman, the author of *Ringleaders and Sidekicks*, has an interesting take on superheroes, specifically Batman, which I'll mention here. She says when little boys watch films/TV shows depicting Batman, they see before them a stoic, strong, silent, man whose face never depicts emotion. He certainly never smiles. Essentially, she suggests Batman has taught boys to suppress their emotions and put others' needs before their own. It's sad but true of our culture's expectations of boys ... Batman isn't the only one projecting this message. However, it is also a great teachable moment for parents who might be sitting on the couch next to their little ones, to talk about why Batman is the way he is and to discuss how he might be feeling. I wonder if poor Batman had many friends when he was a little guy – interesting food for thought about how boys become conditioned to shut down their emotions.

Boy warriors still need lots of help in building emotional and social competencies to learn how to play with and get on with other children. Play is the absolute, best way to build these competencies in our boys.

And for more information on that, I agree with the wisdom from author and parenting expert Ian Grant that boys need the following:

1. **Boys like to explore the natural world in a much more physical way than girls.**
2. **They need to investigate how things work.**
3. **They need balls to kick, things to climb and to be able to pit themselves against a challenge, preferably in your backyard with easy access. (Avoid putting sporting equipment into containers because your son won't be able to find them.)**
4. **They need structure and boundaries.**
5. **They need goals and coaching in how to persist.**
6. **They need a safe environment and a zero tolerance attitude towards ridicule.**

– Ian Grant, *Growing Great Boys* (2008).

> "It is not unusual in our house with three DBs (5,7 & 8) for me to shout 'are you using the drill/power tools?' It is also not unusual to look into the yard and see a cave man-type tool has been fashioned out of branches, rocks and duct tape!" —Wackyboys Mum

The link between dopamine and attention has been the subject of research for many years. Dopamine is created by physical activity, having fun, being creative, problem-solving, learning fascinating new information and having freedom to explore the natural world. Dopamine is also created really easily with screen activity and many researchers are now concerned that excessive gaming and quick entertainment could be re-setting the dopamine receptors in our boys' brains. More food for thought? Could we be contributing to higher levels of ADHD for our children, especially boys and Indigenous children, by not providing them with enough of these opportunities? It seems the further we get from those traditional communities, the sicker, sadder, fatter and more disconnected our young boys are becoming. These little boys have a tendency to grow into being angry, unhappy and unfulfilled men.

> "I wish my mum had not stopped me playing sports." – Men's Survey 2017

As well as the ban on superhero play I mentioned earlier, we are also seeing early years, kindy and prep classes in some places banning tree climbing, outlawing playing 'chasey' and removing the sandpit to be replaced by more mat time, phonics in isolation, more desk work, less free play and homework for 4-year-olds. This is what I call the 'schoolification' of the early years. If I was a 5-year-old boy today, I would be angry too.

Another word on play comes from Daniel Goleman, author of *Emotional Intelligence* and more recently, *Social Intelligence: The New Science of Human Relationships*. Goleman studied the work of neuroscientist Jaak Panksepp.

> **"The primal subcortical circuitry that prompts the young of all mammals to romp in rough and tumble play seems to have a vital part in the child's neural growth. And the emotional fuel for all that development seems to be delight itself."**
>
> – Daniel Goleman, *Social Intelligence* (2006).

This writing validates the common-sense notion that children benefit greatly from experiencing sustained moments of joy and delight. It appears that these moments of delight fertilise the growth of circuitry in the amygdala and frontal cortex of the brain. Panksepp studied the tickling response in mammals, finding that all mammals have 'tickling skin'. In his studies, Panksepp found that children and other mammals were instinctively drawn to adults who tickle them. Apparently the tickle zone in children runs from the back of the neck and around the rib cage. I am sure many of us remember how hilarious it can be to be tickled by someone safe. The circuitry for playful joy has close ties to the neural networks that make a ticklish child laugh. This means our brain can become hardwired with an urge to play, one that hurls us into sociability.

Panksepp argues that many children with hyperactivity, impulsivity and unfocused, rapid shifting movement from one activity to another (as in ADHD), are in fact seeking to activate the joy and delight response. He makes a radical, untested proposal to let younger children 'vent' their urge to play in an early-morning free play, rough-and-tumble recess, then bring them into a classroom after the urge has been sated, when they can more easily pay attention.

The evidence continues to mount validating why movement and play are incredibly essential in the early years, especially in the early years of our boys' lives. Maybe there is a link between the increasing levels of mental illness, anxiety and stress that is being witnessed in our precious teens in numbers that we have never seen before. I believe we need to go back to the basics and bring play back into children's lives – real play in the real world with real children – in our homes, our schools and our communities.

Do we have to wait until we have credible research that validates the strong link between the absence of play and the unwellness of today's adolescents and adults? Why don't we just become bold and start doing it because it makes sense and it is the right thing to do? I firmly believe we will reduce the violence in our homes and communities and online if we restore play to its rightful place.

There are studies that suggest that 'rough-and-tumble play' (this also includes free-range exploration in nature) especially for boys and their dads, reduces violent behaviour later in life. Play fighting, rough and tumble, and even combative role-play, were once considered very normal parts of childhood. Yet today, these forms of play are often misinterpreted as forms of bullying, or a precursor to bullying, and are banned.

Early years' researcher Penny Holland, in her book *We Don't Play With Guns Here*, argues that these forms of play are outward signs of a sophisticated and largely unconscious learning process that helps to build emotional and social life skills. Children learn how to read key facial expressions and body language, and can quite clearly tell the difference between play and the real thing — the 'play code' again.

> *Many boys' lives tend to be micro-managed, over-supervised and hyper-planned, and there is very little freedom and autonomy. The increasing depression and mental illness of our young lads in adolescence may very well be the canary at the bottom of the coalmine telling our modern world that there are some very deep instinctual drives in our boys that need to be nurtured in healthy ways rather than denied and crushed.*

As Gurian explains, the strong drive for external experiences to find self-worth and value is a profound and sacred journey that is at the core of a healthy manhood and begins at a boy's birth.

Just the same as we need to be concerned about the negative effects of our modern world on the healthy growth and development of our girls so, too, do we need to be concerned about how to help today's boys grow into being good men, and not lost souls incapable of empathy, compassion and moral strength. Again, this requires a joint commitment from good women and good men who are committed to the healthy raising of our often vulnerable young boys.

We need to seriously reconsider giving boys back their boyhoods and opportunities for authentic growth in the company of lots of other kids, good women and good men, or we are going to continue seeing more and more 'dickhead' immature warriors wreaking havoc in our communities.

The reality is that our boys will grow into men, and the type of men they become will be based on the guidance they have received from the significant grown-ups in their lives, and on their experiences in childhood and in life in general. All boys, and men, want to be loved, valued, appreciated and respected, and they want to be in effective, mutually caring relationships.

Our home and school experiences shape who we become, and boys deserve to be seen as different in some aspects but just as valuable in our schools — and we need to return play to its rightful place for all children, but especially our boys.

> **"The decline in opportunity to play has also been accompanied by a decline in empathy and a rise in narcissism, both of which have been assessed since the late 1970s with standard questionnaires given to normative samples of college students. Empathy refers to the ability and tendency to see from another person's point of view and experience what that person experiences. Narcissism refers to inflated self-regard, coupled with a lack of concern for others and an inability to connect emotionally with others. A decline of empathy and a rise in narcissism are exactly what we would expect to see in children who have little opportunity to play socially."**
>
> – Peter Gray, *Free to Learn* (2013).

TOP TIPS

- ✓ Diminished opportunities for children's play are negatively impacting how boys are growing up.
- ✓ Intensive parenting sees children with less free time to play.
- ✓ Risk has been drastically reduced in boyhood.
- ✓ Natural consequences and painful moments help boys to learn how to make better choices.
- ✓ Learning the invisible 'play code' in boyhood would help boys later in life.
- ✓ Warrior play can be a helpful and valuable part of childhood.
- ✓ Boys need to make dopamine to stay engaged, especially in our classrooms, and they need movement to do that.
- ✓ Play needs to be returned to its rightful place in childhood.

CHAPTER 10

When boys **MUCK UP**

> "My mum gave me unwavering support in everything that I have ever done, or wanted to do. This includes some bad decisions and outcomes through my formative years." – Men's Survey 2017

Hopefully at this point of the book, the wonderful mums of sons who are reading will have a new understanding and appreciation about why our boys tend to be such poor decision-makers throughout their lives. Notice that I call them poor decision-makers, rather than bad or naughty boys because, technically, that is what they are.

If, with our new understanding, we can reframe some of the unique characteristics of boys that combine as a consequence of their inner biology and biochemistry – the interplay of hormones (particularly testosterone and vasopressin) and their natural need to move combined with an impulsivity that is often unconscious – then we may have different expectations for our sons. Some expectations are passed down in families and are quite simply unhelpful for boys, and yet they can influence them invisibly and deeply. In a way, the expectation that boys are much harder to handle and to raise is a really simple example of an expectation that can be unhelpful. Remember how people responded when I had my third son?

If a well-meaning family member says something like, "Oh, John is just like his dad and he struggled at school, so John will too," they are expressing a low expectation and contributing to the creation of a low outcome for poor John.

Also, when I was teaching I often spoke to parents of high school boys at parent-teacher meetings who held similar low expectations for their sons because their dad hadn't done very well at high school. In a way, this is where boys' school disengagement can become a bigger problem when both parents and teachers support the same low expectations.

I worked with a family where both parents were elite athletes and one of their children had no athletic skills or interest in athletics, and this lad struggled with a strong sense of failure despite being a very capable musician. He believed his musical ability was not a talent valued by his parents.

The wonderful and highly respected Indigenous educator Professor Chris Sarra of the Stronger, Smarter Institute writes passionately about the incredible importance of high expectations in improving educational outcomes for Indigenous students. If we keep colluding in lower expectations for our Indigenous students and many of our male students, we are effectively continuing to support the problem.

Having high, positive expectations absolutely influences performance and hence behaviour in our homes, schools and communities. So, as mums, we need to make sure that we hold high – and yet still realistic and positive – expectations for our sons, so we can teach them and guide them to make better choices. We cannot leave this to chance and hope they pick it up via an exceptional educator in their early years' setting or at primary school. It needs to be a day-by-day commitment that we make. We also need to help other mums come to a better understanding of the power of expectations and of the need for warm, consistent discipline. Accepting the old adage that 'boys will be boys' when they struggle to make good choices sets boys up to fail in so many areas of life. There is no question in my mind that if we have more realistic expectations that are linked to the age and development of our sons, we will be able to be the safe bases that our sons need so they can learn how to make better choices. We also need to recognise that this is a really long-term project and there is no quick fix. Further, we need to recognise that the stronger the attachment and sense of being loved that our sons feel, especially with their mother or the mother figures around them, the easier it will be to teach and guide them on the journey to making better choices.

This means we need to question some of those stereotypical perceptions that still exist about boys. Yes, boys can be more vigorous and energetic and enjoy risky, adventurous behaviour than our girls, however, it is our responsibility to help them realise that they need to respect those around them when they are making these decisions.

Toddlerhood visited briefly – making creative, clever and poor choices

Toddlers are biologically wired to become scientists, adventurers and explorers using all their senses to try and discover how the world works. And boy toddlers, with their extra energy and physical strength, can be really exhausting. When they smear their food all over the wall this, too, does not have to be seen as bad or wrong, but merely your son using his senses to find meaning in his world. When they use a permanent marker to draw you a beautiful picture on the wall or on your dog – again, they are not wrong or bad. Their intention came from a place of love and they were using their 'seeking mechanism' in the way Mother Nature intended. The same goes for when your son unravels a toilet roll – or maybe two or three – and stuffs them down your toilet to find out what might happen. He's not scheming to be bad, naughty or wrong – he is merely using life's greatest teacher – experience – to learn about the world. There was a DB (2) who was fascinated with the toilet and began a game of putting Mum's knickers into the toilet, pushing the button and exclaiming with great enthusiasm, "All gone!" His mum lost around 15 pairs of knickers before he had mastered that experience and he moved on to something else. The next time you have a 'bugger' moment like that, pause, and reassure yourself that your child is a creative thinker with a passion for life who's using experience as a wonderful teacher. I recommend four steps to manage – without using shame or exclusion – situations like this to ensure they don't happen again.

The parental pause

1. Pause and take a deep breath – become present.
2. Enthusiastically lean forward to your son and ask, "Did you do that all by yourself?"
3. Now let him know why the choice he made was one you would prefer he didn't make again. (For example: "We don't play in the toilet because this is where we do poos and wees, and there could be germs that will make us sick." Or: "We don't write on the walls, we write on paper." Or: "We don't put Mummy's knickers in the toilet because then she won't have any left to wear on her bottom.")
4. Finally, involve your son in a lengthy clean-up process that acts as a natural inhibitor or deterrent so he will avoid trying that experience ever again. Never miss this step.

Just beyond the toddler genius stage

Often around four years of age boys can appear to become more 'badly behaved', less responsive to parental guidance and incredibly energetic physically. Over the years I have noticed how many mums have turned to me in desperation during this window because nothing seems to be working with their fierce, busy and very active 4-year-old sons. A partial explanation for this change in behaviour in a significant number of our boys is due to some shifts in hormonal activity, particularly the luteinising hormone, which directs their testes to start making Leydig cells. These interesting little characters lie hidden deep in our little boy's body to play a much bigger role when puberty begins, however, this hormonal shift — whether directly or indirectly — can contribute in some way to this change at this age.

> "After my adventurous and fearless DB (4) ended up in the ED for the second time in four months (broken finger the first time and then a head wound that needed stitching) he said, 'I may as well leave this hospital bracelet on for next time I need to go to Monash.'"
> — Exasperated Mum

From my observations, I have found many 4-year-old boys still struggle with verbal communication and they tend to respond through physical action. This is why I describe boys' behaviour as being *their communication*. Regardless of the reason for this increase in energy and the need for activity, boys from four to six often need a lot more freedom to move, plenty of space to move, lots of opportunities to be adventurous and brave and the chance for plenty of moments where they are autonomous and able to make their own choices — even if they cause themselves physical pain. This window does pass, however, trying to contain little boys who need to be navigating their worlds with energetic action, enthusiasm and very little thought, can be where we are unintentionally damaging our boys and how they see themselves. Mums can find this really difficult because it can be exhausting and frustrating to maintain the balance between being a mean mum and a loving mum. It's a case of dishing out enough parental guidance to keep your boy alive versus giving him enough freedom so he can seize the authentic moments of joy and delight that make him glad to be alive.

If you are lucky enough to have a backyard, fill it with balls of all sizes, bats, ropes and the biggest sandpit that you can fit, and allow your son and his little mates to run wild and free. Yes, they will often do this naked on cold days — please resist your natural mummy instincts to bring them inside and insist they are warm and dressed. Trust me, they will come in when they are ready.

Let me repeat — this highly energetic and frustrating phase of your son's life does pass. There were many times when, before taking the Dent boys out in public, I would first plan to 'run the gunk out of their motors'. Essentially, this meant I wanted to give the boys time and space to be as physically vigorous as they needed to be before we went somewhere where this was going to be impossible. Given that many of our young boys are spending more hours on digital devices than outside running wild and free, it is understandable that we are starting to see high numbers of boys being suspended and expelled when they are four to six years of age.

It is not surprising that many boys struggle with formalised learning in our early years' settings given the restriction on movement. As one mum wrote:

> We are going to an OT each week and I have learned to incorporate large amounts of physical activity into my 5-year-old son's day to help him concentrate at school. I've met with a teacher to discuss ways to make the classroom situation better for everyone. Interestingly, she has found all of the children are better behaved now that she has incorporated extra activities and movement into her class. It is not only my 5-year-old who learns best through movement and an active classroom. I wonder how many pre-primary children are struggling with the 'sit and learn' style and are assumed to have a learning disorder or behaviour issue as a result, just as my son did. It seems quite obvious to me that the current 'sit and learn' model is not working.

To help our boys make fewer mistakes and poor choices, we need to encourage them to understand that there are boundaries in life that need to be respected. Having too many rules can mean they can't remember any of them! A great idea is to have a few clear guidelines for our sons, rather than a long list of rules that they would have little hope of remembering. This technique can be really helpful, especially for our young boys.

It can be helpful to start with three basic rules: 1. try not to hurt yourself; 2. try not to hurt anyone else; and 3. try not to damage the world around you.

The first really important thing for all mums of sons to remember is that the majority – and I mean nearly all – of the poor decisions your son makes that end up hurting something are very rarely intentional choices. Seriously, our little boys do not want to upset their mummies or daddies, or hurt people they really like. And, often, they have no idea why they did what they did.

If we are able to embed these three rules deeply into our boys' psyches from toddlerhood – particularly that hurting others is not OK – then, possibly, we may be able to contribute to the much-needed cultural change around the thinking that it's OK for men to molest, rape and murder women. Maybe if all homes used these simple rules as a guideline then even our girls would stop being so mean to other girls.

What was he thinking? Why boys make poor choices

Recently a close friend shared a story of her 5-year-old son on his second day at big school. She was called by the school to come and collect him as he'd hurt himself. On arriving at school she discovered that her sweet son had chosen to do a backflip off the top of the slide and he'd landed heavily on his back and winded himself badly. When she asked him why he would do that, he said his mate had dared him to do it! What was he thinking?

Another story was about a 14-year-old boy who struggled with ADHD and he decided to graffiti the deputy principal's car. He wrote his own name on the car! What was he thinking?

There was also a 17-year-old lad who thought it was a great idea to skate down a very steep road in the middle of the night while he was drunk. After breaking both wrists and removing an enormous amount of skin, he confessed it was a dumb thing to do and he wouldn't do it again. Sadly, he forgot those words and tried the same stunt a couple of months later and re-broke another wrist. What was he thinking – twice?

During the last winter Olympics, there was some classic teen boy behaviour from 17-year-old Red Gerard who almost missed his event because he overslept after a Netflix binge, then he couldn't find his jacket and yet he still managed to rush to his event and bag an Olympic gold medal. What was he thinking?

As I have explored, boys are still biologically wired to be 'mammoth hunters' or protectors of the more vulnerable members of their tribe, ready to respond to threats quickly.

The hunger for dopamine, the often irrational need for movement and the surges of hormones all play their part in the high energy levels of many boys. Physical strength is ensured with more muscle being present in boys – and physical strength and a fearless attitude have a lot to do with the poor choices your son may make. Even our lamb sons have the same difficulty making good decisions so this process is not influenced by temperament.

To help understand why boys often make poor choices – which often end in injury – firstly let's be clear that they are not doing this deliberately! Their intention is quite simply to 'do' and to have fun and enjoy life by doing 'stuff' while testing themselves to see if they have 'done good'!

So, let's see why "what were you thinking?" might be the wrong question to ask your son after he has done something that seems really dumb to us parents. I have covered most of these things in more depth elsewhere in this book, but just to sum up, here are the main factors involved in poor decision-making for boys.

- **No myelin** – The capacity to make sound, well-thought-out decisions that take into account risk has a lot to do with the maturation of the brain. The fatty white substance called myelin takes until our 20s to fully develop, and this is what helps humans become mature, responsible adults. This process of myelination varies between individuals and there is research that suggests girls develop myelin earlier than boys. So, struggling with planning for the future, motivating oneself, managing impulses and learning from mistakes can take boys until their late 20s or even later – much later. Having no or little myelin impacts decision-making and also our capacity to learn from our mistakes.
- **Boys' behaviour is their language** – Hitting or jumping on top of another boy as a way to say hello or goodbye is quite common and sometimes very painful! 'Aggression nurturance', a term I've already mentioned, coined by Michael Gurian, is a non-verbal way in which boys show affection. The intention is to express his affection, not to hurt! Wrestling and rough-and-tumble play are ways in which many boys connect physically with those they love. So, reframe this behaviour next time you see it and teach your son some less painful farewell strategies, such as high fives. If you have more than one boy in your house, you will notice there is an awful lot of 'aggression nurturance' taking place!
- **Testing themselves** – The invisible self-worth barometer that I have explained in-depth is responsible for many of boys' poor choices because they are always assessing themselves via what they achieve externally. This partly explains why many boys are so competitive and why they keep striving to do better than last time. Hitting targets is a way they do this, so have lots of cushions in your lounge so they don't throw toy trucks. This need to prove his worth to himself is what drives much of a boy's risky behaviour. This also is why many boys often feel they have let themselves down and can get irrationally angry at themselves. And it is also why we need to change the dominant way with which we discipline boys by using a punishment of some kind that usually involves pain.

- **Emotions can be confusing** – Boys don't tend to spend as much time as girls thinking about their feelings, however, they do feel them just as intensely as girls. Feeling like a failure or feeling excluded triggers big, ugly feelings that can often drown a boy, and often he responds by becoming angry and often he expresses that through aggression. The increasing numbers of boys being suspended and expelled in their transition-to-big-school journey – with the current climate of 'schoolification' – may be a result of having expectations of boys that are developmentally inappropriate. We need to look at what is really under the anger - because anger is a symptom rather than the problem.
- **Movement matters** – Movement helps boys create positive neurotransmitters, especially dopamine, and so often boys need more movement than girls and, again, our schools often fail to appreciate this need. Often a boy will be bouncing on your couch while watching his favourite TV program! After prolonged periods of being physically confined, such as when sitting or using a hand-held screen, boys often have a strong biological need to be as active as possible to discharge excess energy in their nervous systems. The need to move, fidget, kick and shove can be a biological need to make boys feel better – not to be annoying or naughty. Prioritise movement in your son's life 'to burn the gunk out of his motor'! Seriously, if you have a social engagement that you need to take your energetic son to, try to find a park where you can have him be very physically active for at least 20 minutes before you go to the engagement and you will really help him succeed at managing to contain his need for movement.
- **Experience is a fabulous teacher** – There is plenty of research that explores how many children learn by doing rather than listening to someone tell them what to do. Boys tend to disengage from situations where grown-ups talk too much, and this includes their parents and teachers. In the chapter on play, I explored how one of the best teachers for our boys is natural consequences, or where a boy learns as a consequence of a real experience. Repeated pain is a wonderful teacher too! This is why boys like to know if they've passed or failed – because it gives them a clear message about their efforts. When school reports use terms like 'progressing', it confuses boys. Being hurt by a wooden seesaw up to three times was a great way for a boy to realise that he is accountable for his choices. Verbal warnings of possible dangers can simply not be heard in their hunger to 'have a go' and test themselves. Celebrate natural consequences even though it may look like you are a lousy parent sometimes!

- **Belonging with the tribe** – We all have a hunger to belong and with boys this is particularly strong, especially when playing. One of the best ways to stay connected is by doing what others are doing – no matter how crazy or dangerous that may be. This is why a 'dare' is such a non-negotiable concept in boy land. To ignore a 'dare' risks being excluded from the tribe. If a boy is a part of a group of boys who feel liked and connected and who have been supported with warm discipline, there is a tendency for them to do less things that are hurtful and destructive – and the reverse tends to happen too. Rooster boys who have low empathy can tend to be the most aggressive as they grow older and they may become bullies in some way or another in their lives.
- **Gaining status** – For a boy to feel better about himself and to be seen as better in the eyes of the tribe, he often will do things to gain credibility and status. Again, this is an inner urge that does not pass the few layers of myelin in his developing brain and can leave grown-ups scratching their heads! This is where some of the most risky behaviours come from – jumping from a taller branch or higher rock and throwing rocks at windows or streetlights. This will become another issue for boys during adolescence – so be warned.
- **Seeking connection not attention** – Even though most boys don't look sensitive and in need of love, affection and tenderness, they are. Biddulph writes about this sensitivity around feeling unloved and abandoned, especially in young boys. Ensuring your son's love cup is full needs to be done in small ways and often – it's even better when done without words and more with actions (see my chapter, ***'Mummy, do you love me?'***. Kicking, hitting and fighting with siblings – more than usual – may be a sign your boy needs more connection. *Sometimes negative connection seems better than no connection.* Notice I use the word connection and not attention because many grown-ups still use the term 'attention seeking' and I believe that is incorrect and disrespectful in many ways.
- **Reducing stress and releasing cortisol** – Because of boys' impulsivity and the need to test themselves physically, they often make poor choices that are seen as naughty or bad. Their sense of failing and letting themselves down also adds a layer to why boys struggle with cortisol overload – and the need to discharge it with a meltdown in the car after school, irrational physical aggression or by running away. Sometimes boys' hunger to have fun – which is a way to release cortisol and make dopamine and other positive endorphins – means they act really silly. This can occur through farting, burping, mentioning silly words, as well as by removing their clothes. Some boys make positive neurochemicals by making

funny shapes with their penises (aka penis puppetry). Others can let the bath run over so they can have a great skidding track on the bathroom floor or use a whole bottle of bath gel in one go. These actions need to be seen as ways of releasing the unique stresses of being a boy and not as a sign of their deliberate intention to make parents really angry. Yes, it is still really annoying and they need to clean up after themselves.

> "I was running late and was a bit angry already when we got in a FULL bus with DB (3) and he picked his nose and ate a huge booger in front of everyone. When I told him (for the 1000th time) not to eat his boogers, he snapped back with: 'I'm hungry, you didn't feed me this morning!'"
> — French Mum

So, Mum, what can you do to help your lad gradually make better decisions when he mucks up?

- Try to see the world through a boy's eyes and practise responding, not just reacting.
- Remember, boys are sensitive and not tough so practise warm discipline not shouting, hitting or shaming.
- Allow him time to cool down and process whatever it was he did that caused you angst — 24 hours is a good time lapse.
- Gently ask what was his intention when he made that choice: "What were you trying to do, hon?"
- Remind him about the three rules and help him work out other ways to achieve what he was seeking without breaking the rules: 1. try not to hurt yourself; 2. try not to hurt others; and 3. try not to damage things in the world around you.
- Forgive him for making a poor choice — often and quickly.
- **Reassure him you still love him** — non-verbally as well as verbally — by 'showing' rather than 'saying' and ensuring that his love cup has more loving in it than it has poo.

A final story I want to share is about a 4-year-old lad who drew a huge lipstick picture on the hallway wall for his mummy. Needless to say, Mummy lost it, despite (she told me) having heard me talk about my steps to toddler genius. She yelled at him and sent him to his room and spent ages removing the mess. Two nights later, while her son was having a bath, he said:

"Mummy, remember the lipstick picture I did for you? Well, I tried so hard to draw you a beautiful picture cos I love you soooo much."

Needless to say, his mum felt pretty crappy in that moment! She realised she had missed his true intention.

> "My mum gave me continual understanding. I am a complex individual with ADHD and have had self-esteem issues. Mum has been incredibly understanding and supportive despite my animosity toward her at times. This has influenced me toward being more compassionate than I would otherwise be. (I am still somewhat lacking in this respect.)"
> — Men's Survey 2017

I think it would be helpful to explore why there is often a mismatch between what a mum thinks has happened and what a boy thinks has happened. When this happens a boy can feel deeply misunderstood and, if he feels misunderstood, he feels disconnected and unloved. This is partly why I am so passionate about building understanding between mums and sons. Let's explore intention in a bit more depth.

Fear of feeling like a failure and a fear of losing status is behind many dumb decisions boys make at school and, when they bring home their sense of disappointment, it is often poor mum who will wear their emotional angst in many different ways.

Here are 20 examples that show the importance of questioning before deciding how to deal with a situation to ensure you really understand why he made that poor choice.

1. A boy was sent to the office after he pushed another boy over in the playground. Why? The boy was defending his sister who had been hassled by the boy he pushed the day before and he wanted to stop him from doing that.
2. A boy was seen running up to greet his friend at the school gate and punched him. Why? Boys often struggle to know how to greet each other and the punch is a form of 'aggression nurturance' or a way of showing how much they like a friend.
3. A boy was playing a vigorous game of chasey and knocked over a girl he didn't see. Why? He was running so fast that he never saw her and it was an accident and he will feel awful for hurting her.
4. A boy stole a book from a school book fair. Why? He saw his friends stealing and rather than lose status, he chose to join in even though he knew it was wrong.
5. A boy who struggled with his mum leaving him in kindergarten, wipes away tears and then turns and gets angry over a tiny thing and throws sand in another child's face. Why? This is the sad-angry

response many early childhood educators see often as many boys are unable to manage sadness or disappointment well so they channel it into anger as it's a more 'accepted' male emotion.

6. A boy began throwing biros and pencils in class. Why? He may have been bored. He may have been trying to impress a girl. He may have been getting worried as he had cross-country coming up later and was scared he'd lose status.
7. A boy has a tantrum about going to school. Why? There's a sight word test and he doesn't know his words. It's easier to not turn up than to turn up and fail.
8. A boy sees his mum waiting at the bus stop to collect him. He races up to her and slams into her leg, hurting her. Why? He is trying to show her how much he loves her and has missed her. He didn't realise it would hurt her.
9. A boy threw a stone and accidentally hit a window. Why? He was aiming for a tree and missed, and never meant to hit the window.
10. A boy was asked to bring in the washing and his mum found some of it in a basket with the pegs still on it later – not finished. Why? The boy really wanted to go and ride his skateboard so he took some of the washing off in a hurry and hoped that would be enough.
11. A boy was asked to vacuum the daddy long-legs spiders and their webs out of the lounge and hallway but he never did it. Why? He was uncomfortable hurting the spiders and felt sorry for them.
12. A boy was asked to get dressed to go to a community event and came out with a very holey T-shirt and dirty jeans. Why? He chose his favourite clothes for such a special event.
13. A boy was asked if he had his jocks on for school – answer 'no'. Why? It feels better without them!
14. A boy was sent to get his shoes from his bedroom and never came back. Why? He either forgot what he was asked to do or, on arriving in his bedroom, he was distracted by some Lego and started playing.
15. On the way to soccer a boy starts getting 'narky' with his sister. Why? He suddenly became hungry.
16. A boy toddler is throwing a mega tantrum in the car for no apparent reason. Why? His sister's foot was resting on his favourite blanket.
17. A boy is not answering his mother when she calls out to him while he watches TV. Why? Boys are often single focus and he is unable to hear her as he is watching TV.
18. A boy cannot find his socks. Why? He is looking in the wrong place as he has forgotten where the sock drawer is.

19. A boy has lost his school jumper – again. Why? He was so intent on playing, he lost all sense of where his jumper was – even forgot he had a jumper!
20. A boy starts kicking his mum vigorously in the leg while she is talking to the teacher at the end of the school day. Why? He had a poo that was due and wanted Mum to hurry up and take him home so he could deliver it.

Often when we see the world through just our mummy eyes we can misinterpret much of our boys' behaviour as being intentional and deliberate and naughty. Of course, there are some children who have a nasty aspect to them and who can choose to do things to deliberately hurt others, however, I have found that to be rare, and often there is a reason for their behaviour. Indeed, in my classrooms and in my counselling rooms, the boys I have found who deliberately hurt others have often experienced significant trauma early in their boyhood.

So, next time you notice a behaviour or event that displeases you, pause and ask yourself, "What is he really trying to say?"

Give him the benefit of the doubt until you have a chance to explore the experience in a quiet moment, maybe in 24 hours' time, and then help him to see the world through your eyes.

Other considerations for poor behaviour in our boys

There are other factors to consider if you are really concerned about your son's challenging behaviour. The more sophisticated we become as a society, the more complicated we seem to make things. Gurian has discovered in his work over the last 20 years that some boys who display oppositional behaviour, irrational moods, poor attention and serious disengagement in school are often struggling with undiagnosed issues on a much deeper level. It seems that genetics, epigenetics and environmental toxicology can be contributing to the genuine struggles many boys have. These things may be contributing to the increasing aggression and violence in boys in the Western world.

Over the years, I have had a number of mums come and tell me about the massive transformation in their son when they changed his diet. For these boys, the discovery of the gut-brain connection – as explored in books such as *The Grain Brain* by Dr David Perlmutter and *Gut and Psychology Syndrome* (also known as GAPS) by Dr Natasha Campbell-McBride and even on ABC TV's popular science program, *Catalyst*, which broadcast a series called 'Gut

Revolution' earlier in 2018 – was life-changing. There is no question our diet has changed with many more processed foods, fast foods and other hidden contaminants. Maybe we need to look more deeply at the health of our boys and explore the chemical and cellular reactions that transpire between digestion and neurochemistry as possibly being a contributing factor to the increasing aggression in our boys.

In fact, there is more and more research coming out that links the state of our microbiome (basically the microorganisms that live inside us) to anxiety, depression and other mood disorders. With rates of anxiety and depression soaring among our young people – particularly our adolescents – it seems it may be worth taking a closer look at the gut-brain link, and definitely taking a closer look at diet where behavioural and mental health issues are present.

And instead of focusing the blame mainly on toxic masculinity and the negative impact of technology, maybe we can consider another factor in the way we understand and manage the angry, aggressively behaving boy.

There is so much research coming out that suggests the additives and preservatives being put into our food – ironically to make it taste better, last longer and make life easier for time-poor people – are contributing to increased illness and poor behaviour in our children. It is not so much the immediate effect of eating food with these ingredients that is concerning, but rather what the long-term, cumulative effects of consumption might be. There are increasing numbers of children developing food intolerances much earlier in life, especially allergies, with some babies being diagnosed with allergies in the first few weeks of life.

I have already mentioned the sensitivity of boys to endocrine-disrupting chemicals and this sensitivity may possibly be behind some of the poor behaviour in our young lads.

For some boys, comprehensive testing in genetics, environmental toxicology and nutrition has shown they have difficulty processing folic acid, or vitamin D or too many heavy metals. Mood difficulties have been linked to poor folate processing. This is why Gurian suggests we need to become scientists for our boys to explore other causes that could be contributing to their aggressive or restless behaviour, rather than assume it is just because they are boys. The ability to concentrate in class and to stay focused and to be capable of self-regulation is much more complex than we used to believe. I certainly worked out in my classrooms that hungry boys are very difficult to teach.

Further, as I said above, our diet has become highly processed and refined, and producers are messing with molecules to create food that we give to our children. There is evidence that certain preservatives in some bread are particularly problematic. The numbers to watch for on the side of your bread packets are 282, 319 and 320. I have had many parents of boys report to me how quickly their behaviour improved once they removed these numbers from their children's diets. I recommend Julie Eady's book, *Additive Alert*, which was updated in 2017, as a quick and easy guide to some of the ingredients we can be mindful about for our sons. She suggests that parents need to take responsibility for teaching children healthy attitudes to high-quality food and she warns of the dangers of too much processed food full of salt and hidden sugars.

The World Health Organisation suggests children have no more than the equivalent of four to six teaspoons per day of sugar (apparently the average Australian has more than three times that!). It seems that sugar can be an environmental toxin for some boys that makes them even more impulsive and aggressive and I certainly had one young son that this applied to. Keeping my 'sugar hungry' son away from sugar in all its forms was a daily battle in our home. However, I took it as my responsibility to prevent rather than blame the impact that sugar had on his behavior.

Just to give you an idea, a 600ml bottle of lemonade contains around 15 teaspoons of sugar, and the same amount of fruit juice contains about 13 teaspoons. Removing soft drinks and unlimited fruit juice from our boys' diets could make a big difference in their behaviour and it is worth giving it a go to see for yourself.

Obviously most fruit juices, soft drinks, low-fat yoghurts, fruit bars and muesli bars are the worst culprits for excessive sugar, often containing up to five times more than the recommended daily intake. Empty kilojoules and passive childhoods are not a good combination for our children. There are lots of great cookbooks and recipes online to help you make healthier swaps for high-sugar items. Perhaps sit down as a family and watch *That Sugar Film*.

Rather than food additives being a sole culprit at times, we need to acknowledge that our environment has changed and we live in a much more contaminated and polluted environment on so many levels. We also live in an environment of high stress much of the time and, for some children, their experiences are beyond stressful and they are living with trauma.

The impact of adverse childhood experiences — trauma and behaviour

As a high school teacher, I met many troubled students. Indeed, one of the reasons I left teaching to become a counsellor was because I had a passion for helping these kids find a better path in life. And it was in my counselling sessions that I heard stories of trauma that adolescents had witnessed or experienced. Some of those traumas included physical, psychological and sexual abuse, extreme deprivation, witnessing violence especially within the home, dangerous bullying and the death of loved ones. It has only been in relatively recent times that we have started to link adverse childhood experiences (ACEs) to behaviour and mental health in children and adolescents.

I have been very concerned for a long time that in our school systems we have tended to punish these kids who struggle rather than help them. Gurian strongly holds the view that the increasing violence, particularly in males – and I'm sure the US experience mirrors what is happening in other Western countries – is linked to trauma experienced between birth and adolescence. It seems that trauma impacts the brain as a form of 'neurotoxicity', which further impacts negatively on the development of emotional and social competence. This is why I have written a whole chapter called ***"Stop hitting, hurting and shaming our boys"***. In fact, this whole issue greatly informs my passion for writing this book and the role that mums of sons can play in preventing and healing trauma, as well as facilitating emotional and social maturity. With more understanding, nurturing and consistent loving care we can improve the outcomes for our beautiful boys.

> **"Boys are coming to school with epidemiological issues from neurotoxins and emotional trauma responses in families and communities."**
>
> – Michael Gurian, *Saving Our Sons* (2017).

Helping boys with conflict

Given that making mistakes is a lot easier for boys than girls, boys will tend to make more. One of the key lessons that we need our precious sons to learn is the difference between intentional mistakes and unintentional mistakes, such as accidents. When boys plan to do something intentional, they will need your warm discipline to realise why it was a poor choice. You can refer them back to the three rules, and they will also need you to help them work out how they can make a situation right. Often little boys who have made an intentional error of judgement will try to blame someone or something else because, in a way, they are trying to protect their sensitive self-worth barometer. Blaming others – even the dog – is developmentally appropriate for young children, however, not for older children and definitely not for grown men.

So how do we teach our sons, when they have mucked up, to accept responsibility and do the right thing?

The first thing is often the most difficult thing for us mums of sons. In the heat of the moment we need to let our son know that when we are both in the emotional 'red room' it is not a good time to talk about the conflict at hand. Indeed, mentioning the need to cool down and take some time to think is really useful. Give them at least 24 hours and at least a night of sleep in between.

In as gentle a voice as possible say, *"Babe, let's chat about this tomorrow after we've both had a chance to cool down and think".* A non-verbal gesture of support would be great but, heck, sometimes that's impossible for an angry mum in the heat of the moment.

I suggest you have this kind of conversation in the same place each time and this is the conversation that you have in this place. It needs to be well away from other siblings and somewhere you will not be interrupted. What worked for my family was the chat on the deck. I would take up a position facing them with my elbows on the balustrade and they would be facing the ocean views behind. This gave them something else to look at if the conversation became too painful and confronting. Trust me, looking into a mamma face that has disappointment or frustration all over it is really hard for a son or a boy who values your love and connection. Then the conversation has some simple steps that, if repeated, will build a structure for your son which he can use for the rest of his life.

If you can build rapport before you have the conversation then you will most likely have a better conversation, so possibly bring a hot chocolate or a juice, or ruffle his hair or say something really dumb. This just creates a little serotonin, the neurotransmitter of calmness.

The five-step conflict resolution process — for when boys muck up

1. Help him know what went wrong (What was his intention?)

Try to let him do the talking by gently asking what he had hoped would happen or what he was trying to do that resulted in the issue you're discussing. Aim to stay silent and yet fully present. Hold the space. Help him to see why the choice he made was a poor one because it would have broken at least one of the three rules. Once I knew of a boy who accidentally broke a neighbour's window. He really couldn't understand why his mum was so upset because he never tried to break the window. Quietly, rule number three was explained, along with the understanding that despite it not being intentional, it was still his ball that had broken the window and it needed to be made better.

2. Help him to make it right

Once your son has recognised his poor choice, give him an opportunity to consider how he could make things right again. Notice, I have suggested that he works out how to make things right rather than Mum or Dad making things right for him. I find this helps boys learn to become more accountable and responsible in the long-term because they are problem-solving their own mistake. It's quite funny that sometimes they will think up something really awful as a consequence. I asked one of my rooster sons once what he thought would be a fair consequence for damaging his brother's skateboard, which he had used without permission. He said he thought he should be grounded for a month … a bit unnecessarily tough perhaps!.

3. Next time?

This is an incredibly important step. You need to work with your son to work out what would be a better choice if ever he was in the same situation again. Remember the little boy who bit the girl who sat on his truck? He would have repeated that behaviour if his mum had not spent time giving him some other information and tools so he could make a better choice. Having conversations about this around the dinner table throughout your son's childhood will help him work out how to make a better choice in many different situations.

4. Then forgive and forget

Given that we mums have amazing memories and we never forget anything, this can be a difficult step to master. We are so often tempted to bring up a past misdemeanour or bugger-up moment. Please do everything you can to avoid rehashing the past because a part of your son will feel you are still disappointed with his poor choice made 10 years ago. Just smile, give him a wink and say nothing.

5. Acknowledge the valuable learning

This last step can be optional, however, I have often found that it has helped my sons to see that life is a long journey of learning and growing. Did I regret putting my finger into a light socket when I was 10? Absolutely. Did I ever do it again? No way. So, again, because our boys tend to learn from natural consequences and experiences that cause them some discomfort, it can be valuable to remind them that life's lessons are not all bad. In a family of four sons, I often found that one son's disastrous muck-up moment, could also become a valuable life lesson for the other sons.

We know that all children model themselves on the grown-ups around them and your son will copy you. At one point I had chosen to stop full-time counselling and focus on writing, running seminars and working as a celebrant at weddings and funerals. One of my sons DB (16) came to me after school one day and asked if he could have a chat on the deck. Now, in our house, that was code for a serious talk. So I headed out and what was really funny was that he was standing with his elbows on the balustrade (where I would normally stand for a serious chat) and I was standing in the position where he would normally stand. He then asked me, "Mum, have you really thought about this decision to give up counselling?" We had a good chat about my reasons and he gave me some really good reasons why I should reconsider my decision based on feedback he had received from some of his friends at school. I thanked him for his concern and, as I walked inside, I had a new understanding about the importance of 'the chat on the deck'.

The mum letter

> *When your sons are in the midst of adolescence, things can get really interesting and they can sometimes find it difficult to really hear you, especially when you are saying something they don't really want to hear.*

Knowing that boys often forget the spoken word, I would write the occasional Mum letter to my boys once they were old enough to understand. I only ever needed to write these letters to my rooster sons because, during adolescence especially, they thought they knew everything and Mum knew nothing. As mums, our well-intentioned and gentle reminders and suggestions are often ignored.

Mum letters address serious concerns — the concerns that wake you at two o'clock in the morning. And my gut instinct would always let me know when I needed to write something. I'm a firm believer in using effective communication when writing such letters. These letters have always been written with respect and honesty and with my heart wide open. I also always use the 'feedback sandwich' approach, which means you start with something really positive, which is then followed by the challenging information and then the letter concludes with another really positive, affirming message that ensures your son knows you love him as unconditionally as you did the week before. A part of the mum letter is that there is no need for your son to ever mention receiving the letter and there is no need to talk about it. It is merely a letter of concern from a loving mum to a strong, feisty son in the hope he may hear the information and consider it.

Here is an example of a possible mum letter to a 12+ boy.

Letter for your DB (12+) when you are worried

My Dearest Son,

I love you more than all the stars in the night sky, more than every grain of sand on every beach in the world and all the hairs on all the bears - I really, really do.

Babe, please take a few moments to read this letter. I know you think I am always worrying, and I try too hard or I am a try-hard(?) but I am your mum and that's part of what parents are meant to do.

Just lately something is different about you and, yes, I am worried. You haven't smiled for weeks, and you are struggling to get good sleep. You are spending much more time than usual in your bedroom and your friends haven't been around for ages. You really seem down and I am worried.

I have been online and checked out some youth websites and some of these things are listed as being a sign that you may be struggling. There is just so much pressure on you kids these days - and too much stress can make you sick. Our world can look nasty and unfriendly too. I also know that you won't want to worry me - and that you might think you will be OK soon - and yet my mum radar is ringing loud bells.

Can we have a chat? If not me, my love, can you please have a chat with some other adult? Any lighthouse will be great. If you want to chat to Dr ... I am happy and I will let you go without me if that's what you want. Or maybe a school counsellor or maybe someone online anonymously such as: Headspace, Lifeline, BeyondBlue or Kids Helpline.

I really want you to let someone listen to you and see if there's anything I can do to help you ride out this bumpy bit.

I have printed off some fact sheets and would love it if you could glance through them.

If you really are OK maybe we could just go for a hot chocolate sundae, shopping or a walk on the beach. Massage? Hot bath with bubbles? Swim with dolphins? Holiday in Monaco or Italy? OK, maybe not the last one ...

Maybe you need a new teddy bear? You know they never hog the bathroom, or pinch the doona or finish your favourite cereal before you at breakfast. They also don't fart.

> Remember that adolescence is a time of intense turmoil and confusion and it will one day get better when your brain finishes growing.
>
> I love you with every fibre in my being.
>
> Your Mum

Once, when my two rooster sons were living together as adults, they each received a letter from me in the mail which contained some Lotto tickets. Neither of them knew that the other had ever received a mum letter – such was the importance of it being a secret just between Mum and that son. When they saw the letters, they looked at each other in horror! Neither of them wanted to open the letter, just in case it was a serious mum letter! We had a really good laugh over it later.

The price of payback

There is one last thing I need to explore in this chapter about when boys make poor choices. Somehow in the historical conditioning of our boys and men, physical retaliation or 'payback' is seen as acceptable and OK. In a way, this physically aggressive action has been seen as justifiable in boy world. We seriously need to deconstruct this perception and expectation. Maybe due to the difficulty of expressing big, ugly feelings, especially in the heat of the moment, when combined with the sensitive emotional barometer of self-worth, payback may seem justifiable. Regardless of possible reasonings behind this pattern of behaviour, all parents need to do everything they can to help their boys understand that conflict can be resolved and injustice can be made right without physical violence. This is why the emotional coaching of little boys, and then bigger boys, is so incredibly important. Giving our boys an understanding of conflict resolution without aggression can happen, especially if they have been raised with the three rules I have already discussed. In the chapter on ***"Building character in our boys"***, I will explore this in more depth.

You will notice that there is no shaming involved in any of these conflict resolution processes that I recommend for mums of sons. Your son may need some very gentle reminders along the way, however, the crucial word here is 'gentle' and with warm discipline, this can even be done with humour. This approach ensures that the love bridge stays strong. It can help your son develop the character traits and a sense of personal accountability and responsibility that you will be proud to acknowledge in him one day. He will also learn about making choices that don't hurt others – towards both boys and girls and men and women. I need to reassure you that warm discipline, especially from mums, is far more powerful than the harsh, toxic punishment that was common many years ago.

> "I farted while driving one day. My 19-month-old son was in the back. He smiled cheekily and said, 'Mummy poo'... His first two-word sentence! So proud ... not so proud of his achievements today though. He ate his own poo and said, 'Nom nom cheese'. I was horrified." — Proud Mum

TOP TIPS

- ✓ Holding low expectations for boys is unhelpful.
- ✓ Toddlers are not naughty, just curious scientists.
- ✓ Boys can be physically more active and rambunctious around four years of age.
- ✓ Help boys learn the three rules: 1. Try not to hurt themselves; 2. Try not to hurt others; 3. Try not to hurt things in the world around us.
- ✓ Boys can make poor choices without meaning to muck up.
- ✓ Use the five-step conflict resolution process to help boys become mindful of choices that hurt and how to make things right again.
- ✓ Boys are unable to process big, ugly feelings when they muck up for quite some time.
- ✓ Practise warm discipline.
- ✓ Keep coaching boys about what they can do next time.
- ✓ Try the 'mum letter' for rooster sons.

CHAPTER 11

Stop **HITTING, HURTING** and **SHAMING** our boys

From time to time I read messages from people who think we should bring back caning to our classrooms to improve boys' behaviour in our schools. It seems their understanding is that by caning our boys we will somehow make them behave better. In my experience, corporal punishment gives temporary compliance at best and certainly ignites further anger and rage within our boys. This is another stereotypical attitude that must be deconstructed and ended.

> "I wish my mum hadn't beaten me, locked me in cupboards, taught me to feel contempt for men including my dad and myself, shamed me around sex and died 24 years ago." – Men's Survey 2017

In my counselling rooms I met many wounded men who were hit and shamed in our classrooms by both men and women. Many times they were hit over trivial issues and often punished for things they had not done. Those who were the product of certain religious school systems that practised corporal punishment often seemed particularly conflicted given that Christianity has strong messages about love.

It is not just men who have been conditioned by these beliefs, as I have already mentioned in parts of this book. Quite recently, I witnessed women in a playground who were observing a young boy who had made some poor choices. They were saying quite loudly, "He just needs a damn good smack!"

> *What is definitely to be avoided is the 'toughen up' stance of last century and the use of sarcasm and shame-based language, which can have lifelong painful, negative consequences.*

I can say without a doubt that all the boys and men I have worked with who have planned, attempted or expressed suicidal ideation, had deep layers of shame. Layer after layer of shame quite simply crushes the life force of our boys and men. For some, the shame just gets too difficult to bare and many expressed to me that the people they loved would be better off if they were no longer around. For some, suicide seems like a way to escape the angst and pain of living with so much emotional pain, especially the shame. For others, the shame can surface over a major loss that may have been prevented if the man had made a better choice, or if he'd had the courage to be emotionally honest or if his pride hadn't been so damn stubborn.

The damaging effects of shaming

Shame is the name we give to the overwhelming feeling that we need to crawl under a rock because we see ourselves as unworthy, unpleasant, dislikeable or reprehensible, and because of this we expect to be judged or rejected accordingly.

> **"Shame is like a knife that sharply delineates the limits of love in every culture, the warning signal that something we are doing risks us being ostracised."**
>
> – Robin Grille, *Heart to Heart Parenting* (2008).

Shaming starts very early and often is created through quite innocent, seemingly innocuous comments from grown-ups and even loving parents. The impossible pressures being placed on today's parents are contributing significantly to more shaming in our children.

- "Stop crying or I will give you something to cry about!"
- "Do you want a smack?"
- "Stop being a sook."
- "Get out of my face."
- "Be a man."
- "What is wrong with you?"

Despite the pressure to try to live up to some family ideal, we must remember there is no perfect child, parent or teacher – never was nor will be. Humans have flaws. Children are evolving and growing, and sometimes in order to master a skill or a competence they will fail often; that's healthy, not bad.

Shaming language implies that a child is bad, naughty or in some way flawed – rather than describing them as a child who is simply learning how to manage and interpret this crazy world. Deep shame is distressing for our psyches and can happen so early in life. Shaming makes it difficult for children and adults to come to a healthy place of self-love and acceptance, and instead leaves a person feeling deeply unlovable and unworthy of happiness.

In my counselling experience with boys suffering despair, depression or even ideas of suicide, I found these lads often feel overwhelmed by their emotions. Emotions were unidentified and unresolved, lying buried inside them. Many of these boys felt deeply flawed and like a failure; they believed that those closest to them did not love them. This deep sense of alienation and feeling separate came up so often when listening to these troubled lads. They were starving for deep, meaningful connection not only with their parents but also with other significant adults in their life. They often felt completely misunderstood. Many schools still use shaming, sarcasm and strong criticism when dealing with poor behaviour, and many boys carry these scars right through life. As I've said, we must remove the old boy code that existed in the 20th century because it is no longer valid; in fact, it wasn't valid then.

Because they are conditioned to hide their feelings, boys may be more vulnerable than girls in terms of their inner world and we must change how we discipline boys.

> *The first step to changing this is to see that discipline is very different to punishment. Discipline is about teaching and guiding our children and punishment is about hurting them in the hope that they will make better choices.*

As I've said earlier, an excellent way to help a boy explore an inappropriate way of behaving is to use movement. When you want to speak about something and you know he could feel potentially vulnerable, take a walk around an oval or up the street while having a dialogue with him about the concerning incident. The movement will help him to feel grounded and safer and as I said earlier it is less confronting and more private than sitting still face-to-face, so he will stay engaged with the communication.

One of the behaviour management techniques that happens in many primary school classrooms around the world is naming and shaming. This means that when a student – most often a boy – has been given two warnings and then proceeds to commit the same inappropriate behaviour again, his name is written in red on the board. I have had many boys tell me how coming into the classroom on a fresh, new day and seeing their name still on the board – written in red – seemed to drain energy out of their body. What is a little bit funny is that a large number of boys are colour blind and so they don't see red very well. Is this possibly Mother Nature protecting them from this technique? I am in no way suggesting that young boys who behave inappropriately in our classrooms should get away with their behaviour. But, what I am suggesting is that teachers use warm discipline and my five-step conflict resolution process (outlined in the previous chapter) to help them learn how to make better decisions.

I have still heard of occasions, in the last five years in Australia, where boys are instructed to sit under the teacher's desk. That is yet another shaming technique that needs to stop. Another one is making a boy stand in the corner facing away from the class with his hands on his head – again this is a shaming and an exclusion technique that does more harm than good. It also does not teach the boy about making better choices, but rather tends to put a label on him that he is bad or naughty.

I once worked with a DB (15) who was still doing extra duties in his boarding school for misdemeanours he had done two years before. This is an excellent way to keep reminding this adolescent boy of his inadequacies. It is not only ineffective, though, it is emotionally dangerous.

> "I wish my mum had not told me I was stupid when I couldn't do my school work. Turned out I had dyslexia!" – Men's Survey 2017

There was once a DB (14) who was having a tough time in a high school I was teaching at. He had shared with me that he'd spent most of his childhood in an orphanage. On his 13th birthday he found out that his real mum and dad lived in the same suburb. As puberty brought the usual extra challenges of increased emotional intensity, the confusion around identity and a hunger to belong, he struggled to fit with the mainstream students. He shared with me that one of the PE teachers had taken to hitting him with a cricket bat during class as a bit of a joke. One afternoon this DB came running into my office to tell me that he had hit the PE teacher with the cricket bat after the teacher had hit him one time too many. He was very distressed and came to tell me he was running away. I reached out and gave him a hug and wished him well. Fifteen years later this, this same DB (now 30) reached out to say hello. He had joined the army and had done quite well and was now running a sporting goods shop. He had wanted to contact me to thank me for being an ally during those difficult years. Just before he hung up he wanted to especially thank me for giving him a hug. He said that he was quite sure that was the first hug he'd been given in his entire life.

> *'Tough love' does not hit or hurt or shame. Giving your son an unpleasant consequence for his behaviour, usually a repeated behaviour as a consequence of poor choices, is disciplining rather than punishing.*

The primary goal of discipline is to teach and guide our sons to make better choices. Sometimes our boys, particularly our rooster boys, need a stronger reminder to reconsider the choices they are making. Removing a privilege, withholding something they value deeply or giving them extra duties or chores, are all ways you can discipline your son without punishing him. I once had to practise tough love on my rooster DB (16) by making his surfboard off-limits for a week because he kept punching his younger brothers. No matter that I understood that the surges in testosterone and the brain pruning in his head could explain his behaviour, I needed to step up and protect the younger brothers. A part of me wanted to cut his surfboard into small pieces at times, however one week – which seemed like the longest week of my life – was long enough for him to refrain from hitting his brothers. This was not a pleasant experience for me or for him, however it was a necessary experience. The only thing that didn't change through that whole week was he had no access to his surfboard. Otherwise, he was treated just the same as his brothers and there was no other punishment inflicted on him. Indeed, I may have deliberately farted close by him a few times so he knew that he was still loved. To be honest, there were many times that I shortened the period of deprivation, often by just a day, because I realised they had seriously taken heed of the message. The look of appreciation and relief was certainly worth that small gesture of kindness.

"My mum went through a stage 60 years ago of believing that the boys in the family needed more corporal punishment." – Men's Survey 2017

I once coached a friendly, enthusiastic boy in one of my basketball teams. He was a delight to have in the team. He came to me one afternoon before basketball training with a very heavy heart to tell me that he would not be able to play basketball again for the whole season. When I questioned him about why, he said his mother was not happy with his grades and he needed to spend more time studying. There were tears in his eyes and my heart ached for him. His mum had broken a part of his heart. Many years later when I met this boy who was now a man, he told me that he was completely estranged from his mother. When we discipline with unreasonable force or too lengthy a sanction, we don't teach, we hurt deeply – we punish. We also create lots of resentment and anger towards the person who created the unreasonable punishment. Trust me, the withdrawal period does not need to be exceptionally long – it just has to be one they would prefer never to repeat.

"When my brother and I were 13-14 we played a lot of different sports. My mum decided we weren't allowed to play ANY sport for a whole year as a form of discipline." – Men's Survey 2017

Mums of sons have told me of times they've cringed in their bedroom in tears as their son's father had decided that the only way to improve his boy's behaviour was with a good belting in the back shed. You do not have to beat your son to improve his behaviour, however, you do need to invest some time and energy into ensuring you have a relationship that is caring and respectful so you can be the teacher and mentor that he needs, when he needs it most. The early stage of adolescence is a critical window where boys can be very easily influenced positively or negatively. The presence of grown-ups who genuinely care about them is unbelievably important. As they are also on the journey to manhood, the presence of good men is, quite frankly, essential for a boy to be able to transition to manhood healthily and effectively.

These men do not need to be fathers – and, let's face it, for many single mums this can be an issue. They can be uncles, granddads, family friends, coaches, teachers, neighbours, the dads of their friends ... the only prerequisite is that they are good role models, so seek them out.

Now, let's explore shaming in more depth:

Examples of shaming

- Deliberately ignoring a boy
- Being sarcastic
- Walking away as though he does not exist
- Rolling one's eyes
- Glaring at the boy with disgust
- Shouting, yelling and swearing at a child
- Freezing a boy out!
- Saying things like:
  1. *You ought to be ashamed of yourself.*
  2. *You naughty boy!*
  3. *You are acting like a selfish brat.*
  4. *Grow up!*
  5. *Stop acting like a baby.*
  6. *Don't be a sissy.*
  7. *You're hopeless.*
  8. *You're not even trying.*
  9. *Why can't you be more like your brother?*
  10. *What are people going to think?*
  11. *Is your name stupid?*
  12. *Stop being so stupid.*

> **"Boys are not necessarily wrong, bad, disordered or pathological, nor are they tough guys who can succeed in life because they are male. Boys and their brains are quite fragile. Not to realise this is to continue approaching men and boys either as presidents or comic book heroes or as inherently defective — rather than who they are: people who struggle in life like anyone does and who need clear and appropriate aid, from the very early stages of their life."**
>
> – Michael Gurian & Kathy Stevens, *The Minds of Boys* (2005).

I once worked with a DB (19) who had had two serious attempts at taking his life. He shared with me that his dad was a controlling man and an alpha male – he drank, smoked, swore, gambled, was a sport freak and was often quite racist and sexist in how he spoke. The DB was more of a lamb on the temperament spectrum. He was a nature lover who enjoyed music, reading and cooking. He said he'd spent his entire life being a failure to his father. He had a clear memory from when he was five years of age of his father taking his special blanket and his teddy bear and throwing them in the fire and making him watch them burn until there was nothing left. He told me that his dad had then turned to him and told him to "toughen up because he was a sissy". His suicide attempts were desperate plans to escape the reality that his father would never accept him, respect him or love him.

Men have told me that these are the three things they really yearn for from their father or most significant father figure in their life. Fortunately, he was able to get the help he needed and he is now a father of three beautiful children, and he is being the dad he had hoped for his whole life. Sometimes, mothers of sons need to invest time and energy in decoding the old male ethos and we need to work hard to convince our sons that they can indeed be accepted, respected and loved exactly as they are.

> "I wish my mum had not been too overbearing and sharing her life stories with everyone, and speaking for me in front of people when I was right there." – Men's Survey 2017

Many rooster boys who appear stronger and tougher are struggling with the same emotional turmoil. They just have an ability to cover it better with a mask. Many times in my counselling room the most important work I ever did was holding a teenage boy so he could sob deeply – possibly for the first time in his life. There was often no need for words, however, the opportunity to own the deep grief, sadness and disappointment in a way that was safe with no judgement, for most boys, was all that was needed. What works best for most girls and women is talking about our feelings, and I have found that can be really confusing for boys. What matters most is helping them identify the main feeling they are experiencing, validate that feeling and then give them a safe opportunity to express it – otherwise their emotions can build up much like a volcano and explode unexpectedly. Around 20 years ago, I discovered the technique of emotional acupressure, which is now commonly known as tapping. This has been an amazing help in my work with boys and men because they are able to release a lot of emotional tension without having to talk about it. I especially recommend the work of psychologist Steve Wells at eftdownunder.com.

On another occasion, I worked with a lamb DB (16) whose mother had been highly controlling and critical and used shaming often. When he finally snapped, after yet another highly critical exchange, this normally gentle boy who was over six-foot tall picked his mother up and threw her across the room, fortunately onto a bed. He then proceeded to punch his fist through two layers of plasterboard all the way down the hallway of the house. He then picked up a cabinet of glasses and threw them upside down. Such was the intensity of the rage that he had held in for 16 years – the suppressed anger had become a volcano that he could not contain any more. Obviously this response is completely unacceptable. This boy has a significant mother wound that could quite possibly cause him problems, especially around female relationships, for the rest of his life unless he gets professional help.

Shame has been linked to a range of issues including anxiety, depression, obsessive compulsive disorder, personality disorders, addiction, eating disorders and even phobias.

American shame researcher Dr Brené Brown says there is an important distinction between shame and guilt, which she feels is essential for parents to understand – and the way we talk to ourselves is paramount. Brown defines shame self-talk as thinking, "I am bad", whereas guilt self-talk says, "I did something bad".

Brown cites a longitudinal research study of a large group of fifth-grade students, which measured whether these kids were using more shame self-talk ("I'm an idiot, I'm a failure") or guilt self-talk ("Boy, I made a bad choice there, I didn't do well at this"). The researchers followed these children into their senior year of high school and found that the kids who were 'shame prone' were more likely to die by suicide, engage in high-risk behaviours and leave school early. The 'guilt-prone' students were less likely to engage in high-risk behaviours, tended to stay at school and apply for higher education, and be more engaged in their community.

Perhaps the most telling part of Brown's and others' research is that the greatest predictor of whether a child will be shame-prone or guilt-prone is the kind of parenting they receive. Brown urges parents to examine their own feelings of shame, watch their own self-talk, and have honest discussions with their kids to set some non-negotiable family ground rules, such as no name-calling between anyone, including parents, and no tolerance for mean-spirited sibling behaviour.

Relational aggression, when experienced repeatedly in homes, definitely creates a tendency for children to do the same to others.

> *The three main forms of relational aggression that we need to avoid in our homes and classrooms are name-calling, put-downs and exclusions.*

Little boys often delight in using rude terms and making up funny names. This is quite innocent because the intention behind it is also innocent. It is when we begin using an intention to hurt and also a different tone in our voice when we do name-calling, that we can do damage. We do need to have many little conversations with our sons around where we have stepped over a line and we have caused someone some emotional pain by calling them names – even if we never meant to cause harm.

Put-downs can also be a part of the boy-man code later in life as a part of teasing their mates. Again, it may not have an intention to hurt, more of an intention to make others laugh, but sometimes it definitely hurts. 'Taking the piss' is very common in boy and man friendships and so mums and dads need to spend some time in conversations explaining the difference to our boys.

As our boys get older, they may be interacting with others via online gaming, chat rooms, via SMS or direct messages and group messages, and on social media. In these forums, they can't see others' faces to know when they've been offended or hear the tone of voice that something is delivered in. It is really important to help boys understand this, and to guide them through this new media (even if you're just figuring it out yourself!). Keep the conversation happening, monitor them and remind them that just as in real life, put-downs, name-calling and exclusion are not OK online.

Often, little boys do not understand sarcasm or put-downs and over time they can learn to appreciate them, however, when they are little they can take these things very personally. Sadly, many older men – particularly grandfathers – practise teasing on boys without realising that it is hurtful and not in the least bit funny. Teasing can be a really bonding experience between good mates and brothers and is sometimes misunderstood by mums, girlfriends and partners. Helping our boys to understand the verbal gymnastics of male conversation and connection can be difficult for mums, however, if their dad or other significant father figures are unable to explain it for them, then Mum needs to.

> "I wish my mum had not spanked me for accidentally breaking a window." – Men's Survey 2017

Having a family mandate or philosophy can be very useful in guiding the family solution-seeking processes I discussed earlier. I really love the large posters I see online and in shops, with some clearly defining the goals and aims of the home such as this one ...

In this house:

We do fairness.

We do honesty.

We do laughter.

We do second chances.

We do mistakes.

We do love.

We do forgiveness.

For boys and dads who tend to be very visual, having such a reminder in full view is a brilliant idea.

While it is crucial to avoid shameful communication, we also need to be mindful of not taking things to the other extreme by offering our boys constant and endless praise. This, too, can be unhelpful.

> "I was having a school morning menopausal outburst when my rock, my macho rooster DB (12), became my calming influence. He casually whipped off my dressing gown (which he was wearing) and revealed his school uniform paired with my high heel boots and he wiggled his hips and turned back to me with a catwalk turn and straight-face pose." — Never-a-dull-moment Mum

Praise and encouragement

In our efforts to look after our children's self-esteem in today's worried parenting world, it seems like many children get stickers simply for breathing! Have you noticed that children don't need to be given a reward for sitting down to watch a much-anticipated movie or to eat ice cream or chocolate? That's because these activities come with a built-in reward, the immediate reward of positive emotion. In contrast, teachers and parents often encourage children to engage in less-desirable tasks by offering extrinsic rewards that deliver an immediate positive emotion that's lacking in the task itself. Of course, this is not what we want – and that's why it is important to set the record straight! We give children chocolate and toys for contributing to housework, stickers for sitting quietly in class and grade 'A's for handing in well-written schoolwork. However successful this type of extrinsic motivation may appear in the short-term, it presents a number of significant inhibitors to a love of lifelong learning. Over-rewarding and over-praising can be particularly confusing for boys. Often it can turn them into praise junkies where they only do things in order to get praise, and if they aren't praised, they can become very angry. Rewards can also quickly become bribes and in the long-term using either will not help your son make good choices on his own.

Research shows quite clearly that giving children stamps and stickers to reward good behaviour towards others actually increases the opposite effect. It decreases their capacity for sympathy and empathy, and can cause children instead to be mean. Dr Helen Street, a social psychologist and co-founder of the Positive Schools Conferences, has found this is similar to the empty yearning for fame, fortune and celebrity. Individuals can be driven towards extrinsic rewards while secretly hating what they are doing. The use of rewards also increases compliance and obedience, which at first sight may seem like a great idea in the classroom. Sadly, in the long term the increase in extrinsic rewards deprives individuals of self-determination. Our rooster boys who are especially hungry for public recognition can struggle with over-praising and over-rewarding even more so than our lamb boys.

> **"A person who grows up getting too frequent rewards will not have persistence because they'll quit when the rewards disappear."**
>
> – Dr Robert Cloninger, cited in Po Bronson & Ashley Merryman, *NurtureShock* (2009).

One of the reasons I suggest that your sons need to do chores around the home without financial rewards is that we are trying to instil in them that families work together. A family that works as a team where everyone helps each other is a really helpful message for your sons to realise. If your son would like to earn some more money because he may have something special that he wants to buy – like new trucks for his skateboard or a surf magazine – then we can encourage that by giving him the option of doing an hour-long task around the home. Maybe he could wash windows or sweep the driveway – no matter the task, it needs to take roughly an hour and will have a monetary reward. By doing this we are teaching our boys that things have value and they need to respect the value of things. They need to also take responsibility and put some genuine effort into earning anything extra that they want which is above the normal family financial arrangement. Please don't pay your sons to do everyday chores.

I deliberately chose not to pay my sons any pocket money. So one afternoon I noticed rooster DB (8) walking down the hallway eating lollies. I stopped to ask him where he had got the money from to buy the lollies, and this was his explanation:

"Mum, I had a really good idea. I thought that if I cut some flowers from your yard and some from the neighbours' yards [without asking them I might add] and made bunches of flowers, then I could sell them to the neighbours to get some money so I could go to the shop and buy some lollies."

I immediately knocked on my neighbours' doors to apologise with my son, however, we were all quite amused with his financial nous. He now works in a global investment firm!

Please do not be disillusioned, praise can still work provided we don't overdo it.

Praise works best when:

- It is specific.
- It is sincere.
- It is not excessive.
- It is to do with effort rather than achievement.
- It is intermittent.
- The reward is within context, and not too big or expensive.

If we always keep in the back of our minds that boys are hungry for our acceptance, respect and love then we can keep filling their love cups more effectively using acknowledgement. Rather than praising, the art of **acknowledging** our sensitive boys is incredibly important. This is more about letting them know, "I am noticing you and the choices you are making". Some of these suggestions have also been included in the chapter on ***"Mummy, do you love me?"***

Acknowledging kids positively (or practising positive noticing)

1. Smile at them.
2. Wink at them.
3. Say, “Hello” and use their name.
4. Say, “I’m glad to see you.”
5. Suggest, “Let’s go play together.”
6. Ask them to show you how to do a puzzle.
7. Give them a pat on the head or back.
8. Hug them if appropriate.
9. Ask about their favourite toy.
10. Play a hand or clapping game with them.
11. Hold their hand.
12. Say things like:
    a. “Thank you for helping me clean up the toys.”
    b. “Thank you for being kind to your brother.”
    c. “I noticed you washing your hands after going to the toilet.”
    d. “I know how hard it is to be patient when you play with others.”
    e. “I noticed you using your quiet voice – well done.”
    f. “I saw you brush your teeth without my asking.”
13. Sing songs with them, especially their favourite ones.
14. Cuddle up and watch a favourite kids’ program with them.
15. Pretend to be an animal, a truck or a dragon.
16. Find them or call them and say, “Hi.”
17. Make them laugh. Lots.

You will notice that by acknowledging our sons or practising positive noticing with them, we are very much focused on strengthening their attachment and bondedness to us in a loving, supportive way. This is incredibly important. It will fill our son’s self-worth barometer and it will remind him that many of his actions are positive and even helpful. Again this takes us back to connected parenting and attachment. The more loved our boys feel, the more secure they feel, the calmer and happier they are and the better they will behave. It is not complicated stuff, is it?

I cannot reiterate enough that we need to challenge the stereotypical beliefs that suggest that if you want boys to behave well, you have to punish them when they don’t. Hurting our boys with physical punishment and verbal abuse may bring temporary compliance but it will ruin the relationship and create emotional angst that will need to be expressed at some point in time.

> *We need to stop being mean and cruel to our boys and focus our energies on building supportive relationships that are warm, fair and firm so we can teach and guide them to make better choices and be accountable and responsible when they don't.*

The buried anger and rage that hides deep inside many boys can manifest as serious aggression and disrespect for figures of authority later in life. It can also be a driver to find ways to keep it hidden with addictions, poor motivation and irrational fear of failure. Sadly, mental illness, especially depression, is another way a damaged boy-man can find himself struggling later in life.

> "I had just hurt myself and my eldest son DB (5) ran off to his room and grabbed a soft toy to comfort me. After I made a big deal of how sweet that was of him, my middle son DB (3) held out his hand and said, 'I've got something for you too, Mummy'. I said, 'Oh, how sweet, what is it?' He grinned. 'Booger,' he said, and threw it at me. The three of us collapsed about laughing, my sore leg forgotten". — Mum of Three Boys

I deliberately called this book *Mothering Our Boys* rather than *Mothering Our Sons*, because I know that many boys' and men's lives have been altered positively by the influence of someone else's mother.

> *Aware and caring women can really impact boys who have a tough mum.*

In 2016, I reconnected with a young man who had been a part of one of the basketball teams that I had coached. He saw me across the room at a function and made his way over with a big grin on his face. I recognised him instantly and remembered that he had been the only child of a mum who had some significant mental health issues. After we made the usual rapport-building chat he dropped his voice and said he had hoped he would run into me one day because he wanted to thank me for two things that I had done. The first one was that he wanted to thank me for a particular basketball move that I taught him how to do down the middle of the keyway because that move had helped him become a valued basketball player over many years. We laughed that he could remember that that had mattered so much. And then he leaned closer to me and told me about something I had forgotten. Apparently, one day at school when students were coming down the stairway towards the canteen, I had put my hand high up on his back and held it there for a few moments. I am prone to positive touch and sometimes it does happen quite randomly and intuitively, so although I did not remember, I did not find it surprising that I had done this. He said he had been having a really bad time in his life as his mum was being really difficult and unpredictable and he had felt very alone. He said that warm touch on his back on that tough day was something that quite simply gave him hope that he wasn't alone. He had tears in his eyes as he thanked me. That was when I realised that mums of sons have a responsibility to watch out for and nurture the sons of other mums who may be unable to nurture and care for their sons as they need.

> *Make your home welcome to your son's male friends and fill their love cups with genuine concern and affection, because you never know when their cup is empty.*

We have welcomed a number of other mums' sons into our home over the years and, yes, it does add to the chaos, it increases the food bill and it certainly increases the washing, however, we know that when boys are able to find a safe place inside a mother figure's heart, they will be transformed.

My sons were surrounded by many loving mother figures and I am eternally grateful for the connection and kindness that these women offered to my sons, and continue to offer them to this day. You can never have too much mother love as a boy.

> "I've been brainstorming with my mum for about half an hour about what I wished she hadn't done and neither of us can think of a single damn thing." – Men's Survey 2017

TOP TIPS

- ✓ We need to change the belief that boys need to be punished to get them to behave better.
- ✓ Shaming is common with boys.
- ✓ Deep shame causes significant damage emotionally, mentally and psychologically.
- ✓ It is important to reassure boys that they are not bad or naughty, but rather they often make poor choices and this can be improved.
- ✓ Mother-love and acceptance can change boys' lives positively (even from mother figures who aren't related to them).
- ✓ Over-praising is not helpful for children.
- ✓ Acknowledging our boys positively can help them learn how to make better choices without hurting them.
- ✓ Boys need to do chores to learn how to be part of a family.
- ✓ When mums are warm, fair and firm we can teach and guide our sons to make better choices and to be accountable and responsible when they don't.

CHAPTER 12

Avoiding the **MOTHER WOUND**

> **"Unresolved issues in a man's relationship with his mother are profound sources of trouble in a man's life."**
>
> – Michael Gurian, *Mothers, Sons and Lovers: How a Man's Relationship with his Mother Affects the Rest of His Life* (1993).

In the opening chapters of this book, I mentioned that we all tend to carry scars from our childhood, and most of those scars are fairly benign and can actually become a source of building family linkages rather than destroying them. My sons quite happily reminisce about my failures as a mum, particularly the times I threatened them with a wooden spoon if they did not go to sleep. I would often take a wooden spoon up to their bedroom and, yes, I have been known to break a couple on the edge of their metal bunks. I honestly admit that I forgot their lunchboxes numerous times and was known to call them by the wrong name often and, yes, I even called them by the dog's name occasionally. I have failed to attend the school assembly that I was helping my son prepare his item for because I got the wrong day. I have taken the wrong boy home from a birthday party and I have left one of my sons at the pool after swimming club – so I am far from a perfect mother of sons. Maybe, because I never strive to be perfect, my sons were more accepting of my failure moments. Maybe it made failure easier to embrace as a boy – who knows?

A deep mother wound is not formed from these experiences. Serious disruption to the 'secure attachment' that is optimal for every child with their key caregiver – whether biological or not – is quite different to occasional challenging moments. There are three types of insecure attachment that are commonly known as avoidant, ambivalent and disorganised and these are the types that seem to be most often underneath a mother wound. These categories of relationship were developed by Mary Ainsworth – a student of the father of attachment theory John Bowlby – and have been explored by many parenting researchers and experts including Dr Gordon Neufeld, Dr Stanley Greenspoon, Dr Fraser Mustard and Dr Margot Sunderland, just to name a few.

Mothering can be seen like a triangle with these words:

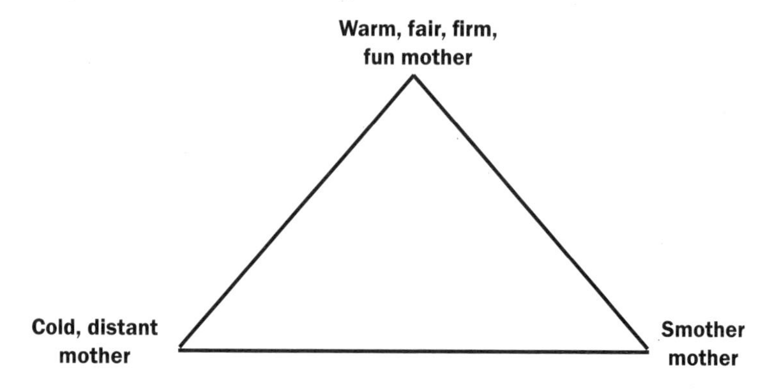

It took me a long time to come to the realisation that having a smother mother was almost as destructive for a boy as having a cold and distant mother. Remember a mamma who smothers her baby or toddler with kisses, hugs, tickles and raspberries is not a smother mother – that is a mother working on secure attachment! A smother mother is one who over-invests in her son's life and, indeed, is a mum who enmeshes her life with her son's life. Some mums substitute their sons as a form of intimate partner rather than a son. Seriously, a son needs a mother who is a parent and who can hover somewhere between mean and loving.

I was once at a barbecue where I witnessed a smother mother and her son. The mother was a teacher at the school I was working at and when her 12-year-old son came up to her at the barbecue she asked him if he had put his undies on. She then properly reached inside his tracksuit pants to check if he had, indeed, put his undies on – in front of all of us! I was gobsmacked and, quite frankly, did not know where to look.

> "Mum would do everything for me as a child which didn't allow me to be independent. Consequence is I sometimes don't have the tools or the confidence to do things myself." – Men's Survey 2017

A smother mother takes away her son's accountability and his need to grow up and accept responsibility for his choices. She will often do his homework and is often at the school complaining about any minor indiscretion that may involve her son. The sons of smother mothers are often bullied because they have been unable to build the emotional confidence and buoyancy to manage their own lives. They are often quite needy emotionally and when not around their mother, tend to hover close to female teachers hoping they will look after them until they can be back with their mother. There are times when boys realise that their mother is smothering them and they are incredibly powerless to push back from that out of a fear she may abandon them. In a way it can create a Catch-22 situation. At home, these boys tend to be like little kings who have to do nothing – no chores and no responsibility. They are often pandered to and get anything they want. Smother mothers tend to envelop their boys in Bubble Wrap so they never feel the bumps and bruises of life. Later in life, these boys find it really hard to separate from their mums and, indeed, many of them never leave home. So, there really can be too much love – and what tends to work best is for sons to have warm, fair and firm mothers who can also be fun.

> "I walked into the lounge room to find two of my boys giving each other shoulder rides. After a gentle reminder to be careful with each other, I saw a well-planned swipe at one of the innocent book-reading brothers on the couch, from the boy on the bottom, with the leg of the boy on the top. I pleaded, 'Please stop hitting your brother with your other brother' … Words I didn't think I'd ever say. I had to laugh at myself." (DBs 5, 6, 8 and 10)
> — 4-Boys-R-fun Mum

The smother mother relationship can impact sons later in life as well. In mature, intimate relationships with women, men can often be triggered when they feel they are being smothered or over-controlled by the woman they love. Often they have no idea why they become so angry and defensive. This mother wound can be triggered when well-meaning mums tell their good men how they should do things because it implies that their way is not good enough. I have long been reassuring couples that there can sometimes be a 'mum' way of doing things and a 'dad' way of doing things and, while they are different, they can both be acceptable. After years of such criticism, many men can feel completely emasculated and they can exist as almost a shell of a man.

Sometimes, a boy who had this kind of mother experience can struggle with intimacy in a few different ways. They do need and yearn for love like everyone else, and at times they will miss their partners when they are not around. However, often when their partners return, they feel 'trapped' and hanker after space again.

> "I wish my mum had not been really over-protective until I hit my mid-teens." – Men's Survey 2017

Men can often feel smothered in a relationship when they are unable to sustain their friendships with other men outside the committed relationship. I have frequently listened to men express how suffocating it feels when they are not allowed to be away from home for any length of time. Needless to say, these relationships seldom survive long-term.

Every human has a need for individuation and separation, and holding on too tight can feel suffocating.

When a son finally leaves his boyhood behind, hopefully some time in his 20s or even later when his prefrontal lobe finally grows, it is advisable that he walks out of his mother's home with both his testicles intact – metaphorically speaking. I have worked with many men who feel their mother has one testicle and their wife has the other and that he can never please either. The art of letting go of your sons is coming up soon in this book.

So, how does the cold and distant mother-son relationship impact our boys later in life? Sometimes it creates an incredible yearning for love and tenderness, and yet they can find that terrifying as well. A boy who has had a cold, distant mother has a seriously armoured heart and can struggle to open it as an adult because he can struggle with deep feelings. Not only can he find them uncomfortable – he can find it hard to share his deepest loving feelings with the woman he loves because he is wary of getting too close to his partner in case it becomes too much. This mirrors how he felt around his mother and he may risk getting hurt again.

If this boy has been able to spend time around a warm, fair and firm mother or mother figure it can make a huge difference to his understanding that not all women are as emotionally frigid as his mother.

> "I wish my mum had not said that I was a mistake." – Men's Survey 2017

There is another possibility for men who have had the emotionally unavailable mother and that is that they will attract a woman who will abandon them just like their mother did. Falling in love can happen even if you have had a frigid mother because our primary instincts, when combined with our hormones, can make the phenomes of being attracted too strong to resist. We know that falling in love is the easy bit – staying in a committed relationship is quite different. What can happen for men who had a cold, distant mother relationship is that when the honeymoon period wanes or when his partner gets to be less loving and attentive – for example due to the arrival of a new baby or new work commitments – this can trigger terrifying, irrational fears within the man that he is about to be abandoned again. This can come out as rage or escapism where a man can use his addictions to compensate for the pain in his heart, generated by the thought of being abandoned again. Either of these reactions will make the relationship difficult to sustain.

When we carry a father or mother wound, it goes far deeper into our adult psyche and soul, and it often unconsciously impacts our relationships negatively. In my counselling work, I found that many boys and men tended to stay very loyal to their mother despite having experienced major painful moments that caused them enormous heartache. Metaphorically, boys and men who carry a mother wound will tend to struggle significantly in connecting closely and emotionally with women.

> *Some men with a mother wound can find it difficult to be the tender, loving father towards their children that they want to be because their heart seems to be frozen.*

This often-irrational defensiveness can be triggered around figures of authority, especially school teachers and female bosses. It does not take much 'to poke the bear' that is a mother wound and often that happens unintentionally. There were times in my counselling days when I was asked to work with a boy who had shoved or pushed a female teacher over quite a minor verbal communication. Other times I found that boys with a mother wound could be incredibly disruptive in classrooms with female teachers and yet behave really well in classrooms with male teachers and have absolutely no idea why they behaved this way.

If there are times that the man in your life is irrationally defensive or angry, one possibility you could explore is that you may have poked his mother wound. In a way, the 4-year-old boy inside your grown man is still yearning to be accepted, respected and loved.

Without experiencing a positive mother-figure relationship, a boy can struggle with his relationships with women and especially his intimate relationships later in life. One of the main reasons for writing this book is to help prevent more little boys from experiencing mother wounds because I know that the wounded heart of a boy can become a defended heart as a man. This means they find it difficult to open and receive love, and even harder to give love, and these are essential traits when forming intimate, safe relationships.

In my experience, men who have a significant mother wound tend to struggle much more in their relationships. It is often an irrational struggle that can be incredibly confusing because the boy is desperately yearning for love and affection, while the grown man continues to get angry because he is not getting that love and affection. Some family violence can stem from this inner war. The men simply lash out and attack the woman they love in an attempt to punish their mother for not being the safe, loving maternal presence they needed.

"I wish my mum had not tried to control me and my family and not listen to anything I say. Her way or the highway!" – Men's Survey 2017

I still remember working with a 50-year-old man who had struggled with alcoholism his whole life. When he told me his story it made sense to me that addictions can help men manage their mother wounds. This man had been born in Africa to a well-to-do family, which meant the mothering was done by nannies, rather than his mother who tended to spend most of her time at the tennis club. This was culturally normal at the time. Sadly, for this little boy, if his mother noticed that he was developing an attachment to a nanny she would have that nanny removed and replaced with another one. So, what tended to happen was that he was repeatedly abandoned emotionally over and over as a young child. Not only that, when he was five years of age he was sent to boarding school around 50km away from the family property.

This shy, little boy struggled with the tough boarding school routines and he was hit, excluded, made fun of and shamed daily. Dealing with this incredible tension and fear meant he developed a stress-related speech disorder and his anxiety manifested in bedwetting, nail biting and much crying. He simply learnt to harden his heart and he remained at that boarding school until he was 14 years of age. His family moved to Australia and, as soon as he could, he moved as far from his mother as possible. His life had been one broken relationship after another and the only comfort he found was in alcohol. He had been an incredibly hard worker and was seldom without a job and he financially supported the two children that he had fathered with two different women. Meeting and working with this man touched me deeply. I used emotional tapping in my therapy work to help release unexpressed emotions from deep within his nervous system and I noticed that when tapping on his K-27 – a position on the chest – it felt like I was tapping on solid rock.

Indeed, I was aware that armouring the heart is a process many children learn to ensure their survival, especially in traumatic relationships and environments. I had never felt such a deep armour before. Over many months and many honest hours of sharing really painful experiences from his childhood, and also releasing the intense grief he held around his mother, this man's chest gradually softened. In one of the last visits with him, there was laughter in his eyes and hope in his step and he was heading off to an alcohol and drug withdrawal facility to detox from alcohol. His mother wound was still there, however, nowhere near as deep as it had been, and I seriously hoped that in time he could find a way to trust opening his heart, possibly for the first time ever.

In a research study led by Wayne State University in Detroit into the relationship between sexual assault and alcohol consumption, the researchers found some common characteristics among a significant number of male perpetrators of sexual violence against women. These were that thesc perpetrators commonly held these attitudes and beliefs:

- traditional gender role beliefs
- acceptance of rape myth
- hostility towards women
- acceptance of force in interpersonal relationships
- alcohol expectancies regarding sexuality, aggression and disinhibition
- stereotypes about women drinking alchohol
- alcohol as a cue for consensual sex.

Each of these characteristics would likely have been formed by these perpetrators in their early life based on their family, cultural and religious values. Obviously their life experiences come into play, too, and many perpetrators are commonly victims of childhood abuse themselves – so the cycle continues until something (or someone) shifts. They also commonly have poor social skills and lack empathy, which has been linked to poor attachment.

The reason I mention this study in this chapter is that by avoiding a mother wound we may be able to reduce the possibility of hostility towards women and this could be a small step in changing the culture that currently persists around women and sexual abuse. If we are able to teach both girls and boys that physical aggression and force are unacceptable in any situation, we take yet another step forward in this journey of positive change. Alcohol has a lot to answer for in homes and communities everywhere when it is used irresponsibly and excessively.

Some men who have a mother wound seek a woman in their life who can be their mother. They seem to be attracted to women who are good at mothering in a traditional way because they are still yearning for that nurturing. For some men, the only love they received from their mother in their childhood was that she cooked for them, and so meeting a woman who enjoys cooking can feel like a match made in heaven. Sadly, what can happen is that over time the relationship changes from one of man and woman, to man and mother, and that is seriously not good as it can blur the lines of intimacy. Sometimes men surrender their independence and accept becoming voiceless — just like when they were little boys with their mum — and this, too, can be unhealthy.

> "I wish my mum had not constantly been negative, cruel, made trouble and set family against each other. I will never understand why she has caused so much damage and continues to do so." – Men's Survey 2017

There are also aggressive and violent men who not only have a mother wound, but they tend to transfer their rage for their mother to their female partner because they grew up witnessing their own father (who likely also had a mother wound). Sometimes this is learnt from their father, however, often it is the 4-year-old son inside the grown man who's still desperately trying to express his anger and frustration at not being able to reach his mother's heart. These men often set impossible expectations of their partners — and in a way they're mirroring their own inability to have met their mother's expectations. Some men become incredibly possessive and completely dominate their women ensuring they have no power and no choice — again, just like what happened to them when they were little boys.

I really want to make the point here, particularly for any woman whose son may have a father who is an angry, controlling, perhaps violent man. **Please know that biology does not equal destiny.** There is refuge and there is hope, no matter how far away it may seem at times.

Firstly, if you are in a situation of family violence, I would urge you to seek help to ensure that you and your children are safe, and to get some support. There are countless support services and, in Australia, you can start by calling 1800RESPECT or visiting their website. I know this is a HUGE issue but it's also a darkness in our society that has had a very bright light shone on it in recent years and I think the less we all tolerate living with it, the greater dent we will make in this problem over time. Asking for help is a first step.

Seek out other wise, caring women in your community to support you and your son if you are struggling: is there a loving teacher, aunty, next-door neighbour who your son can reach out to and spend some time with?

As for your son, yes, he may have witnessed or been a victim of violence but that does not automatically mean he will grow up to be a violent man. We now know, thanks to studies into our brain's neuroplasticity that we all have the capacity to change the way we think and act — it is NEVER too late. Statistics are not certainty. Time and time again in my counselling work, and even now in my work as a speaker, I have met countless men who have broken the mould. Despite their fathers being violent or hateful or distant, these men have sought help and chosen a different path and worked to become wonderful partners and fathers.

One of my favourite examples of a man who defied what seemed to be destiny is Josh Shipp, who's a hugely popular American youth and motivation speaker (check out his talks online, especially his ones on "Just One Caring Adult"). When he was 14, Shipp – who had been in and out of foster homes all his life and made it his mission to get kicked out of all of them – swallowed a bottle of pills to end his life. He failed, thankfully, and ended up with yet another foster family. This time was different. He had one caring adult in that family who did not give up on him – even when he ended up in serious trouble with the police – and this turned his life around. Shipp is now hugely in demand, has spoken to more than two million teens in live events and runs online mentoring for teens, parents and schools around the world.

Never give up hope.

Having said all that, my focus in this book is on the mother-son relationship. I have deliberately left this chapter to later in the book because by now I have already explored many of the ways to prevent giving your son a mother wound. If we can imagine that mothering is on a continuum, it can really help to understand how we can avoid giving our sons any significant wound of any kind.

How to avoid the mother wound in boys

1. Ensure emotional and physical nurturing when they are under five.

From the early chapters you will now understand so many ways to meet the attachment and nurturing needs of our sensitive, and often fragile, boys. Little things can become big things quite easily. Filling those love cups and building those love bridges will ensure that your son has a strong connection into your heart. Of course, he knows there will be days when your heart is closed – this could be due to exhaustion, illness, too much stress and a myriad of other reasons that come from living in an uncertain world. He needs to know that there are times that the women he loves will be emotionally unavailable. What he needs to see is the return of the open-heart from his mum with an explanation that he may be able to understand. We need to reassure our sons that they are not responsible for their mother's happiness because that is a burden too great to bear for a little boy. Loving attachments and love bridges can be built at any stage of your son's life – boys are very forgiving and welcoming of the hope of a more loving relationship. I have seen this happen time and time again in my counselling rooms. One of the things that can be a sticking point is that mums often find it hard to forgive, as opposed to our sons who find it easier. I am completely convinced that with more awareness around the fragile early years of our boys' lives, we can ensure that more mums and sons are able to build the warm, safe relationships that will support them right through life.

> "My DB (3) was really into singing rhyming words. They didn't always make sense but it was a fun thing we always did together — until I sent him to get me some corn in the fruit and veg shop one day and at the top of his voice he shouted, 'Corn, corn, corn, I love corn, and Mumma loves porn!!!!'" — Red-faced Mum!

2. Avoid shaming, criticism, ridicule and rejection.

I am pretty sure that if you explored my earlier chapter, "***We need to stop hitting, hurting and shaming our boys***", you will have seen how damaging these things are to boys of any age. It can be really frustrating for mums of sons to watch them make the same dumb decision over and over again. Remember how I explored the topic of "what was he thinking?" in Chapter 10? There is so much power in loving your son after he makes really poor decisions – especially when he hurts himself. To be honest, this ability for mums to warmly embrace our sons' muck-ups, mistakes, moments of failure and crushing defeat may very well be the key to lowering the suicide rate for adolescent boys and men. If we follow those simple steps every single time, while holding our hearts open to our boys, they will learn that they can love themselves when they fail. Essentially, this is what loving unconditionally really means, doesn't it?

We really need to let our warriors know that it's OK to fail provided you get back up, brush the dirt off and get back on the horse. We need to remove the outdated belief that in some way it is better for a warrior to die than to publicly lose. This is why we need to find as many true stories of good men who have failed badly, especially in the public eye, and who have rebuilt their lives to an even better place as a consequence of their actions. We need to see failure as almost a test or a rite of passage that can help boys and men grow and conquer their own sense of inadequacy.

There are some fabulous stories and videos online that show examples of boys and men overcoming adversity and/or failure. It is worth searching some of these out to share with your sons. For example, Ed Sheeran has given a great speech about how he started life with a port-wine stain birthmark on his face, a stutter and thick glasses, but used music to overcome these differences and now celebrates difference, while being regarded as one of the world's coolest and most-loved musicians. Jimmy Stynes, the late AFL footballer, is another well-known, much-loved and highly respected sportsman whose inspirational story around turning failure into victory is well worth sharing with boys, especially AFL fans. There are so many stories out there of men who've overcome adversity ... John Green, Nick Vujicic, Derek Redmond, Stormzy, Lionel Messi, Mick Fanning ... to name a handful.

YouTube footage of the Burrumbuttock Hay Runners shows 200 long-haul trucks loaded with hay heading from New South Wales to drought-affected areas in Queensland. More than 200 truck drivers and their support crew – 99% of them men – gave up a week of their lives to bring this life-saving support to struggling farmers.

Our sons need to see stories like this often so we can counteract the negative stories that seem to saturate our 24/7 media cycles. There are endless stories of the wonderful, brave men in our health services, our fire and rescue services and in every single community around the world. There are a good, decent men everywhere who have chosen to live rather than die when life dealt them a difficult hand.

> *I need to make a special mention about how damaging criticism is to sensitive boys. If we can remember that every little boy is striving to find some form of success in his endeavours to fill his self-worth barometer, then it should be quite easy to understand how destructive criticism is in his life.*

When this criticism comes from his mum over and over again it can create a mindset that ensures he will give up really easily any time he is challenged. The language a boy hears in the first few years of his life becomes his inner critic for the rest of his life. Making fun of boys when they fail, being disrespectful when one of their choices may create an embarrassing situation – especially in public – is especially dangerous and damaging to boys. This repeated insensitivity to a boy's emotional world can create a toxic relationship that will be impossible to mend later in life. A boy who has been frequently criticised by his mother will tend to become a highly critical man. This means his ability to be optimistic, enthusiastic and hopeful is severely diminished because a negative mindset has been created.

The most damaging way to break a boy's heart is via public ridicule from either of his parents or anyone he respects. It is particularly heartbreaking for a boy when he is ridiculed by his mother.

3. Have good expectations of your boys – that they will become co-operative, kind and gentle.

There is no question that having positive, realistic expectations around our boys and their tendency for impulsive and adventuresome play will change the way we respond as mothers. When we see a boy's poor choices playing out in his behaviour patterns, we need to consciously stop viewing boy behaviour as bad, naughty, stupid and inevitable.

We need to remove the language that is so commonly used around boys, even when it is not intended to be hurtful. We need to also be loud advocates and boy champions who constantly celebrate the beautiful traits of our precious boys. We especially need to challenge the perception that little boys tend to be bad or naughty or stupid and that their bad behaviour is a form of inevitability. Together we can do this and our young boys will have a much more improved potential to grow up to be good, loving men and not harmful predators or immature jerks.

> "I wish my mum hadn't made it difficult for me to separate from the mother/son relationship and become a married man." – Men's Survey 2017

4. Improve your understanding of how boys see the world.

When mothers of sons are able to change the lens with which they view their boys so that they focus on understanding and insight, it is so much easier to meet the unique needs of our boys, especially during times of conflict and confusion. If boys are raised in homes with warm, fair and firm mothers who are able to help them navigate their confusing emotional and social worlds, so many of the statistics that I shared at the beginning of this book would improve drastically.

5. Acknowledge gender strengths and accept and support gender vulnerabilities.

When mums of sons are able to accept and embrace the fact that both genders are equally fabulous and that neither is better than the other, it will really help transform those subtle messages that our boys pick up very early in life. If mums are able to invest time and energy in educating both girls and boys around some of the differences that can cause challenge and misunderstanding, it would really help those adult relationships later in life. Encouraging messages of respectful relationships regardless of gender is something every mum can do in her home with warm wisdom and guidance. Teaching and modelling values such as compassion, honesty, integrity, cooperation, gratitude and kindness in our homes will ensure that tomorrow's children are raised by wiser mums and dads — good-enough, imperfect, committed parents.

6. Support the need to individuate and become a separate grown-up — i.e. a man.

You do not have to be a perfect mother to raise a healthy son. However, no matter how much we love our sons we must never lose sight of the fact that we must let them go so they can continue on their journey to manhood as individuals, as Mother Nature intended them to be. From the moment your son starts walking, he is beginning this journey with his tiny steps. Dr Arne Rubinstein explores in his excellent book, *The Making of Men*, how the healthy maturation of men needs a boy's psychology to evolve into a man's psychology. This transformation cannot be left to chance and both mother figures and father figures play a significant role in the finishing of our boys so they don't grow up to be jerks.

Rubinstein describes the difference in these psychologies as:

Boy psychology:

- I seek acknowledgment.
- I want it all for me.
- Power is for my benefit.
- I am the centre of the universe.
- I believe I am immortal.
- I take no responsibility for my actions.
- I want a mother.

Healthy man psychology:

- I seek that which I believe in.
- I share with my community.
- Power is for the good of all.
- I am just part of the universe.
- I know I am mortal.
- I take full responsibility for my actions.
- I want a relationship with a woman.

Steve Biddulph writes about the need to educate boys to avoid toxic masculinity, and I completely support his position and his passion. In adolescence, your son will continue to step backwards from you as he searches for his own identity, turns towards his peers and friends, and also begins his sexual awakening. Your son will need to find good men to walk beside him on his journey to manhood and when mums support this fundamental need in our boys, boys value and appreciate it even if they are unable to express it. You must let him go. I can reassure you, that for some sons, this is the hardest thing you will ever have to do. When you let them go, completely untethered to you, completely free, something really beautiful happens somewhere down the track. You will meet your son as a grown man and you will see in his eyes that the love he has for you is still in his heart.

The importance of other mother figures

Boys who have a mother wound are not destined to live a life that is complicated by difficult relationships with the female sex. The presence of a warm, caring mother figure – whether she be biological as in an aunty or a grandmother or non-biological as in a family friend, neighbour or teacher – can be enough to reduce the negative impact of a mother wound. In a way, a relationship with a woman whose heart is open to a boy carrying a mother wound can restore the broken heart within him.

In many traditional indigenous communities the grandmother holds not only the wisdom of the past, but she is the figure of authority for both boys and girls. I have met many boys over the years who, despite a really difficult beginning with their parents, have been raised to be good men by a grandmother. As mums of sons you will meet many boys over the years, and I ask you to be mindful of the boys who look sad and lost. Step forward and be an amazing 'aunty', even if you're not related! Show them what female compassion, kindness and love looks and feels like and you may change their life positively forever. I remember one teenage boy who came to live with us for a while after a family conflict. A few months after moving in, he came and told me that I did "this mothering thing" really well. When I asked him what he meant he said, "It's just so fun and easy and calm living in your home – there's no real stress and drama."

Please open your heart to as many boys as possible – just in case they have a mother wound.

> *If we want boys to grow up to be capable of giving and receiving love from a partner, especially a female partner, they need to have experienced how it feels to have been able to have an open, undefended heart.*

I have seen massive shifts happen in mid- to late-adolescence when a caring, warm female teacher has shone a beautiful light of positive regard onto a boy who had never known it before.

> "I wish she were able to take more of a parent role, in relation to healthy challenge and guidance, rather than parent me as an equal."
> – Men's Survey 2017

> "I wish my mum had not been so often emotionally unavailable and aloof. Led to many feelings of being disapproved of that weren't necessary." – Men's Survey 2017

TOP TIPS

- ✓ Every boy benefits from having a warm, fair and firm mother.
- ✓ A mother wound can impact a boy throughout his manhood.
- ✓ Being a cold, distant and emotionally unavailable mother to a son can create a mother wound.
- ✓ Being a smother mother who is overly invested in her son's life can also create a mother wound.
- ✓ There are six key ways to avoid creating a mother wound in your son:
    1. Ensure emotional and physical nurturing when he is under five.
    2. Avoid shaming, criticism, ridicule and rejection.
    3. Have good expectations of your son that he will become a co-operative, kind and gentle young man.
    4. Improve your understanding of how boys see the world.
    5. Acknowledge gender strengths and accept and support gender vulnerabilities.
    6. Support the need to individuate and become a separate grown-up – i.e. a man.
- ✓ Open your heart to as many boys as possible – just in case.

CHAPTER 13

Helping **BOYS** understand **LOSS** and **DEATH**

"I just wish my mum had not died." – Men's Survey 2017

Significant loss experiences of any kind hurt. The separation distress that many of our young children experience is a good example of this because, in the eyes of the child, they have lost connection with the safest grown-up they know. Given that sensitive boys can struggle with feeling safe and loved, then any loss experience that occurs early in life needs to be a wonderful, teachable moment for mums to help their sons understand why it hurts so much.

You will witness just how distressed a boy will become if you have left his favourite rabbit or blanket at day care or, worse still, lost it. Because that rabbit or blanket was a major source of comfort to that little boy, the absence of it is quite frankly terrifying. The loss of such a powerful comforter triggers the primitive brain and the fight-flight response because it really does feel like a potentially life-threatening moment for our young boys.

The most significant loss experience that will challenge you in life is the loss of someone you love dearly when they die.

> *So often, as loving mums, we want to protect our children from death and we avoid dealing with it, but unfortunately we are actually protecting them from a vital learning and this will come at a great cost later in life.*

Coping with significant loss and death is a crucial life skill that children can benefit from experiencing while they are still children. I have met many people over the years who were told that their family dog had been sent to a farm and that was why he wasn't in the family home any more, only to find out many years later that he had been put down by the vet because he was very unwell. In a way, farm kids get to see and become familiar with death simply because animal deaths naturally occur over time in a farm setting. I still vividly remember my 15-year-old brother sobbing in the shed when his pet joey (a baby kangaroo) died, however, no-one spoke about it or went to soothe him. I hope that today we can better help children understand death, including losing their much-loved pets.

When we lose someone we love dearly, it is a catastrophic injury to our heart and the pain is extremely uncomfortable and unrelenting. It can be like the worst pain of all to experience because there is no quick solution or remedy that can fix it. The death of a loved one can also make us feel weak and powerless – both things that can cause boys to behave with anger and aggression, rather than surrender to deep sadness. On top of that, the grieving process is a chaotic and emotionally overwhelming time in our life and the mixture of emotions can make us feel very unstable and out of control. Any time we feel out of control, the primitive brain is triggered again because of the threat to our survival. Grief is not just about sadness and bereavement, it is a time when irrational feelings like anger, disappointment, confusion, guilt and powerlessness all search through our mind and body. It makes everyone feel pretty awful and so our emotionally vulnerable boys can struggle deeply when they are grieving. Our sons need to see their mums and dads (especially dads) cry when someone special dies so that we normalise that crying is a very normal and healthy way of expressing grief and sadness for men and women. Even though seeing their parents cry is healthy, it can also frighten our little boys. It can be really helpful to give your son some ideas about what he can do to help you when you are sad or crying, because he will want to be helpful. Maybe he could find the tissues, hold your hand or give you a gentle tickle on the tickle spot high up on your back.

When we give clear messages that our big feelings – which are incredibly valid, normal and are a healthy part of the grieving process – are somehow wrong or bad or, worse still, a form of weakness, we may very well be setting these boys up to struggle with knowing what to do with the same feelings later on in life. So many men that I met in my years working around funerals and in palliative care are terrified of feeling grief, and many have learnt the art of freezing these feelings deep inside them. Sadly, buried feelings of deep grief have a tendency to turn into depression, or workaholism or emotional withdrawal from people they love. In other words, we need to teach our boys today that grief hurts and everybody cries.

> "I wished my mum had talked about how she was feeling when her son, my brother, was killed in a work accident." – Men's Survey 2017

You may remember that I have mentioned how guinea pigs can help our rooster boys learn to be gentle and kind. Well, these lovely little creatures can also be fabulous teachers for our boys when it comes to death. I suggest guinea pigs because they tend not to live as long as cats or dogs so the lesson can be learnt early. What we do know is that if you tenderly stroke a small animal, you will increase the capacity to connect lovingly with it and so if you have a guinea pig that your young son pats a lot, he will fall in love with it. When it dies, his heart is going to hurt and he is going to feel those big emotions that come when we lose someone we love. This is the teachable moment about, what is death? The concept of death is important for young children to understand and we need to be mindful not to use phrases like 'passing over', 'going to sleep' or that God came and got them. I have worked with some pragmatic little boys who have been terrified to go to sleep because when Nanna 'went to sleep' she ended up in a coffin in the ground, and some children worry that God is going to come sneaking into their bedroom and take them away just like God did to Nanna. Please use the words 'dead' and 'died' to your little children, especially your boys.

> "My DB (4) and I were talking about death and that when you die you watch over the people you love from the stars. My son said to me, 'Mummy when I die I will watch you all the time, even when you do a poo!'" — Amused Mum

Farewell rituals

I strongly recommend that you have a funeral for your guinea pig so your children can begin to build a template for understanding what happens after a death when a human dies. A shoebox can work really well as a coffin, and if you explain that we are preparing the guinea pig for their last journey, they may have something special they would like to put in with their pet — often a little truck! We need to teach our boys that a funeral is not just about saying goodbye — it is also about being grateful for the life that has been lived and it is a reminder to celebrate the gift of life that we still have. Please don't bury the shoebox too deep with your first pet funeral because there have been many pragmatic boys who have needed to dig up the guinea pig a few weeks later to see that it is still dead. The death of the family guinea pig allows your son to be able to explore death and to learn that grief creates emotional pain that eventually fades and goes away. They also learn about the need to dispose of the deceased's body reverently and that some things bring comfort, like ceremony, prayers or leaving flowers at the grave. This builds a valuable template for future death experiences, and builds resilience and the ability to recover, which will be needed later in life if and when they experience a major loss.

Having children at (human) funerals can be incredibly helpful for grown-ups. I clearly remember a two-and-a-half-year-old grandson running through a chapel and patting on his Poppy's casket declaring loudly and proudly, "This is my Poppy's box!" He brought smiles to everyone's faces and he reminded everyone that the true legacy of his grandfather was right there in his grandson. It was a really beautiful moment.

There will be many quiet pillow chats after the death of your guinea pig as your son will continue to come to terms with death, grief and recovering after such a painful event. We need to remember as mums that no matter how much we want to, we cannot take our son's emotional pain away after he loses someone he loves. We do need to teach him that family will surround him and support him and love him when he cries or possibly uses his behaviour to express how awful he feels.

Boys who lose a loved family member or a close friend can really struggle for a couple of years after that death. Even when a well-meaning mum can ask them how they are doing, they actually want to protect her from worrying and will often deny that they're not doing so well. It sometimes helps to keep tabs on them via their friends. What is important is that you know that they will be grieving for a long time and that under that male mask, a boy's heart is hurting.

There is a strong linkage between a major loss experience later in life and male suicide, and this is why we need to educate our boys early about grief. We need to teach them that grief hurts and it takes ages to get better.

We need them to know this is normal and that there is nothing weak or wrong about them. Grief can make you feel incredibly powerless and I'm sure this is one of the reasons why men can struggle so much with it, sometimes finding it too hard to bear. The 'mammoth hunter' and the 'deer hunter' can be brought to his knees by grief and, in some strange way, that can make men feel even more like a failure.

Other forms of loss

Grief is not just reserved for death. Boys experience grief in other ways as well. If a boy moves to a different school or town or his parents' relationship breaks down, a grieving process will be triggered and it can be really confusing because there is no dead body but the feelings of pain can be just as deep.

Separation from family

A number of years ago I received an email from the mother of a 12-year-old boy who'd begun boarding in an all-male school in a large city. Her son had a very close and, as she described, 'chatty' relationship with both his mum and dad. When the parents delivered their boy to the boarding house, they were required to attend a seminar run by a 'boy expert' who outlined what their boy would need in the transition away from home to boarding school.

This expert recommended as little contact as possible, preferably none in the first three weeks. His theory was that the boys needed to not be distracted by contact from their parents while the school was busy creating fun activities like rollerblading, movie nights, sporting events and trips to the beach to enable friendships to be formed. This recommendation is a total denial of the emotional challenges first-time boarding students experience because they are grieving deeply not only for the parents, but also for their homes, their pets and also for the community they lived in. This can take weeks, even months, to overcome and it is often described as homesickness when, in actual fact, it is genuine grief and it needs to be respected and acknowledged. We can prepare our sons for this process, however, denying it is going to happen and then making it difficult for a grieving son to communicate with the safest people in his life beggars belief and displays an ignorance around grief and loss. So, why would this school recommend no contact with mums and dads? I am thinking that the staff may believe that by distracting the students, they would avoid the tears that may come when the boys hear the voices of those they love on the phone.

Avoiding and denying emotional grief in boys is part of the problem with angry men later in life. This is a complete denial of the grieving process that is occurring for every single boarder. Avoiding and denying these painful emotions teaches boys that they must bury and suppress their feelings in order to succeed in life. This is so wrong and smacks of the old male code that boys need to be toughened up.

A loss event is always followed by a time of grief as the uncertainty and discomfort of the change process flows through the conscious and unconscious parts of our minds. This then triggers thoughts often based in fear, which create emotions including sadness, anger and deep longing for what was safe and secure. When we feel vulnerable or out of our comfort zone, we yearn to be close to those we love the most for comfort, for reassurance and to remind us that this period of grieving will gradually get better.

> "I wish my mum had not shut down after death of my brother."
> – Men's Survey 2017

There are many reasons why today's children are less resilient than they were many years ago and we need to bring that understanding into our conversations around transitions from home whether it be the early years, into secondary schooling or even leaving home for further education or employment. Education and information about this time of uncertainty – and acknowledging that it can be much more debilitating than a patch of homesickness – months ahead of time and again as they prepare to head off is important. When I was counselling full-time I was often busy in the first term of the school year helping the more sensitive 13- to 15-year-olds overcome this separation from their families, their homes and their communities. Many cried themselves to sleep every night for up to three months.

Every child processes loss differently so, remember, no one size fits all. I encourage these boys' families, especially mums, to stay in touch, to send messages of love and connection including care packages.

Relationship breakdown

In the case of separation or divorce, losing the woman you love and your children is one of the worst griefs that a man can experience, even if he has been the main reason why the relationship ended. This incredible sense of powerlessness, when combined with deep regret, can end up in rage. Sadly, many women have lost their lives as a consequence of a man's grief which has turned to aggression. This is why we need our boys to understand what happens after we lose something we love. Fortunately there are now many organisations – which did not exist a number of years ago – run by men to support other men during these difficult times. Men do often process grief differently to women and talking often makes many men feel worse. Often men need significant time to process the big, ugly feelings and it's important to note that Mother Nature has often been an excellent ally.

> *It is not only grown men who struggle with grief. There is a particular vulnerability in our teenage boys when their first love ends. Their first intimate loving experience, which includes the first time they open their hearts to another female, is incredibly powerful.*

To have that experience end with the incredible intensity of emotions that is unique to adolescents, can have devastating and catastrophic consequences. I have anecdotally heard of a number of teenage boys who have ended their lives because the pain was simply too much to bear and the rejection was also too much. This is why we need to build education and experience in understanding loss and death very early in our sons' lives.

Allowing the grief and moving through adversity

My own sons experienced several deaths of family and friends in their adolescence. Even though they experienced intense grief and sadness, my sons have become very familiar with death and funerals. They know what is the right thing to do, they know how to be respectful and they have become completely comfortable around the strong emotions that funerals can evoke. They have been among the pallbearers at grandparents' and cousins' funerals. At one of the funerals for a very popular young lad, it was ironically heartening to see so many teenage boys sobbing honestly and openly, and holding each other and supporting each other. There is hope for the next generation of men if these are the young lads who are coming forward. We can only gain in confidence and competence with experience. We certainly cannot do it by keeping young boys ignorant and unaware in the hope that we are protecting them.

There are many times in adult life when major adversity can knock us flat on our faces, whether that be a loss of a relationship, a job or person that we love. Loss can strip us bare to our very foundation. I've heard of many men particularly who have used the ocean and nature and, in particular, surfing to find themselves again in time after walking through the pit of grief. The ocean has a way of holding a safe space for men to explore the depth of their deepest pain and confusion. For male surfers, knowing that out on the waves there have been moments of exquisite joy that made them glad to be alive can often be the silent motivation that gets many men back on their feet, back into life and back into living. Often this pilgrimage of deep exploration has happened as a solo journey.

Of course, the same experience can be provided by any of Mother Nature's special places – for some boys and men they may find a safe space out hiking, bike riding, mountain biking, climbing, birdwatching, kayaking, fishing, snorkelling or even gardening. The healing power of nature can be felt simply by being present in nature.

Hope really matters when recovering from a significant loss and I have met many boys who did not know that the crushing grief they felt especially from a broken-heart loss of a mother or lover, does ease in time. We need to keep reminding our boys that the cycles of life will repeat many times and that even though bad things can happen to good people which can bring you to your knees, these things will pass too.

> "While watching me get ready for work, my DB (6) was sitting on the bathroom vanity watching me intently. I stopped and looked at him and he said, 'Mum, when you die can I have all your makeup so I can give it to my woman'. I laughed and said, 'Of course you can'."
>
> — Blessed Mamma

Talking to children about life after death

I have a strong belief that children under 10 years of age benefit from being supported in the belief that when we die a special part of us continues on to a beautiful place. Those who have a faith already share this information with their children. However, those without a faith may create a potential emotional challenge for their children that can cause deep emotional distress if ever they experience a sudden death.

Having a metaphor of hope can be especially helpful for little boys who are generally quite pragmatic. My explanation is that the imagination protects and insulates children from the pain and challenges of the adult world. If they can imagine that this wonderful place exists, then it brings them enormous comfort if a death occurs. They will say things like, "Nanny must be with Spotty now, Mummy"; or "I hope they still have chocolate and ice cream in heaven because Poppy loved them!" Those parents who have no belief in the continuation of the soul or human spirit or essence of a loved one can be reassured that when their child gets to be older, they can discover their own truth. It's much like discovering that maybe Santa is not a real being; it will never take away the positive spirit of Christmas. There comes a time when the magical time of childhood is tainted by reality, however, a little magic supports young children during a vital stage of their lives. I have found that having this metaphor for little boys creates lots of interesting conversations, which are often very humorous, and these moments of lightness in the midst of grief can help everyone cope better. I do remember my DB (8) coming to me soon after my dad had died suddenly from a heart attack and asking me how far it was to heaven. He wanted to know if it was further than London. I had to tell him I didn't know because I hadn't been there yet. Gotta love our little boys as they work out the practicalities of life.

If you would like to learn more about children and how they process death, please feel free to visit my website (maggiedent.com) and find the "common concerns" page on death and loss. There is an article I wrote for *Kindred* magazine called, 'Death Through the Eyes of a Child', as well as some other resources I have created to support children through grief.

If you have a loved one who is unwell and unlikely to live, please be openly honest with your son in an age-appropriate way. I do encourage you to take your children to funerals and graveyards so you are making them familiar with the reality of death, dying and recovering. Thankfully, many boys will want to have a funeral for a dead beetle or a dead crab and, yes, they are still wonderful opportunities to explore death. Unless they have experienced emotional intimacy through safe touch, their heart won't hurt the same way and they will get to work that out to you.

Coping with significant loss and death is definitely a vital life skill that children, especially little boys, can benefit from experiencing while they are still children. Young boys need these life lessons as early and as often as possible to ensure they can become a capable warrior when death knocks at their door — because it will.

I would like to close this chapter with a poem I wrote many years ago, dedicated to all those parents who have lost a child through miscarriage. This is a loss many families have faced — and it can be such a difficult journey navigating your own grief while explaining this loss to your other children if you already have them. This poem is for you and I hope it offers some comfort.

Gentle Little One

You were with us for such a short time
and yet you have touched our lives in so many ways.
You are a gift of the love
between two special people,
a gift to show that the miracle of birth is not
something small or ordinary,
it is a miracle.

You are a symbol of togetherness
and connectedness of those we love.
This powerful symbol has activated
and deepened the love and affection of
those who really matter in our lives.

You are a blessing of all that is good,
beautiful and special in life.
This blessing will remind us all
of the fragility and sacredness of the
gift of life.

Little one, beloved son of ours
we thank you for the gift, the symbol and the blessing
of your tiny life.
May we all keep these special reminders
deep in our hearts, minds and souls.

Journey softly, little one.
Until we meet again, go with our love.
Farewell for now.

— Maggie Dent, 2005

> "My mum was a wonderful gift to us and our children. At her thanksgiving service, friend after friend stood up (they all seemed to think they were her best friends!) and spoke about her humanitarian love for life and influence on their lives. I don't think I've ever know someone who was so consistent in their character and values ... in both public and private. My own children just loved sitting with her for hours cooking, making play-dough figures, or drawing ... BTW, my mum actually died five years ago quite unexpectedly after a short battle with brain cancer."
> — Men's Survey 2017

TOP TIPS

- ✓ Any loss experience will trigger grief.
- ✓ Pets such as guinea pigs can give our children a gentle first experience of death.
- ✓ Grief triggers our primitive fear of survival.
- ✓ All children need to experience loss as young children rather than be protected from it.
- ✓ The big, ugly feelings that grief can bring can be very frightening for boys especially.
- ✓ Help boys to learn that the pain in their heart will go away.
- ✓ Take boys to funerals and cemeteries, and speak openly about death in age-appropriate ways.
- ✓ Coping with death and loss is a life skill we need to teach our boys before puberty.

CHAPTER 14

A **GOOD DOG** can help raise **BOYS WHO CARE** more (PS and some cats)

"I am grateful to my mum for always being there for me for anything, for being able to talk to her about anything and not judging me at all. Unconditional love." – Men's Survey 2017

The four Dent lads, now fully grown men with three of them also now loving, awesome dads, are better men because we had good dogs as a part of our lives. I'm sure all good-enough parents try to love their children unconditionally, however, sometimes our face just twitches and we can't pull it off. I believe the only creature on earth who can love our kids, especially our boys, completely unconditionally, is a good dog. Seriously, they wag their tails and greet our children joyously, even after they have wet the bed, hit their sister, blocked up the toilet and refused to eat their dinner. It makes no difference to a good dog; they just keep exactly the same loving happening. A good dog never waivers and greets every moment of your children's lives with the same amazing, unconditional, positive regard.

Without even realising it, the presence of our family dogs — particularly one called Jessica Claire — has shaped parts of the boys' psyches, minds and hearts in positive ways that we humans, quite simply, could not.

Our feisty, bossy Fox Terrier, Jess, could never be exhausted by the antics of four Dent boys. One of their favourite games when they were younger was to entice her to attack our hose – just like she would attack a snake – and once her jaws were locked on, they could swing her around in the air. She loved the game. I had seen her swinging around on the clothesline as well, with her brothers hanging off alongside her.

She was a really smart dog in so many ways. Some nights she would divide herself between all four boys and sleep two hours with each without even needing a watch. There were some mornings when I went to wake up my sons that I would find her little head next to a boy's head on a pillow.

What else can a good dog do for the boys in your home?

- As parents we really try not to have any favourites, however, we know that sometimes some of our children are easier to live with than others – especially families with 'roosters', the high-energy, self-important, opinionated and power-hungry children. Dogs never have favourites and they love equally. A good dog can meet our children's natural exuberance and excitement without any effort. They can chase, run and jump insatiably when we grown-ups have collapsed on the ground hours ago. I enjoyed many a calm cup of tea while Jess ran the gunk out of my sons' motors – she could dispel any excess cortisol that was in their system beautifully. I wrote two of my books with Jessie's little head on my feet because I think she thought I needed some company. I miss her as I write this book.
- Having a good dog can teach our children responsibility – my boys had to take turns to feed Jess and pick up the dog poo. There are some lessons in life that may not be pleasant, however, they are essential to have in our kitbag before we leave home.
- Every human being has a burning desire to feel that they belong, that they are wanted, and that they are loved. A good dog shows how much they value every person in their family. Jess could get very excited whenever we returned home from school. However, it was something else to watch her as she ran round and round the lounge room, barking with joy, running over the couches to show one of my boys who had just returned from university for the holidays how much she had missed him. His face showed an expression that I couldn't have inspired, even though I knew he had missed me too. Maybe I needed to do some laps around the lounge as well?
- We all need to find safe comfort when life gives us a working-over, like when we make mistakes, fail exams, or struggle to complete a task as well as we wanted to. There is nothing like a good dog to come home to after such a day. Jess would always know when one

of the boys had had a lousy day at school and she would follow him and, when he sat down, she would be on his lap. Silently he would stroke her and hug her, and soon he would be feeling better and happier. She never got it wrong.

- A good dog also can teach empathy and compassion so much better than us humans. Once, Jess was hit by a car and she was at the vet's — not seriously injured, however, injured. We were all very worried and sad. Something magical happened that day. My two rooster boys — normally emotionally tough, self-absorbed and with very little concern for anyone but themselves — comforted their two lamb brothers with kind words of reassurance. I am not sure this would have happened if one of their brothers had been hit by the car instead of Jess!
- A good dog can quite simply be a boy's best friend. They never tell lies, they never dob on you, and they never tease you. They just like hanging out with you, no matter how you're feeling. Some days that is the sort of mate a boy really needs, especially after a day spent 'battling' on the frontline at school.
- A good dog will also give your children the capacity to understand death, loss and the journey of grief. This is one of the toughest journeys any of us can travel in life and to experience it deeply as a child, when your beloved dog dies, is sadly a great preparation to building resilience and capacity for future major loss experiences, including traumatic events.

> "I am a mum of three sport-mad boys so my house is very loud and there's always a ball being kicked! I have so many funny moments but my most recent one is from my DB (2) who certainly does rule the roost! As I served him a lovely homemade meal his reaction was 'Oh yuck!!! Dog poos!'. Well, no, son it's not dog poos, it's rissoles!"
> — Clearly-not-a-chef Mum

One of the very best teachers you can ever add to your family is a good dog. My four sons are better men, sons, partners, mates and fathers because of Jess.

Thanks Jess — runt of the litter — for the love and lessons you taught us all. We still miss you.

Jessie made such an impact on our family that I wrote a book about the wisdom that she taught us all, called *A Dog's Life Wisdoms*. This is just one of her teachings:

8th Wisdom — Show your love without words.

Words can lose their meaning and power over time especially in our closest relationships. We dogs have always known this and that's why we show how much we love those we love rather than tell them. First we wag our tails, we wiggle our bodies and often we simply put our chins against our loved one's arms, legs or even shoulders if they are sitting down. I also like snuggling close by on the couch and, better still, in the bed because that's a fabulous way to show how much I love those closest to me. For some dogs like me who are lucky enough to be allowed on the main bed, spooning is a very special way to show love without words.

— Maggie Dent, *A Dog's Life Wisdoms* (2016).

NB: Please — if it suits your life circumstances and your family — give serious consideration to getting a puppy or a good rescue dog. It is a bit like bringing another child into the family. The need to accept the responsibilities as well as the potential joys is paramount.

Life lessons from cats and other animals

We also had a ginger moggy called Ginger Megs for 12 years. Some days she could be a really loving cat, you could pat her, she would purr and everyone would be filled up with endorphins. Sometimes, this gentle loving experience would end abruptly when she suddenly pounced up and leapt at you with her claws — seriously like a 10-point injection! This happened a number of times over the years and each different son would look at me with confusion asking what had happened. I had to reassure them that they probably didn't do anything to make Ginger Megs do that — she had simply changed her mind. I often said that having Ginger Megs was good preparation for living with women later in life as we can be a bit prone to randomly changing our minds as well!

Seriously, any fluffy pet can help your son become a more loving and gentle man. I can remember very clearly on the farm having a pet kangaroo, and one of my older brothers was its main guardian. As a 15-year-old grumpy and moody teenage boy, he took incredible responsibility looking after our pet kangaroo, including feeding it during the night. I can still vividly remember the night that Joey died — he had caught some sort of infection. I crept down to the shed to see what was happening and I could hear the deep sobbing of my older brother and I knew that his heart had been broken. That's when I first realised how much love a boy can have for a pet.

> "My mum taught me to have empathy and that it was OK to show emotions." – Men's Survey 2017

At some point in time, the youngest Dent lad somehow ended up with a white rat. Initially, I was not very impressed as I wasn't very fond of mice. But over time I grew to really like this rat because it had character and was very clean. Sadly, it had a traumatic accident and died and, again, my youngest learnt great lessons about sadness and grief. Incidentally, I have been much more comfortable around mice ever since.

Some boys develop bonds of friendship with lizards and pet snakes and birds, and I'm sure that every single time they develop a friendship with something else they are improving their capacity to become a good friend. So many boys are losing these opportunities because they are overly engaged with the digital world. A pet is a wonderful opportunity to draw them out and help them enjoy real physical contact, responsibility, empathy and love.

> "I get so emotional listening to 'The Lion King' music with my DB (3). One day I said to him, 'I love this music so much, it gets me right in the heart'. His reply: 'And I love this music so much it hits me right in the eye!'"
>
> — Laughing Mumma

I have had some families tell me that they could not have a pet full-time so they shared a pet with another family, and I think this is a great idea. This way you are able to enjoy the benefits of a pet without the full-time responsibility. This means that going on holidays without your pets is a lot easier and you share the costs for their upkeep and care. Meanwhile, they are still being amazing teachers for your children.

One last message about good dogs: I have found that one of the best therapies I can suggest for a boy who is being bullied badly at school, or who has experienced a different form of trauma, is a puppy. It can quite simply be a life-saving move. For boys who have an additional challenge such as autism or ADHD, a loving pet can make a world of difference in so many ways. In some of our more challenging schools, therapy dogs are making an enormously positive impact, especially for low-achieving boy students.

TOP TIPS

- ✓ Dogs can really love unconditionally.
- ✓ A good dog can help calm stressed boys.
- ✓ A good dog can teach compassion and empathy better than humans.
- ✓ You can teach responsibility with a good pet.
- ✓ Dogs can become your son's best friend.

CHAPTER 15

FUN, food and **FARTS**

> "My DB (6) informed me that his friend had seen the movie 'Fifty Shades of Grey'. I told him I doubted it, as it's only on at the movies and you have to be over 15 to watch it. 'Well, his mum must've lied and said he's small for his age.'" — Gobsmacked Mum

It took me years as a teacher and a mother to really understand why having fun, eating food and farting were such important factors in the mental and emotional wellbeing of boys. When boys of any age feel overwhelmed or become confused about why they make such poor choices – which sometimes result in them hurting themselves, hurting others or damaging things in the world around them – it creates stress in their bodies. Neuroscience now tells us that stress is largely a flooding of the hormone cortisol, and anyone who has that happening will know it doesn't feel very good. So, essentially, what is happening with so many little boys is that they have worked out that the fastest way to get rid of cortisol, or to move the stress they are feeling, is to find a way to have fun, eat something or fart. Indeed, for some young boys, being silly can be a way of coping with anxiety, not just stress.

A huge motivation in writing this book is to improve relationships between mums and sons so we can reduce the stress boys feel when they are misunderstood, confused or punished for things that had no intention behind them to hurt or harm. Being calmer can help boys be kinder and less prone to angry outbursts especially irrational anger.

> *So, if you can lighten up a little and be a bit more ridiculous, you will have a son who has less of a need to discharge the stress he feels, as well as a happier home.*

> "My mum taught me how to cook and look after myself."
> — Men's Survey 2017

Neurotransmitters that help us feel good like serotonin, dopamine and other positive endorphins can be triggered really quickly through fun, food and farting. It has been found in studies of heterosexual relationships that one of the things that can attract a woman to a man is the capacity for them to laugh together a lot. Laughter triggers all the best positive neurotransmitters and is, indeed, a form of intimacy in its own way. Mums who learn to use humour with their son who may be struggling, will tend to have a stronger and warmer relationship with him.

Dopamine feels fabulous for our boys. It is the neurotransmitter that stimulates attention and engagement, and it feels really good when it is flooding through our bodies. In a way, boys are dopamine hunters! They cannot have fun without their friend dopamine!

As I mentioned in Chapter 9, fun, physicality, being creative, challenged, learning something interesting and having freedom to explore outside are all healthy activities that create dopamine. However, dopamine is also produced when we are rewarded for action — and this is something the screen world delivers in spades (for us and our boys!) so we need to ensure our boys are not getting their dopamine fix exclusively online because then it can become habitual.

> "When my third DB (13 months) laughed out loud at me burping, it sent his two older brothers DB (8) and DB (5) into hysterics. I've learned that farts and burps ARE funny and no amount of pleading or begging will convince them otherwise, nor will it stop nearly every conversation being turned into something to do with poop/bums/toilets." — Mum of Three Boys

Having fun when you are a poor verbal communicator is one of the reasons why boys practise aggression nurturance, which I have mentioned several times and which essentially means they use their body to communicate connectedness and affection with others. Boys tend to understand this non-verbal communication, however, girls can find it confusing and confronting. Again, it is not acceptable for a boy who is trying to show that he likes a little girl to go and hit her or shove her. The first time this happens is an opportunity for mums to explain why that is not acceptable and give him some other strategies that he may use next time.

This physical nurturance includes hitting, slapping, wrestling, punching and any other myriad of activities that ensure that physical connection happens. Throwing things at each other is a more remote way of aggression nurturance, and throwing cushions, balls, soft toys, clothes and even food can be seen as incredibly fabulous ways of connecting with a boy you like.

Sometimes boys make poor choices about what they throw and they cause harm rather than connection, which can make them feel really lousy. Feeling really lousy can make them feel vulnerable which can then make them feel angry, and sometimes a physical fight will ensue that will confuse the boys even more. There is a big difference between mock fights and real fights and essentially that is why rough-and-tumble play needs to be considered as a valuable part of the boy's growth and development.

Rough-and-tumble play with Dad or a father figure can be incredibly bonding and, at the same time, can teach boys about being too rough and about how to avoid hurting the other person.

The biological need for boys to be physically active is why having fun for boys often requires physical exertion and boisterous play. Games of 'chasey' are particularly valuable for boys as they discharge negative energy and fill themselves full of good dopamine – they are a great mood changer. When these games also evoke loud laughter, they are pure gold for our boys who can find the world a bit confusing at times.

The need to be spontaneously ridiculous could be seen as a type of coping skill for managing stress, rather than a sign your son is incredibly immature. I am quite sure there are many mums reading this book who have a male partner who can still do some incredibly immature things in the hope of making you laugh!

There was once a DB (6) who had a little boy over to play. Unbeknownst to his mum, he had found some condoms in his parents' bedroom. These became water balloons and when his mum went outside to bring in some washing, she was a little concerned to see burst condoms all over the ground!

Another hilarious play experience happened when a couple of boys found a packet of thick sanitary pads in the back of the laundry cupboard. They had a fabulous time peeling off the sticky bit at the back and plastering them all over the wall in the hallway in a pattern. Sometimes, our boys just want to play together, often very physically, and have fun regardless of what they play with.

The power of laughter

An essential component of having fun is laughter because it releases wonderful feel-good endorphins and neurotransmitters instantly throughout your whole body. Boys are always looking for laughter and lightness in their lives and while some days it will drive us almost crazy, as mums of sons we need to recognise that this is incredibly important.

> "Upon farting rather loudly, my son at all of two reassured me, 'It's OK Mum, I didn't fart, that was my booster rocket going off!'" (DBs 2 and 5)
>
> — Lone Ovaries Mum

Laughter shared between two people brings those two people closer together in an incredibly joyful exchange of delight. It does more than that too.

Laughter:

- transforms emotional states
- stimulates endorphins and creates wellbeing
- increases levels of serotonin
- is a key coping skill, especially for boys
- is an anti-bullying strategy
- encourages lightening-up in serious moments
- is a bonding experience when shared in groups
- builds inclusivity and connectedness, and secures friendships
- releases tension and stress
- is a key element in effective communication, especially in close relationships
- is an antidote to violence.

In global resilience studies, having a sense of humour is recognised as being a very valuable life skill. It is a huge protective factor in schoolyards where it can protect children from unwanted harassment or bullying. There are so many benefits that can be gained on many levels from laughter.

Laughter can transform negative emotional states faster than almost any other strategy or technique a parent can use. It is unfortunate that a sense of humour does not arrive in a box underneath the Christmas tree; it would be so much easier than cultivating it as a child has to do, along with so many other life skills.

> *Given that laughter is such an important way for our little boys to discharge excess energy, particularly stress, we need to make it a priority to help our sons develop a sense of humour that is respectful.*

There are times when young boys use inappropriate humour in certain circumstances. Risqué or 'shed' humour has a very important place in the Australian psychology as do our 'larrikin' depreciatory humour and language patterns. Culturally we tend to 'put things down' or deflate compliments. For example, "Wow, you have scrubbed up pretty good tonight darling!" can be an Australian compliment that is genuinely meant to be kind. An overt compliment like, "Wow, you look amazingly beautiful tonight!" could get you a quick kick in the knee! This cultural nuance needs humour and without it, people can easily take offence. Apprentice tradespeople are sometimes the brunt of antics and pranks by older staff. Some young lads are asked to find the left-handed screwdriver or the black and white striped paint. If a young lad does not understand that this is a form of joke, he can feel really shamed when his workmates laugh. So it is really important that we prioritise helping our little boys to learn the complexities that are a part of a sense of humour.

> "Our two nieces were staying over. We sent the two girls and our two boys off to get ready for bed. The girls cleaned their teeth and put on their PJs. Our boys had a wrestle instead and I ended up changing 'sharted-on' sheets as a result! Boys!" — Mum with a Nervous Twitch

When humour isn't funny

The sad reality is that part of the old male code is supported by sexist and racist humour, which is very common in some parts of the bloke world. If we are to raise our boys to be respectful to girls and women and other cultures, we need to start when our boys are very young. This means that we lovingly coach our sons when they repeat sexist jokes that are disrespectful to women and denigrate them in any way. Humour is an incredibly strong bonding pattern among men and male humour can definitely often be a bit gross or inappropriate when shared in front of women. Helping our boys realise that there is a time and a place for being a bit gross, and for shed humour or paddock humour, is crucial for our boys. If we start helping them realise this difference early in life then we are giving our boys a better chance at knowing how to make appropriate choices using humour.

Sharing simple riddles and jokes with young children is an excellent way to nurture a sense of humour. There will be times when the children share a joke that is a little inappropriate and it's important to avoid shaming or overtly sanctioning their attempts – especially publicly. One of my sons – who was in Year One at the time – came home busting to tell a joke at the dinner table. It went like this:

"Mummy, what's the difference between a light bulb and a pregnant lady?" The answer was: *"Well, you can un-screw the light bulb!"*

Needless to say, his older brothers loved the joke and he had no idea what the joke was about. He was just passing on something he had heard at school.

> "Our son DB (4), youngest of three boys, has always been fascinated with his penis. I overheard him telling my mother-in-law, 'You rub it like this and it feels good. You should try it sometime Nan'." — WB Mum

One way to encourage laughter and lightness in the home is to have fun fact books, joke books and riddle books beside the toilet. This is a place that everyone has to visit and having some material that builds a sense of humour is making very valuable use of this little room. These books often combine humour with interesting fun facts and can be educational as well as entertaining. A few of my favourite lines from our toilet joke books are:

"No man has ever been shot while doing the dishes."

"Five out of four people have trouble with fractions."

"If one synchronised swimmer drowns, does that mean all the others have to?"

"What happens if you get scared half to death twice?"

"Marriage is the chief cause of divorce."

"Be careful not to be too open-minded – your brains might fall out."

By reading these books and sharing the funny bits with family, children can learn the nuances of joke telling and of being humorous. This is a very important part of communication among friends and family. Only practise can improve anyone's ability to be humorous. I can still remember wondering what was wrong with me during my teenage years because I didn't seem to be able to 'get' jokes; I just missed what was funny. I still remember feeling quite stupid as well.

The capacity to laugh deeply and in an uninhibited way is another life skill that takes developing. Children who feel safe and valued can even fall over when they get an attack of giggles or laughter. Lightness and laughter can calm our boys when they are struggling. A positive gauge of the wellbeing of a child can be how often they smile and laugh. It is something that is very difficult to fake as children – if they are unhappy or frightened, their face shows it. As adults we need to treasure these exquisite moments of joy.

> *On the first day of school, a first-grader handed his teacher a note from his mother. The note read, "The opinions expressed by this child are not necessarily those of his parents".*

I recommend that parents use props and puppets to increase the levels of lightness in the house. Witch's hats can warn children that Mum is feeling grumpy and her tiara will help children know she's feeling happy. Puppets can cheer up any place; they become metaphors that can help with communication so powerfully. I know teachers who have the clean-up puppet, the quiet time mouse, a Tigger puppet for exercise time and the serious owl for proper chats about values. Be adventuresome and lighten up, and your children will come with you. In the process you, too, could make your spirit and heart happier, and help your stress levels dissolve.

Laughter and lightness in homes and classrooms shows safety and connectedness. Sharing some time with your son watching funny videos online especially about funny cats, dogs, or fainting goats can be a special time. Sharing laughter can be one of the strongest ways of holding a loving bond with your son. When they have left home and moved in with the next most important woman or partner in their life, you can still share any funny moment that you find via a text message or email, or sharing a meme on social media. I still do this today.

> "DB (5) had just seen some sheep shearing being done after a visit to a farm with his class. He came home, gently dragged the baby of the family over to the jolly jumper ... I could hear baby goos and gaas and funny 'shearing head motor noises' from the kitchen and was wondering what on earth was going on. When I walked into the room I saw a baby in a growsuit being turned over, then legs and back being 'shorn' on the floor under a 5-year-old in his Bonds singlet and shorts leaning over her into a jolly jumper, 'shearing' her with a hair brush. I asked DB what was going on, and without even looking up, under strained breath, he said, 'Just shearing the sheep Mum'. Ahhh, life with boys!!"
>
> — 'Shearing'-the-baby Mum

One last message on the topic of humour that's important to teach boys is that there is a difference between when we laugh *with* people and when we laugh *at* people. This is a difference many boys find really difficult to distinguish and, indeed, many adults also find this difficult. Be mindful to spend lots of time teaching how words can be helpful or hurtful, and that making fun of people is breaking the three main rules.

I have always been an enormous fan of the pun and, sadly, I think it's disappearing from the English language because so much humour now is in a visual format. So, for any mums who are fans of the pun, here is a selection to bring a smile to your face.

1. *He bought a donkey because he thought he might get a kick out of it.*
2. *A chicken crossing the road is poultry in motion.*
3. *The Energizer Bunny's been arrested, charged with battery.*
4. *A skunk fell in the river and stank to the bottom.*
5. And… *I was wondering why the baseball was getting bigger, then it hit me!*

Food

Food is so much more than fuel for our little boys' bodies. Given that young boys tend to have faster metabolisms for all sorts of reasons, they often find themselves hungry. What is really interesting is that it takes a very long time for boys to realise what hunger feels like – they just know it makes them feel awful, and angry. I have worked with teenage boys in my classroom whose behaviour after lunch has been pretty appalling. Often, I would find out, they had missed lunch or had forgotten to bring money to buy lunch. So, from very early on in my teaching career I would keep spare fruit in my room just in case I saw a boy who was behaving uncharacteristically poorly and perhaps simply needed something in his stomach. Again, being hungry triggers cortisol just the same as feeling excluded, misunderstood or unfairly treated – they all create a physical and emotional discomfort that a boy wants to get rid of as soon as possible. Having easily accessible and nutritious snacks close by at all times is something all mums work out as being a 'must' pretty early in their mothering of sons.

Some boys can also struggle with thirst because it triggers a similar response, but not quite as intensely. Always having water and spare food nearby is just sensible, preventive mothering and it is always a good place to start when your son is starting to have an emotional outburst, meltdown or tantrum – or all three happening at once. Boys do get hungry quicker and a paediatric dietician once recommended to me that mums need to keep an awareness around ensuring that boys are getting enough protein because it does help stabilise blood sugars. Boys seem to be more sensitive to additives and preservatives, and possibly this suggestion around protein could help as it makes common sense to me.

> "Quickly popping into the shops after school pick-up to grab a couple of things, I gave my DB (9) the three litres of milk to hold, and told him to wait near the checkout while I grabbed the bread. As I emerged from the aisle, all I could see was my son standing in a massive pool of milk. 'What happened?' I asked. 'I was balancing the milk on my head'. Needless to say, I didn't ask any more questions." — Happy Mum

When your boys are having a growth spurt, the amount of food they can eat will have you shaking your head often. The key windows of particularly vigorous growth spurts are also the times when there are significant hormonal shifts and changes – often involving testosterone – happening. When these things happen simultaneously, your son's need for good quality and increased quantities of food will be something he has very little control over. Ensure there is high-quality cereal and good quality bread in your house 24/7, and that includes in your freezer. Please be careful to read the sugar and sodium levels of the cereal you are buying. Most cereals should be in the lolly aisle of our supermarkets due to the high sugar content. I've known a starving boy to eat a kilogram of yoghurt in one sitting when he is experiencing a growth spurt. No, he has not had time to think about anyone else in the house who may need that yoghurt – his starvation that drives the cortisol means his single focus is on ending the pain in his stomach!

The ritual of food

There is something else about food that I have discovered over the years. Food memories and food rituals have a strong tendency to build belonging. Certain foods that have been cooked repeatedly in your home will bring incredible comfort to your son. The smell of favourite foods cooking can instantly shift your son's cortisol levels after school, without you having to say a word.

> *When a boy has a mum who can understand and appreciate that there can be a special relationship between her son, her food and her heart, she can be filling his love cup to overflowing, especially at some of his most challenging times.*

My two rooster sons have both shared how they once packed their bags to run away from home because they had not been able to get their own way. Both times I had noticed what was happening and, luckily, was able to put on a roast lamb dinner as they were making their getaway. Seriously, both times they returned home because they could not run away if there was a roast cooking! Baking at home can build invisible bonds to your son's heart, and baking while he is hovering at your elbow can also be a bonding experience. One of the best ways, I found, to coax a teenage son out of his bedroom was to bake a cake using the mixmaster which he could hear from the bedroom. Licking the leftover mixture from the bowl and licking the beaters is still something my sons enjoy today – even as grown men – when they visit.

> "At the breakfast bar one night, Master DB (2) wasn't keen on eating his dinner. A muesli bar sat idle nearby on the bench, which he became fixated on, and demanded to be given. I told him, 'Eat your dinner and then we can discuss the muesli bar'. After eventually eating his dinner, his gaze returned to the item on the bench. 'Mum, now, we need to discuss this muesli bar!'"
> — Speechless Mum

There are some lamb boys who find that food is one of the absolutely best things in their lives. These quieter souls are often the nature lovers, the animal lovers and the food lovers.

From age two, most nights before he had his last kiss, one of my lamb sons would ask, "Mummy, what's for dinner tomorrow night?" I knew from this that food was one of his greatest loves in life, and it still is today.

If you have more than one child, try to remember each child's favourite food for times when life is challenging for them. This could be exam time, relationship stress time or severe outbreak of acne time, to name just a few. Sometimes, just having a favourite food when you're having a tough day can make everything seem better.

I firmly believe that our strongest food memories that trigger endorphins in adulthood do so because the person who baked them frequently when you were a child, loved you deeply. Funny thing is that there is some research that supports that. As your sons grow into adolescence, help them learn to cook their favourite dishes and ensure that your pantry is not full of junk food so that they learn to eat healthily and responsibly.

Farting and other anatomical wonders that make boys laugh

> "My son then DB (5) was chatting to me in the bathroom while I was drying myself after a shower. He asked thoughtfully, 'Mum, were you sad when your doodle fell off?' I replied, 'Sweetheart, I was born a female so I've never had a doodle'. He smiled at me sweetly and shook his head, 'Oh Mum ...', as though I had no idea what I was talking about." — Confused Mum

Boys have a fascination with the human body especially bums, penises, poo and farting. This is normal and mums of sons need to be careful that we don't display our disapproval of their endless fascination with these things. Let's be realistic, as women we don't have external genitalia so we really can only guess what that must be like. Maybe if we look a little more deeply under the need to create so much laughter and delight around the physical body, we would see that this is a way for our boys to avoid being too serious. And so, could it also be seen as a coping skill to help boys manage stress? There is no question that holding a penis in a warm hand can be very calming and reassuring for little boys. Our job is to make sure they choose to do this soothing with an understanding of private versus public.

My fabulous dad was my hero and he was a master farter. This meant he could do farts that changed in tune and, once, I witnessed him walking from the top shed to the bottom shed farting each step of the way. He did not know that I had seen him and when I suddenly turned up behind him, he had the biggest grin on his face. You see, when success can come from such a minor skill, you can learn a new appreciation for how difficult it is for our warriors to find success in their day-to-day worlds. Seriously, you will have your son come and tell you how proud he is of a certain fart that he did!

> "In response to my, 'I love you more than all the stars in the night sky, more than all the fish in the ocean, etc.' bedtime ritual, my DB (4) says, 'Mummy, I love you more than all the poos in the toilet!' Naw!" — Poo Bum Mum

Having a successful poo and doing a fabulous fart are achievements that really matter to boys. Your son will often come and tell you what his poo looks like – no matter how many times you tell him that you do not need to be updated on his poo performance!

I once had a DB (7) who came and played at our house reasonably often. I noticed that he never flushed the toilet after he had done a poo and so I asked him one day, "Why?" His answer was so sweet. "My mum likes to look at my poo!" I replied, "Well, I don't, so when you're in my house you need to flush your poo. Thank you so much".

Your son could have many discussions with you about the fact that his fart does not smell bad. So, from an old mum with years of experience at trying to convince my sons that their farts do smell pretty awful, give up the need to argue and save your breath for something more important. I still have my adult sons occasionally tell me that their farts smell like roses!

> "Overheard in the corridor, boys in one of the bedrooms: 'I love you Riley ...' I'm thinking — oh, bless — I literally hold my hands over my heart with pride and am bursting with love. Then the statement continues: 'I love you Riley ... that is why I have to fart on your head!' I have to sneak away so they don't hear me laughing and go and write this in my notebook — I have pages of similar, just waiting for their 21st birthday parties!" — I Am That Mum

Farting in the bath is another delightful experience that many little boys and men seem to enjoy. Nothing delights them more than multiple farts in the bath because they make even more bubbles! Sometimes farting in the bath has ended up with a little poo arriving too – and, rather than being horrified, the boys thought it was additionally hilarious!

I need to offer a warning to mums who have multiple boys to stay for a sleepover, particularly teenage boys. Having farting competitions and even discovering the wonder of 'the blue flame' while with their friends are often the norm. My suggestion is, the following morning do not ignite a naked flame in the room where the boys slept. That faint blue cloud of a night full of boy farts could cause a catastrophe that you would prefer did not happen!

I think I mentioned earlier, that for my 63rd birthday this year, one of my birthday cards explored the different sorts of farts that exist. Seriously, as we read that card there were tears of laughter from our whole family and I will keep it and read it again and again when I need to have a good dose of good humour to lift my spirit.

Despite our sons' delight and fascination with farts, we do need to teach them that there are some expectations around intentionally farting in public. Accidental farting can happen to anyone and that just requires an authentic apology.

> "A few years ago I was feeding my then DB (2) some dinner in the kitchen nook. My eldest DB (4) walked in farted loudly right in front of us, looked at me and said, 'You're welcome,' then walked out." — Flatulent Mum

I am going to repeat that I do think mums need to fart more if they have sons. It is a powerful, non-verbal way of connecting to our boys using one of their favourite methods of communication. As I've emphasised throughout this book, a well-timed fart can transform a mood — it can say, "I'm sorry", and it can remind a son that he is still loved. This can be particularly helpful when your son is in early adolescence and has become less communicative.

Hopefully, now you may have a new understanding of the importance of fun, food and farting in your son's life. They can be sources of joy and delight and a way for our little boys to help cope with and manage being boys who can find communication difficult at times. Heck, given our boys used to have complete freedom in a natural environment for around eight years of their lives in the company of loving women who were comfortable with them being little warriors — is it any wonder that they can struggle living in our 21st-century world full of restraints and unrealistic expectations? I think I feel a fart coming!

> "Taking a shower with my DB (6 months) and DB (2) sitting waiting (not too patiently) for me to finish, I 'gave up' and jumped out of the shower to have DB (2) look at me horrified, but with an obvious effort not to alarm me. He burst out, 'Mummy, your willy fell off!' If I ever needed a reminder I was the sole lady in the house there it was." — Amused Mum

TOP TIPS

- ✓ Boys try to avoid the stress hormone cortisol by making positive neurochemicals.
- ✓ Having fun makes boys feel better.
- ✓ Dopamine is made with physical activity, especially via vigorous play.
- ✓ Laughing makes boys feel better.
- ✓ Boys need help to develop a sense of humour.
- ✓ Boys need to learn when humour is inappropriate – and to laugh with people, not at people.
- ✓ Food makes boys feel better.
- ✓ Food is a wonderful way to create rituals and memories that our boys will carry with them for life.
- ✓ Farting can make boys feel better.
- ✓ Mums can learn about the power of a well-timed fart.

CHAPTER 16

Building **CHARACTER** in **OUR BOYS**

> **"Character is shaped by life experience and cannot be seen from the outside or from physical appearances. It cannot be judged by prizes and accolades. Nor can it be judged by age or culture. Character can only be ascertained from how a person lives and interacts with others."**
>
> — Maggie Dent, *Nurturing Kids' Hearts and Souls* (2005).

It seems that in this busy, ever-changing world we may have lost sight of what is really important in raising our children. We focus so much on the grades our children achieve and their physical, sporting, musical, artistic and mental abilities that we seldom recognise or celebrate their humanity and the depth of their unique character. It is only when we see an absence of this dimension that we bemoan the fact and complain about our young people. When we see senseless violence against the old, the defenceless and the innocent we are horrified. When we see young people hopelessly addicted to alcohol, drugs and other forms of self-harm we are saddened. We see young people living lives that are aimless, with no purpose or meaning, and we wonder, why? The digital world has a dark side that many believe is corrupting the natural innocence of children far too early. Given that many boys are impulse-driven and take longer to mature and make better decisions, as I have already explored, then we need to focus on exploring how to build a healthy character in our boys.

Our competitive, selfie-driven, consumer-driven world holds sporting heroes and actors in places of high status and value regardless of their true character. The media shares many stories of badly behaved sporting heroes and celebrities, and these stories can influence our little boys into thinking that behaving badly is something to aspire to. It is a little sad that the media, including magazines and social media, sensationalise these stories of badly behaving people because they believe that is what sells their magazines. If only the media would share as many stories of fine, upstanding sporting heroes and celebrities who act with honour, respect, concern, unconditional regard and the courage to hold ground when confronted with choices that compromise being true to self.

Indigenous communities historically focussed on the development of the character within their children as well as their physical growth. Responsibility for the development of a child was shared by everyone. Physical growth was important and children were taught new skills when they were ready. They were also taught the gifts of the spirit and the heart. These are what we loosely term values, virtues, social manners and etiquette. Without these templates, young people are often unaware of how to behave and what to value; they basically live a life that is code-less. The early years of boys within these communities tended to be spent around the women, learning ways of caring, sharing and helping the young ones and the elderly. When the boys would transition to being around the men, the mentoring and teaching in the ways of being a man would be taken very seriously. So, in a way, boys were constantly being guided and shown how to be sensible, cooperative and respectful.

According to developmental molecular biologist John Medina in his book *Brain Rules*, you can create moral maturity in most children. There are many definitions for what moral means and probably the most accepted one is that "morality is a set of value-laden behaviours embraced by our cultural group whose main function is to guide social behaviour". This seems to have a lot to do with the strong evolutionary requirements of social cooperation, a concept that Charles Darwin promoted alongside competition in his famous work. According to research, it seems moral awareness is a universal characteristic that is innate to a degree and, of course, then conditioned by our social and cultural influences.

> **"A willingness to make the right choices — and to withstand pressure to make the wrong ones, even in the absence of incredible threats or the presence of a reward — is the goal of moral development. Which means your parenting objective is to get your child to pay attention to and align himself with his innate sense of right and wrong. This takes time. A lot of time."**
>
> — John Medina, *Brain Rules for Baby* (2010). www.brainrules.net.

Medina says that families who raise moral kids tend to follow fairly predictable behaviours around rules and discipline, generally following three very simple steps.

- Clear consistent rules and rewards
- Swift punishment or deterrent consequences
- Explaining the rules.

Even though Medina has used the word 'punishment' or 'deterrent consequences' – which sounds like a parent needs to be a controlling adult, forcing children to submit to adult will – he means that children need some guidance or a gentle deterrent to prevent repeating behaviour that is unhelpful or unwanted. This can include showing a child what behaviour is fairer or kinder – rather than what is right or wrong – or getting the child to clean up a mess they have made. This helps them learn that they are accountable for their actions and at the same time, we respect their childlike need to experience the world as a *child* – think putting every Band-Aid in the house on at once, smearing Dad's shaving cream on the floor or painting the cat.

If a boy bites another child, picking him up quietly and walking away from the wounded child is a form of deterrent consequence that you can follow up with a calm conversation about treating others fairly, i.e. emphasising the rules of your home.

Understanding emotional competence is also important and reading Daniel Goleman's book was a significant milestone for me. Finally, a well-recognised and respected expert was exploring the emotional domain of us mere mortals. *Emotional Intelligence* is still seen as groundbreaking work and the knowledge Goleman brought into prominence has changed many things: the direction of people's thinking, education and consciousness. Howard Gardner probably coined the actual term 'emotional intelligence' in his book, *Frames of Mind*, in 1993.

So what are the key characteristics of emotional intelligence?

Emotional intelligence

- knowing your emotions and feeling states
- managing your emotions
- motivating yourself
- having an ability to accurately empathise with others
- handling relationships
- having the ability to not be swamped by your emotions

- believing in your ability to cope
- persisting in the face of frustration
- having impulse control
- being able to delay gratification
- feeling hopefulness.

These are the characteristics of healthy emotional intelligence. A person with emotional competency would, for example, have patience in queues, resolve conflict without verbal or physical abuse, be capable of loving, caring relationships, overcome setbacks quicker than others and enjoy being themselves most of the time. Emotional competence reduces the need for physical aggression and defensiveness. Emotional illiteracy and social incompetence starts early in life. Indeed, there is a high incidence of transference of low patterns of coping and resilience that is quite easy to discern by three or four years of age. When these patterns continue long-term, the damaging effects can be very debilitating in later childhood, adolescence and adulthood. I am sure you know some grown-ups who have not yet developed a mature emotional competence and who still throw adult tantrums from time to time. I know I can still struggle with impulse control some nights around chocolate!

Daniel Siegel, in his excellent book *Mindsight*, explores emotionally mature behaviour as being a function of the middle portion of the prefrontal cortex and it has the ability to coordinate these essential skills:

- regulating our body
- attuning to others
- balancing emotions
- being flexible in our responses
- soothing fear
- creating empathy
- having insight
- having moral awareness
- using intuition.

While many of these attributes are similar to the characteristics Goleman describes, the ability to soothe fear, create empathy, and to have insight and moral awareness, seem to suggest a deeper level of emotional and social capacity can be nurtured in our children. Siegel argues that due to the plasticity of the human brain, we can build emotional and social awareness and competence at any time in life. However, the best time to build this awareness is in the first years of life. Knowing that building the neural connectors takes time to form, it will help parents to understand why children – especially little boys – can take quite some time before they are able to learn how to make better choices.

One example that shows what can happen when such social and emotional awareness is not built in the early years comes from a study of some of the American teenagers who committed mass murders in their school environments in the early 1990s. The study showed that what these teenagers, who were all boys, had in common was that when they were children, they had little opportunity to play and were largely ignored by those around them. They felt ignored, even ridiculed, in their homes and at school, and the emotional wounding and scars these experiences left on their sense of self-value was obviously deep. Compounded with a fascination for violent movies, guns and weapons, there was little possibility of a positive solution to any conflict occurring in their lives.

The final straw that breaks emotional restraint is often small and relatively insignificant. A traumatised young person may perceive that the only solution to their continued pain is to take drastic revenge for every painful experience they have ever been through. The need to pay back or seek revenge when you have been wronged as a boy is something we really need to focus on preventing as soon as we see it the first time. Many ex-partners – mainly women – are killed every year and so often there is a revenge element to the crime. Emotional illiteracy is common among many of our worst perpetrators of crimes that hurt others and this is something we can help build in our little boys before they become men who hurt others – intentionally or otherwise.

"My mum taught me warmth, empathy, love and manners. Sorry, couldn't separate the four." – Men's Survey 2017

Given that women are traditionally more emotionally savvy, then the role of us as mothers in building a good basis for future emotional competence in our young boys would seem to be obvious. With great patience, we can help our little boys understand emotions – and all emotions are valid. Emotional literacy can be difficult for boys to develop, especially in the early years when they are biologically wired to be physically active, curious and impulsive. As I explored in the chapter on ***"When boys muck up"***, so often their intention is not to muck up! This is why I encourage the use of the three rules – so we can explore how little boys make poor choices and why they need to learn to reconsider a choice they have made.

Of course, it is not just young boys who struggle with making poor choices – early adolescence can also be pretty frustrating, especially for mums who are trying to guide their boys to grow in a sense of responsibility and accountability. Indeed, developing a sense of those two important traits is a really big part of building good character in your son, especially in our rooster boys. Empathy can help boys make better decisions when they meet personal conflict. I firmly believe that boys often respond to physical violence because they know no other way of 'fixing' the problem. Having those pillow chats or quiet chats in the bath or on the deck about how someone else may feel when your son has made a poor choice are incredibly important in building a sense of empathy. In the past, little boys were simply hit, hurt or shamed when they made poor choices, and they weren't given any help in understanding how to make better choices.

> "My DB (1.5-year-old) toddler had been having all the big emotions in the kitchen and, after a failed attempt to negotiate with him during his tantrum, I told him I would be waiting for him in the lounge room when he was ready. Next minute, from the lounge, I hear his frustrated, stomping feet followed by his broken, sad voice calling out, 'Mummy, man down, man down!' When I went back into the kitchen he was lying on the floor in a huff."
> — Amused Mum

Many children who behave as bullies have problems with empathy. This emotional competency is mainly learnt through life experience and with the guidance of a caring adult. Despite research findings to the contrary, play fighting has come to be seen as a disturbing facet of childhood and one from which children need to be saved. This shift in parenting could be contributing to boys being less able to negotiate tricky social situations later in life and getting into serious trouble by misreading the social cues between play and a real threat (remember I wrote about that in Chapter 9?). Children need to learn the many invisible codes of behaviour that provide life skills. This learning is being eroded by the current attitude towards demonising normal childhood misbehavior. Children are meant to make mistakes with the choices they make because they are children – this is how they learn. The less boys play with other children, the less often they have opportunities to develop emotional and social literacy. Play really matters!

Given that we know that the brain anchors memories more strongly when powerful emotions are present, it makes sense that if we are to build the capacity for our children to be empathetic and able to tune into other people – and to not be narcissistic, self-indulgent little brats – then we need to model and demonstrate endless moments of empathetic connection with them. If your intention from the word go is to build the ability in your son to be kind, compassionate and caring, then this intention will direct and guide the choices you make as a parent. Whatever we prioritise, guides the choices we make as humans. Even if your baby or toddler does not understand your words, they will certainly know what the tone of your voice, your facial expression and what the type of touch you are using means. This is one of the reasons why pioneering paediatrician and educator Emmi Pikler encouraged the 3Rs as the foundation for her approach to caring for young children: **responsive, reciprocal, respectful** care. If these three characteristics are present in 80% of our interactions with our babies and toddlers, then they will develop the social and emotional intelligence to be decent people.

> "Mum has throughout her life volunteered in or been involved in community events/activities/associations/etc. ... and whenever I've volunteered she has been interested and actively supportive of these activities." – Men's Survey 2017

Boys can definitely learn how to be more caring and empathetic by watching the significant grown-ups who are a part of their world – this includes family, neighbours and definitely teachers. There are a number of ways children can learn and practise the gift of concern for others and to discover the benefits of loving service. Nothing warms the cockles of my heart more than reading stories about school students who do a wonderful community service such as raising money for needy charities. For modelling service and community spirit, here are a few more suggestions:

- collect papers or mail for a neighbour when they are away
- care for friends' pets when they are away
- take soup to sick family, friends or neighbours
- help elderly people with tasks like shopping and gardening
- make crafty gifts that cost little and give them to people in need
- bake cookies, scones or muffins for people in need, or for birthdays
- take small gifts of gratitude to teachers and carers
- phone and send cards or letters to thank people for their kindnesses
- share toys and the like with friends
- practise random acts of kindness to others
- help with family chores without being asked
- send rainbows of love and kindness to people and countries in need
- smile lots
- say hello to people at school or in the community who seem sad or lonely
- give a gentle shoulder rub to family members or friends

- leave a loving note on a family member's pillow to share why you love them
- with permission, gather blankets for a blanket drive
- knit a scarf and donate it to a charity
- pick up broken glass on the road or path
- give family and friends a hug
- welcome new students into a school.

Another good way to build character in children and teenagers is to watch an uplifting movie or documentary with them – always checking for age-appropriateness guidelines before choosing a film. Chat with them about it afterwards, discussing what happened and the choices the characters made. Here are some golden oldies (check the ratings!):

Dead Poet's Society

Good Will Hunting

Alaska

Life is a House

I am Sam

Pay it Forward

Stand By Me

Forrest Gump

Braveheart

Lion King

Shrek

Soul Surfer

Karate Kid movies

Reading picture books that explore empathy is another way of building the understanding in little boys. We have a recommended list available on my website.

For older boys, a fantastic book to check out is Ben Brooks' *Stories for Boys Who Dare to be Different*, which offers short stories about men, past and present, famous and not-so-famous who "went on to make the world a better place through compassion, generosity and self-belief", as the back cover says. The book is beautifully illustrated, too, and includes a wonderful diversity of men.

Building character in our boys is not just about what we teach them, it is about our boys being heard safely, without judgement. So often in my counselling rooms I heard the back-stories around a major conflict that had seen a boy be punished harshly – stories that these boys were never given a chance to share. We must let boys have a voice, because if we don't, they simply stop trying to communicate their confusion, their misunderstanding and their vulnerable feelings. They tend to create an inner voice that acts as an internal enemy of themselves: "I am bad", "I am useless" or "There is something wrong with me", are just some of the voices that form in their minds.

Clark Wight, head of a private junior school in Western Australia and a wonderful boy champion, shared in a presentation his belief that:

> **"We as teachers and parents need to listen to boys' voices. It is an opportunity to de-construct the 'boy code' – old rules that favour male stoicism that make boys ashamed about expressing weakness, vulnerability and their own emotions. It is about giving boys an opportunity to use their 'voice', to enable us to give the consistent attention, empathy and support they truly need and desire, as well as to give parents and teachers some tools to try and understand our sons and students even better."**
>
> – Clark Wight, *A Time to Connect: Being 10 and Moving Forward* (2005).

Emotionally literate men who have a capacity to be aware, conscious and committed to leave the world better than they found it, are incredibly important in the shaping of our boys' character, and fortunately there are plenty of good men around. There are many organisations that are helping dads become the fathers they really want to be, and positive fathering is definitely becoming an overt way of being in the lives of men. Helping our boys work out what is the right thing to do in any given situation, regardless of how difficult it may be, is really the secret to building a positive character in your son. Helping him to identify that having a conscience matters and that he needs to trust his own instincts about what is the right thing to do is vital – especially when he may have to stand apart from his friends from time to time. Hopefully this means that good men will no longer stay silent when other men are being disgusting and disrespectful to others, especially children and women. The change is slowly happening, and encouraging your son to know how to be fair and how to be kind will certainly help.

> "My mum has given me insight, the ability to question." – Men's Survey 2017

The power of kindness, fairness and gratitude

> "I am grateful for my mum's kindness because it has helped me to become a kind person, too." – Men's Survey 2017

Kindness matters

What is kindness?

Kindness is the capacity of an individual to act from a place of genuine concern for oneself and others, and it includes the qualities of empathy, compassion, generosity and consideration with the intention of making a positive difference in our world. Being kind is a choice made from the belief that every action influences others, and it honours our deepest, invisible motivation to have value and worthiness in our lives.

Compassion and kindness have the power to touch deeply and this often ripples through the world around us; showing kindness invites others to be caring in turn. This is a universal reality that has great power. Many people have been touched by the kindness of others after the global disasters we've witnessed recently (and regularly). Kindness was the most powerful pathway to teaching I knew in my own home and in the classrooms where I taught adolescents for 18 years. It is great that science can now prove what wise, caring Elders have known for a very long time.

Interestingly, there is still a perception that boys need much firmer discipline in order to learn how to behave better. This is linked to the old code and must be questioned wherever possible. As I have stated already, kindness allows a boy to feel safe and valued and research around attachment – whether primary or secondary attachment – shows that feeling safe and valued increases the natural motivation of children to follow their significant grown-ups' intentions. Kindness also helps the primitive brain to feel safer and less reactive, and that certainly helps little boys in social situations where they feel threatened.

The effects of being treated fairly and with kindness have been shown in studies in neuroscience, to make a significant difference to the way the brain integrates, and subsequently, to how individuals feel and behave. When we are treated with kindness, it allows our nervous system to relax and the pleasant sensations from endorphins, often serotonin and sometimes oxytocin, to flood our body. It makes us feel safe, valued and connected. Stress and distress have significant effects of how children and adults interact with the world.

> *When we are kind, we don't take advantage of our power, or of other people's vulnerabilities. Instead, we seek to comfort, encourage and strengthen those around us. The strong sense of belonging that comes with being treated with kindness is tangible and powerful.*

It removes the distance between individuals from 'them' or 'us' to 'we'. Treating others as we would like to be treated is an ancient way of building character and human understanding. Medina explains the astonishing skill called 'deferred imitation', which develops rapidly and which research shows exists in a 13-month-old child who can remember an event a week after a single exposure. When we know this, we can appreciate how important it is to model kind, caring behaviour in front of our babies, toddlers and young children. If we have never been treated with kindness or fairness, we simply will be unable to treat others the same way.

The modern world has somehow grown a culture of individualism, insensitivity, selfishness and even cruelty. We really are living in the era of selfies and many of the selfies taken have had a filter added to ensure that whoever is being photographed looks perfect. Yikes! The pressure to be perfect rather than authentic is very real in the 21st century. As social beings, a primary need of all humans is human intimacy and connection and I believe so many of the social ills of our world – increasing violence, bullying, alcohol and drug abuse, mental illness and suicide – come from a place of disturbing alienation, social exclusion and separateness. If we can build a strong culture of caring, based on kindness and fairness, our children may find the world a different place when they become adults. This culture needs to start in our homes and then flow into our schools so that every child can be influenced and shaped by it. I would argue that this culture of caring needs to start with us mums.

We can help our little boys come to understand the importance of kindness through our actions and through the stories we share with them. Babies and children who are raised with a culture of care, compassion and kindness will treat others the same way, and they will expect to be treated that way throughout life. This all stems from early life experiences that build up 'filters' or a particular lens through which we see the world. If we only experience disrespectful and unkind interactions with our significant caregivers, then that is how we will behave towards others. This is why I am so passionate about changing the way we discipline boys as compared to girls. All our children need to be treated with significant loving care and guidance rather than being hit and hurt. Just because we love children does not necessarily mean they feel loved and valued. The code of kindness and fairness will ensure that children will feel the love, and with this primary human need filled, it will allow children to have the energy to grow and flourish. Again, on my website you can find a list of good picture books that explore kindness that could help you with your boys.

Fairness matters

> "My mum taught me how to be respectful and valuing everyone for who they are no matter what walk of life." – Men's Survey 2017

Being fair and kind are essential for building healthy, happy relationships from childhood to adulthood.

Dr Matthew Lieberman and Dr Naomi Eisenberger in their paper on *Social Cognitive Neuroscience: The Pains and Pleasure of Social Life* explored how powerful social exclusion is on individuals including children. Using brain imaging, they found that when a person experiences rejection or social exclusion, they experience a form of physical pain. Children who have poor attachment to their parents will struggle to connect with other people. This sense of pain may explain why it is so hard to get children to return to school after they have experienced a serious conflict that made them feel rejected or left out. The other interesting thing the researchers discovered was that being treated fairly activates the same parts of the brain as having our basic needs met like eating, coming in from the cold or eating chocolate. It triggers the pleasure response. This may partially explain why young boys can become physically aggressive when they are excluded from games or they don't have a friend to play with. This shows how painful and destructive punitive punishment and shaming is on our boys especially when it is repeated – often. Their little bodies get flooded with stress hormones and they are triggered by their survival brain to fight or escape.

> **"Being treated unfairly activates the social pain and disgust circuitry. In our evolutionary past being accepted and valued by one's group is important because it means access to critical resources for survival and thriving."**
>
> – Matthew Lieberman & Naomi Eisenberger. 'The pains and pleasures of social life: A social cognitive neuroscience approach.' *Neuroleadership Journal*. Retrieved 20 June 2018 from http://www.scn.ucla.edu/pdf/Pains&Pleasures(2008).pdf

These research findings reinforced my personal belief that a meaningful life is determined by how safe, loved and accepted we are as an individual. What may seem small and unimportant – like someone playing 'Round and Round the Garden', or blowing raspberries on a toddler's tummy – profoundly shapes how attached or bonded a child feels to their significant carers. We are much braver to make mistakes if we are still valued after we mess up! Every decision we make as a parent, grandparent or teacher needs to respond to the inner response our children have to how we treat them. If we meet our children's core need to know they belong, they matter and that learning and growing is what they are supposed to do – and we treat children with kindness and fairness – we can improve every child's pathway of potential. They feel attached in a loving way. When our little boys are feeling attached, they want to lean in towards us and their nervous systems are able to be calm and open.

> **"It is widely understood that people learn by example. But adults who are respectful of children are not just modelling a skill or behaviour; they are meeting the emotional needs of those children, thereby helping to create the psychological conditions to treat others respectfully."**
>
> – Alfie Kohn, *What to Look for in a Classroom and Other Essays* (1998).

A golden secret to disciplining with fairness and kindness

Seeing the world through the eyes of our children is the secret to being the respectful, considerate parent you really want to be. One of the most significant benefits I gleaned from studying neuro-linguistic programming (NLP) many years ago was an awareness that beneath every behaviour is some form of positive intention. Sometimes, a child may bite another child because they are feeling crowded and overwhelmed, and they're trying to create some space for themselves. Sometimes seeking serotonin, we eat too much chocolate, so that we can calm down and be nicer human beings.

Next time you approach a conflict with a boy of any age try to ascertain what it is he wanted to happen as a consequence of the choice he made. Sometimes a child will hit a child because they want that boy to stop hurting another child. The reasons they may give you will be very childlike and when we see through their eyes, we can often witness what they were really trying to do. I wrote pretty extensively about this in Chapter 10 so revisit that if you need some more suggestions for understanding what your son is thinking.

The primitive brain, with its flight-fight response, is easily triggered in our little mammoth hunters – our boys – when they have unmet needs like tiredness, hunger, thirst or a deep sense of being emotionally disconnected from their most significant grown-ups. So often, a parent's punitive response to a boy's poor choice or inability to cope, simply floods their little brain with the stress chemicals that make everything worse. This form of authoritarian parenting often unintentionally teaches a child about submission/dominance.

> *If we are committed to raising a child who will know how to use fairness and kindness later in life, then we need to avoid having a parent-child relationship that is based solely on power and control.*

I am not suggesting that our little boys do not experience discipline when they make poor choices repeatedly; I am simply saying we need to avoid 'punishing' them as the main way to get them to make better choices.

Remember that there is no 'perfect' in parenting but being mindful will definitely help you make better decisions as a parent. However, there is no guarantee that you will get it right every time. Even if we just pause most of the time when our children do things that make us feel frustrated and annoyed – and be grateful that we have the opportunity to be parents in the first place as so many people don't. Hopefully by building a better understanding between mums and sons, we may make parenting them a little less reactive and a little fairer. There will be times when we will respond abruptly and from our exhausted self, and that is completely normal because there is no perfect.

Compassionate and respectful 'now' parenting allows both the parent and the child to be valued and respected. Next time you have a teachable moment with your child, even if it involves a spectacular tantrum, when you reflect on that experience a couple of hours later after a nice cup of tea, ask yourself my three questions for compassionate parenting:

1. **Was that fair?**
2. **Was that kind?**
3. **What has that taught my child?**

If you are not happy with your answers, simply plan a different response next time. There is no need to beat yourself up, think dark, negative thoughts or eat the whole family block of fruit and nut chocolate; you simply allow your higher brain and your heart to guide you to making better choices next time. I do recommend that you have a quiet conversation with your son many hours after the conflict and tell him you are disappointed with the way you responded because it was not fair and possibly was disrespectful. I can guarantee that your son will forgive you instantly. You are also modelling apologising for making a poor choice and being accountable for that choice and these attributes will definitely help you build a healthy character inside your son.

Gratitude matters

> "My DB (4) after a day in reception [an early years' class] comes out to greet me. He says he has a present for me and reaches into his pocket and pulls out a live millipede. I say thank you very much and ask how long it's been there. He says, 'Since play time Mummy, he likes it in my lovket'. This poor little millipede had spent the day in his pocket. I was very grateful but asked that we put him back in the leaves which he happily agreed to!"
>
> — Naturalist Mum

Let's be honest – no one likes an ungrateful child! We definitely seem to be noticing an increasing modern phenomenon of increasing ingratitude, entitlement, narcissism and a more self-centred perception of the world! So, why does gratitude matter?

Researchers within the field of positive psychology have been carrying out a lot of research around human behaviour and it would seem gratitude definitely does matter. Fostering gratitude improves wellbeing both emotionally and physically and, in one study, the group who practised gratitude reported being more supportive around other people, as well as that they were sleeping better and feeling happier within themselves.

Essentially, laying the groundwork for gratitude in the early years by showing a high level of warmth and empathy to children is important and, for our little boys, possibly even more important because expressing themselves verbally can often be something they struggle with.

Sadly, we can't just nag our boys into being grateful! We know that when our significant grown-ups model genuine gratitude, our boys are watching. Gentle reminders definitely still have a place in nudging our children gently to remember to say thank you.

> *Teaching our children to be grateful for gifts is one thing and teaching our children to be grateful when people give us time or an action that has helped us, is also really important.*

Being a volunteer in an organisation or helping out a neighbour in need are simple ways of teaching your son about gratitude especially for those less fortunate than yourself.

I spent a number of years as a volunteer in a hospice and I know it taught me some seriously big lessons about gratitude. Simply being grateful for my health and for the prospect of a life that was still possible for me were lessons in gratitude I have never forgotten. I may have been known to have conversations with my young boys about the importance of being grateful for your health, especially when I would come home after another one of our clients had died.

When I was an at-home mum, I had the boys help me bake biscuits at the end of term to give as thank you gifts for their teachers. We did not give biscuits to all the teachers that my boys had and that also involved me having conversations with them about value and respect. Some teachers simply had made life difficult for the students in a particular class and it was OK not to bake biscuits for them. I felt they needed to learn authentic gratitude, not gratitude that is compulsory.

Sometimes we can teach our boys to be grateful for what they have, for what they've received in life, in a reverse way — by actually getting them to give things away. At times we decided to donate some of their toys to a charity for children who come from vulnerable families. I made sure they washed and cleaned the toys so that they looked brand new and we also wrapped them as gifts in wrapping paper. By donating to children less fortunate we were indirectly acknowledging how grateful we were for being more fortunate.

So, yes, gratitude does matter!

> "Never been a dull moment in my house with my DB (22) 'cyclone son' and his friends who often apologise for giving me all my grey hairs especially through his risk-taking teens. But, so far so good, he is growing into a compassionate, family-oriented, hardworking, caring young man who tells me whenever I speak to him how much he loves me and how he is grateful for everything I've done. Just as I hoped and prayed he would as this is what society needs more of. I laugh to myself as his loving girlfriend now patiently experiences his whirlwind ideas/plans with his childhood friends included in them!"
>
> — Lucky, Grey-headed Mum

We can build character in our boys and we need to prioritise this well before puberty starts. Having a sound base of values and expectations is a very slow process and mothers have a really big part to play in this through endless conversations, modelling and (as I said earlier in this chapter) choosing to expose our precious boys to stories and films that show examples of good character in other boys and men. It is important to help our little boys to understand that there is a right way and a wrong way and that despite sometimes making the wrong choice, we can still hold our hearts open to them as they make amends. Please help any boys who are a part of your life, not just your own son, learn about kindness, fairness and gratitude because it's not so much who teaches them, as to whether or not they have learnt about the power of these wonderful attributes of character. It is OK in your conversations with a young boy to affirm that you are committed to helping him grow up to be a good man with a strong character rather than a jerk or a creep who has a weak character. When the significant father figures – and please note I did say father figures as I know many children don't live with their dads – in their lives are singing from the same song sheet, our boys have a much better chance to grow up to be good men, not perfect men, but men who have a character that helps them navigate the world with genuine compassion, courage and integrity.

> "Mummy finds a crusty, dead frog on the patio and kicks it away. My DB (3) finds said frog and brings it back to Mummy. 'Look Mummy! He's special'. 'Oh, yuck darling! Put that down, it's dead and very yucky'. DB (3) tosses it onto the grass. 'It's not yucky Mummy, he's special.' DB (3) bends down to inspect dead frog. 'Oh, hello froggy. You sleeping?'" — Grossed-out Mum

TOP TIPS

- ✓ Building character needs to be an intention when raising both girls and boys.
- ✓ It is really important to develop emotional intelligence gradually throughout boyhood.
- ✓ Picture books, storybooks, films and documentaries can help build character – and enable conversations about values and expectations.
- ✓ Helping our boys, especially our rooster boys, develop empathy is incredibly important before adolescence.
- ✓ Practising gratitude is good for our wellbeing on many levels.
- ✓ Teaching the importance of kindness, fairness and gratitude will help build good character in your son.

CHAPTER 17

Sons and love, **HEALTHY SEXUALITY** and relationships

> "I took DB (4) to have a little ice cream treat one day. I felt so in love with him in that moment so I said, 'I love you', and without taking his eyes off his ice cream he replied, 'I love chocolate'." — Like Mother Like Son Mum

We all want to raise our boys to be capable of having healthy, respectful relationships where they are capable of giving and receiving love and of being sexually intimate. Despite the wide reporting of sexually predatory behaviour of some school boys, sporting stars, politicians and film celebrities, the vast majority of boys and men are capable of loving their intimate partner respectfully.

Many years ago when I was counselling full-time I worked with a man whose wife of 25 years decided she wanted to end the marriage. They had five children and he was devastated, and the ending had blindsided him. After the first session I gave him John Gray's popular book *Men are from Mars, Women are from Venus* to read before I saw him again. I didn't agree with everything Gray wrote regarding the differences between what women and men want, however I felt it was a good starting point for this confused man. When he returned to see me, he sat down and said, "Why didn't someone tell me this stuff? I could have done this if I had known". What he was saying was that the ways and means of living in a meaningful, respectful and helpful relationship with someone of the opposite sex was something he had never given any thought to before now.

> *Human relationships can be difficult, even when they are still healthy because every individual sees the world differently, has different perceived ideals and different personalities.*

A long-term committed relationship between a man and a woman that includes having children has many highs and lows, which can confuse men particularly. Falling in love with someone can be pretty easy, especially with all the wonderful neurochemicals that come with being attracted to someone. Sadly, this stage does not last forever and the transition into a stable, caring relationship – with its decline in the excitement of being newly intimately connected with someone – can take time to adjust to. The arrival of children and the change in the parents' relationship can cause more confusion and stress, especially if there is poor communication between the couple. When couples can identify the challenges they experience and work towards overcoming them together, relationships tend to grow more solid rather than shatter into pieces. Sometimes, when the relationship is unable to find a respectful, caring equilibrium, it can be better to end it.

> "I wish my mum had not remained in a marriage with my father and [had been] courageous enough to believe she was worth better."
> – Men's Survey 2017

The biological drive to be a deer hunter – meaning to be the dominant provider in a family – can be one of those 'single-focus' times in a man's life that can undermine relationship. There is a strong unconscious drive in most men to provide physical abundance like a home and sound income to the woman they love, especially when she becomes a mother. This drive can be so strong that they spend extremely long hours away from home trying to do this job to the best of their ability. This means that sometimes mothers are left unsupported for long periods of time with little children, and that can be a source of conflict between a mum and dad.

I once met a mining engineer in the Pilbara of Western Australia at one of my dads' seminars a number of years ago. Following the seminar, he came and asked me if I had any suggestions on how to manage the phone conversations he had with his daughters when they cried because they missed him. I asked him how long he had been away from home – home was the Sunshine Coast in Queensland, on the opposite side of Australia. He said that he thought he'd only been away a couple of months but he suddenly realised while I was speaking that he had not been home for eight months. He paused and said he had simply lost track of time and not noticed how long it had been because he was so focused on being the best deer hunter possible. He had a large house on the Sunshine Coast, he had a boat fully paid for and another house in the Pilbara, and yet he was still working incredibly long hours away from his family. This good man started to tear up and then he said:

"I have just realised I need to be around my family and so I am quitting my job and heading home. My girls are four and six years of age and they need a dad. Thank you for the wake-up call, Maggie."

When we are raising our sons it is so important for us to talk about relationships rather than just love and sex or else we miss preparing them to be capable of living in a loving, caring relationship, which they yearn for just as much as women do.

> "Love the caring nature of big brother DB (3) to little brother DB (2). 'Don't drink any more bath water, I just did a biiiiiig wee in here.'" — Happy Mum

Helping our dads and father figures

Unless our son's dad/father figure is being intentionally abusive – either physically, emotionally or psychologically – we mums can really have a role in helping to maintain and nurture positive relationships between the two. Dads have often told me how they regret mucking up their relationship with their son because they didn't know how to do fathering better. This was mainly because when they were stressed, tired, overworked or feeling misunderstood they defaulted to the way their own tough father would have behaved. As mums, we can help to glide over these bumpy times by explaining to our sons and their father figures why they are unable to manage conflict better. The following is a blog I have written about how to do this.

When fathers are tough, inflexible and unloving

Over time I have been asked many times by mums about what they can do with the men they love who make choices in their family that seem harsh and uncaring.

Many of these mums have said they know their husbands and partners are good, loving men but they just seem to react in many situations from a place that is certainly not their heart. These women genuinely want to help their men become the fathers they know these dads want to be.

In particular here, I am addressing the father-son dynamic as father-daughter relationships can be very different. I am also specifically writing here for those mamas in a relationship with a father figure whom they live with.

To begin, I need to tell a story that is based on one I heard many years ago in rural Australia.

Once upon a time there were three 14-year-old mates who had been friends for a number of years. Sometime in the previous year they had come to like playing golf. On most Saturday mornings they would meet at the golf club, get their fathers' golf sticks from the buggy room and play at least nine holes of golf before the main competition started late in the morning. This pattern of behaviour had been happening for almost a year before something went horribly wrong.

On this particular Saturday, after the boys got back to the club room and they were putting the golf buggy and sticks back into the buggy room, they started a harmless shoving and pushing game – for want of a better word. One of the boys grabbed one of the golf sticks and pretty soon they were pretending they were fencing. This game then led into a random game of trying to hit each other with the golf sticks. They damaged a few of the walls where the golf stick cracked the plaster. Then, somehow or other, the light fittings were smashed and some of the lockers were also hit and damaged in the senseless, mindless game-gone-wrong 15 minutes of insanity.

When one of the club members who had arrived early for the competition walked into the room, the boys stopped suddenly. The boys' fathers were called and the boys were made to sit on a bench outside the buggy room facing the car park where many other members were now arriving. The members were obviously very unhappy with the vandalism and damage.

Soon the first father arrived and as he got out of his car he slammed the car door. As he came up the path towards where his son was sitting, he began shouting abusively calling his son "a bloody idiot" and asking him how he could be so stupid. When he reached his son, he physically took him by the shoulders and shook him vigorously while continuing to shout in his face. He then shoved his son in the direction of the car and again slammed his car door as he drove off in a furious haste.

The second father arrived and as he got out of his car he also slammed the door. As he came up the pathway towards his son his face was black with a silent fury. When he got near his son he swung and hit him really hard over the head and then he began shouting the same shaming abuse as the first father. As his son began to walk towards the car, his father shoved him so hard from behind the boy sprawled onto the path. He then dragged him to the car. He also slammed his car door and took off in a furious haste.

The third father then arrived and, unlike the previous two fathers, he did not slam his car door. He walked up the pathway towards his son and held his arms out to his son and gave him a hug. He whispered something to him and then with his arm around his shoulders he guided him carefully back to the car and they drove off quietly.

An hour later the third father and his son returned to the golf club. They had been to Bunnings and purchased all that was needed to repair the damage that had been done. The father and son worked all afternoon patching the holes and repainting. They repaired the lights and then, when they were finished, they quietly left.

When I was told this story it affected me deeply because in my counselling rooms I so often had to hold a boy who had had a similar experience as the first two boys did with their father or father figure after they'd made some seriously poor choices.

They had been so shamed and wounded by their dad's behaviour and they never forgot that sense of being a huge disappointment to their father. Many still carried that wound far into adulthood.

Were the first two fathers bad men? No. The first two fathers had done what they thought was the right thing so their sons could learn that they had made a mistake. They thought they were teaching their sons not to vandalise other people's property. And it is highly likely that their own fathers would have managed one of their less-than-perfect moments with a similar response. Sadly, rather than feeling they made a bad choice, their sons were left feeling they were wrong, bad or flawed. This is shaming and it has a way of making individuals feel worthless and incapable of being loved.

The father who chose to support and love his son and to teach him that when you make a mistake you need to make it right, most likely had a loving, warm father when he was a boy the same age. Or, maybe not.

Chip off the old block

How do we help the dads in parent-land who have had the tough father who was often critical, sarcastic, blaming, shaming and possibly physically punitive?

The experience of having such a father has created some really strong memories in the part of our brain where we store procedural memories – the memories of how things were when we were kids. I have written a lot about how boys and men are often single focus and that they are in one place in their brain while women can be in many places in their brain. So, for a dad to respond from his procedural memory is quite understandable. In a way it's like he has a box in his brain that holds the information about how to be a father, particularly around his son. Not all men who had a tough father react this way and for some they have included in their parent memory box some of the ways that their mother parented — ways which were more loving and supportive — or they have learnt other ways to be a better dad.

So, back to the original dilemma for the mums out there who struggle to know how to help their man change the reactive and negative way that the dad in the house is being a father.

Let's start with one obvious fact — no one likes being criticised or told what they're doing wrong! For many men who have experienced harsh parenting and punishment as boys, their natural defence is to protect themselves by getting angry and defensive or by withdrawing and ignoring.

Giving constructive and helpful suggestions needs to be carefully navigated so as not to trigger the boy-wound that was marinated in shame and self-disgust.

Go gently with love and compassion.

Some suggestions:

- Never question a father figure in the heat of the moment, especially if the children are still present.
- Choose a good time and suggest: "We could have a chat soon about how to manage some of the tricky things that come up in our home because I think we could do a bit better". Emphasise the 'we'. The metaphor of being a parent team is really helpful.
- Start by reminding Dad about all the things he does that are wonderful and helpful before you begin the conversation.
- Make sure you use 'I' words not 'you' words. "I noticed yesterday when you were trying to get the kids in the bath that you kind of lost it a bit — I heard you call them stupid idiots ..." Then pause. Wait. Let him think.
- Then you could say something like: "Name calling, exclusion and putdowns all hurt no matter what age we are". Remind him of the three rules that the family are trying to implement.
- Reassure the dad that you have also done the same thing, and you are just checking how he is feeling because you have found when

you speak like that you're often exhausted or stressed. So ask him with great love, "Are you OK babe, hon?" or whatever your term of endearment is. Wait.

- If he says he's OK and he just lost it, you don't need to say anything else because he will already be disappointed in himself.
- If it feels right, check whether he has apologised to the kids yet?
- Reassure him that he is not his dad and that he can be the dad he wanted when he was a boy or a teen. Giving him hope is really important!
- Chat about some other hot points that you've noticed in family life of late and write them down and then suggest you have a family meeting soon to see if you can work out some solutions with everyone's input.
- At another family meeting, both parents can ask their kids to suggest to them three ways they could be a better mum or a better dad. Give them some time ... and accept their suggestions with grace!
- I would give him a gentle tickle in the tickle spot high up on the back as you finish a conversation, or give him a hug or a huge pash. Reassuring your man that your relationship is good despite this issue matters.
- The conversation is then finished. It does not need to be brought up again. It is done!
- Trust me, your man will think about that conversation for the next couple of days.

Often in my dad-only seminars, I have dads who come each year to the same seminar because each year they need to be reminded of the positive choices they could make. This is because even with their best intentions they often forget a great idea that they had taken away from last year's seminar. Remember, their memories are not as efficient as ours and they forget stuff – often really important stuff – mostly unintentionally.

Sometimes it can be helpful to remind them gently that they may have forgotten to connect deeply with one of the children – it is not deliberate and more often than not they are grateful for the gentle reminder that is given with love. Talking about the ways in which we can build micro-moments of connection have helped lots of dads become closer and more loving to their kids.

I've had a number of dads also tell me that they can get angry and upset when the children are behaving badly because in some way they feel like they're failing their family. Often, they can take it quite personally and they then sadly react in a very defensive way because they think it's their fault.

How else can we help the defensive dad who's had a tough father become more loving, respectful and connected to his children?

There are some fabulous articles written by men in the Manhood Project, Fatherly.com, the Fathering Project and the Good Men Project websites. Sometimes finding an article or podcast or the like that could be helpful and copying the link and sending it to your children's dad can be helpful.

Perhaps they would also enjoy some light-hearted YouTube clips, or online posts from people such as the Kiwi 'How to Dad'. Another good channel on social media that shares sound wisdom is 'DadMum'.

Other great books to explore are Steve Biddulph's *Raising Boys in the 21st Century*, *The Making of Men* by Dr Arne Rubinstein and Michael Gurian's wonderful work. *The Australian Man Up* series is another excellent documentary to watch.

> "DB (6) asked me if boys talk more than girls. 'Maybe when they are little, but not when they are older.' 'But Daddy doesn't say much at all.' I asked him if I talk more than Daddy — 'Yes! Daddy talks for 1 second and Mummy talks for a million seconds!'" — Loved Mum

My 'Maggie Moment' YouTube clips have also become a favourite with many dads because they're only short and usually tackle just one thing at a time, and that's important. I know that there are good dads who, after being to one of my Boys, Boys, Boys seminars, said they found it so helpful they brought their brother and mates to the next one.

I have written a small book called *Some Secrets for the Modern-Day Mammoth Hunter*. This was written mainly for rural men as that is where our suicide prevention work was focused and it does contain some swear words, however, some men have said it has been a helpful reminder about how to be a good man, husband, partner and father.

This is a great time to be a dad as the social norms are changing, however, some dads can be resistant to changing because of adverse childhood experiences (ACEs).

That reactive place can be such a powerful influence on how we parent and it happens quickly and spontaneously. In a way, a dad can't be what he hasn't seen.

These 'tough' dads can also be reluctant to seek professional help because it can feel like a threat to their masculinity. It would be great if we could reframe that perception to one that suggests that owning vulnerability can be the most courageous act around. Many relationships break down because couples struggle to become a healthy parent team, and negative parenting choices from either parent can create so much conflict that one parent may choose to end the relationship in order to protect their kids! If you suggest your man seeks professional help, please make sure you avoid making him feel like a failure – instead help him feel he could be even better – and maybe happier – and that you have his back.

Lastly, make sure you notice and acknowledge the good moments of your man's parenting journey – don't over-praise or he will be suspicious. We all want to be a 'good-enough' parent and we want to raise our kids to be caring, decent human beings and that goes for mums and dads – whether they live in the same house or not. Changing unhelpful habits is never easy, however, it can happen when managed in a caring, supportive way.

> "I always tell my friends with young sons that the best thing about parenting teenage boys is the humour factor. The lengths that they go to and the level of creativity astounds and amuses me to no end. Yesterday my DB (16) son purchased an air horn with the sole purpose of scaring the life out of his much younger siblings. The whole house is quiet before bed and boom! He scared the living daylights out of his siblings and fell on the ground with laughter. After he'd filmed the whole event of course! And I just laugh right along with him!"
>
> — Amused Mum of Three

When relationships end

If you decide to end your committed relationship with the father of your children, do your best to ensure you honour his place as the biological father – provided he has not been abusive in any way. Avoid speaking negatively about him and work with him as a caring, cooperative co-parent as best as possible because that relationship technically does not end.

My sons became good men thanks to the involvement of their dad, stepdad, their grandfathers, uncles and so many other good men in their school and communities. Their mum, aunties, grandmothers, girl cousins and positive mamma figures also played a huge part in who they became. The more good men and good women our boys are exposed to from birth to adulthood, the better. One day your sons want to have their parents – whether still together or not – to help them celebrate their significant life moments, completely comfortable that they will do so with respect. It can be done and, yes, it does take emotional maturity to do it well, however, the benefits are so worth it.

The last important life lesson to teach our sons is that committed relationships in the Western world are based on free will, not force or compulsion. Even in a legal marriage between a couple – whether heterosexual or same sex – it must be of their own free will, which means no-one owns anyone! If a parent's relationship breaks down, so be it. Parents still don't own their children. Their lives are not ours to take. They have their own lives, futures, needs and relationships separate from you. They are not pawns in any misguided game of payback or revenge. They have the right to live free from fear and violence.

When making decisions after a break-up always focus on what's best for the kids and ensure they are heard when making those decisions — no matter how difficult it may be personally.

Avoiding our sons becoming creeps

When boys and men behave in disrespectful ways towards girls and women, especially using sexism, they are being creeps. This is the word Steve Biddulph uses and I feel it is very appropriate because they are not necessarily being bad men, rather they are acting immaturely by being thoughtless and insensitive. Sadly, behaving this way – especially in early adolescence when boys are desperate to belong – if left untethered and not questioned, can become ingrained attitudes. Rosalind Wiseman, in her excellent book *Ringleaders & Sidekicks*, explores the power of peer pressure on teenage boys. The conditioning of the old male code is still very strong in high schools in the Western world. Wiseman says these invisible rules about how-to-act-like-a-man put pressure on boys who have been raised to be respectful.

To stand up against sexism and racism and any other form of social injustice, especially if the dominant boy group thinks it is a part of being a man, could see a boy being ostracised and/or labelled as gay. As a former high school teacher I can attest to this behaviour and no matter how many times I questioned the boys about it, it continued especially in early adolescence.

> *The hunger to belong is very strong in early adolescence especially, and many young boys are quite prepared to sell their soul, give up their integrity and walk on their values, just so they can stay within the group.*

It is important to simply know that this is a common phase to be mindful of as your son heads off to high school.

Given the #MeToo movement, there is an increased sensitivity and a growing awareness around how unacceptable this behaviour is and that is a good thing. However, we need to be realistic to realise that this culture is embedded in many layers of society and that change will come gradually. No matter how difficult this cultural change may be, mums of sons have an important role to play. This may be a time where you consciously choose films to watch at home that show adolescent boys being respectful towards girls particularly – and hopefully by now you would have been making helpful suggestions over many years when watching TV shows or online videos. Hopefully you will also help your boy come to understand the difference between being fond of someone, being in love with someone and just experiencing lust about someone. Even though it may seem to have been a waste of time in your son's early adolescence, trust me those values that are embedded by many, many conversations over many, many years are still deep within him and they do tend to resurface as he gets older and gradually emerges from adolescence.

The online world has unfortunately given fuel to the creep factor in our boys and men. There is absolutely nothing wrong with admiring a beautiful woman – however, how you express that admiration respectfully needs to be a conversation that we mammas of sons have. Thanks to social media, our boys are getting plenty of exposure to pictures of scantily clad young women – often these pics are posted by girls they know, posing in very sexy poses (but that's a whole other book!). This can be a tricky window for mums of sons because our conversations about being respectful when they see these images often fall on deaf ears, as most teens question what we well-meaning parents are saying. Positive lighthouse figures can be incredibly helpful here by affirming the same messages. We simply *must* keep telling our boys and girls that many decisions we make while we are a teen, we can come to regret. Once we mature and grow our prefrontal, our choices change. We need our boys to know there is no way it is acceptable to make rude or disrespectful comments about how a girl or woman dresses or looks – just no way, not online, not offline, not even in private messages. That is not only a sign of immaturity, it smacks of arrogance and superiority.

> "DB (5) asked me, 'Mum am I like an octopus?'. I answered 'No. Why?'. DB5: 'Cos they have "testicles" too — just eight of 'em'!!!" — Laughing Mum

Pornography encourages female submission without explicit consent and the ease with which pornography will find our sons – without them even looking for it – is really unhelpful in raising a boy who is respectful to girls and later women. To curb the growth of this creep culture that is often driven by peer pressure needs both mums and dads, and our schools and our communities, to all have the same intention to educate and redirect our boys during their formative years.

> **"Our boys are nothing if not morally fragile, from the inside out. And there are ways in which our boys are simply more vulnerable than girls to moral instability. To neglect this fact is to neglect our boys."**
>
> - Michael Gurian, *The Good Son: Shaping the Moral Development of our Boys and Young Men* (1999).

Both our girls and boys are being marinated in a culture of sexualisation from very early in life and no matter how hard we try, they are constantly being conditioned to look sexy and to use their bodies to gain acceptance and approval. So often we see completely inappropriate messages on children's clothing that reinforces gender differences, not to mention the creep factor. Do everything you can to protect your children and deconstruct these messages that they see over and over again.

Indeed, I believe that the journey to protect your son from becoming a creep starts, again, as early as possible. Fortunately there are many excellent picture books that start the conversations around self-respect, body awareness and consent. A really good place to start is with the picture book *No Means No!* by Jayneen Sanders. If we have any hope of counteracting the coercion and force that is present in so much of the pornography where women's consent is not sought explicitly, we need to start young. So many of the chapters in this book are already building the social and emotional awareness of our boys, and so reading many of the books about being respectful, especially around other people's private parts, will simply anchor this perception deeply in our boys before they reach puberty.

Many years ago I met a woman called Holly-ann Martin at a conference in Katherine in the Northern Territory and I have watched as her advocacy and education around child protection has grown nationally and now internationally. I encourage you to check out her website, safe4kids.com.au, as she has books and resources that will definitely help in lifting this positive awareness of respectful behaviour from childhood.

My absolute favourite first book for your son's education around sexuality is *Secret Boys' Business* by Rose Stewart, Fay Angelo and Heather Anderson. This is a really easy-to-read book with lots of pictures, which are not too threatening! It is great for boys from eight plus and seriously would be great to give to any teen boy because they think they KNOW everything and sometimes they really want to check up on the facts. For everything about boys and puberty, this is your go-to book!

Another fabulous expert in the field of sex education is Cath Hakanson of sexedrescue.com. Hakanson has an incredible ability to take the cringe factor out of sex education. She even has a resource that helps you learn how to respond when your boys ask awkward questions by giving you scripts. Avoiding the questions or giving benign answers will not help your boy to grow up with an understanding of healthy sexuality. It is best to start soon and look for teachable moments from early childhood. The birds and bees chat is not one chat, it is many chats.

Without emotional and social competence, individuals will flounder in relationships. I have worked with many women who struggled with emotional honesty, especially with themselves. As I have explored already in this book, the importance of boys playing with other children – both girls and boys as often as possible in their childhoods – is the best way of building an understanding about how to get along with others.

I have had many mothers talk to me about their sons who became committed online gamers even before adolescence. These boys argued that they were not drinking alcohol, smoking, being delinquents or being disrespectful to girls while they were gaming in their bedrooms. However, the years that they spent in their bedrooms rather than in the real world had come at a cost. When these boys finally emerge from their bedrooms around their very late teens or early 20s and step into the party scene they flounder. Many of them struggle with male communication because they have not developed an understanding of healthy teasing or of the non-verbal communication cues that many men use when out socially. Not only this, but they have not been around girls in social situations and have absolutely no concept of how to start conversations or how to even ask a girl out on a date or for a dance. I know of many boys who have ended up with social anxiety and who have simply retreated back to their bedrooms. This is why I keep stressing that we must keep a balance between the virtual world and the real world, and as mums we need to be very strong to ensure this happens. Having regular sleepover evenings, camping trips, fishing trips, football trips, surfing trips or trips to music festivals are all ways that we can keep boys growing socially and emotionally.

I recommend some other books that can help to have those conversations with your sons about love and sex in adolescence. The first is *The Secret Business of Relationships, Love and Sex*, again by Heather Anderson, Fay Angelo and Rose Stewart.

The second book I recommend is *Love, Sex and No Regrets* by Elizabeth Clark. This is a bit like sex therapy for teens and it explores how sex can be special rather than demeaning or about dominance as depicted in pornography. *Dating and Sex: A Guide For the 21st Century Teen Boy* by Andrew P. Smiler is another book that is a good resource for teen boys. It's an extensive guide to relationships and safe, respectful sexuality for themselves, and with others. Smiler also explores gender stereotypes and sexual orientation in a straightforward, easy-to-understand way and there is no other book quite like it that can help our lads navigate this bumpy time of transformation. For other ideas, check out sexedrescue.com.

> "I was driving in the car and the conversation went like this: DB (3.5): 'Mummy, I've got a woody ... Daddy says if your doodle is hard then it's called a woody!!'. Me: 'Really? Wow! Well ... that's what happens to boys sometimes'. Son (proudly, praising me for my knowledge): 'Good girl, Mummy!'" — Outnumbered Mum

One message that I think is really important to give our boys — particularly in our 'pornified' culture — is that if you want to become a decent man then you need to nurture your own sense of humanity and decency. There is a pervading perception out there that men simply exploit women or are seeking sexual conquest rather than seeking authentic connection. This stereotype can be quite confusing and damaging for our adolescent boys in particular, because it can make them feel like sex is not supposed to be a mutually positive experience, which can offer an emotional connection as much as a physical connection. When boys don't respect their sexual partners, it strips them of their self-respect. Everyone loses. Surely, as mums of sons we want our boys to experience a rich, loving sexuality. Respect is an ideal that in traditional communities is extremely valued and something that would be tested in your rite of passage to become a man. Thankfully, the reverse is also true. The more that you respect and value girls and women, the more you can come to respect and value yourself. If we remember the inner barometer of self-worth and how it is such a strong part of being a boy or a man, we may appreciate how important self-respect and doing well matters. This is just one of the reasons why I devoted a whole chapter to building character in our sons. This is also why we need to focus on developing this as an invisible code within our boys well before the bumpy ride to manhood begins.

Effective, intimate relationships are about teamwork rather than about who is the deer hunter – the main provider – and who is the primary caregiver at home. Now it is more about: Have we created something that works for us and our family? As the gender stereotypes continued to peel away, I have hope that our families will mirror this new paradigm of working together to ensure that both grown-ups who are the parents of children are able to have their own needs and dreams met through mutual cooperation and support.

> "My mum was a full-time worker and she did everything around the house as well. I wish she had shared the load more – encouraged Dad to help and taught us three boys to be more independent. I really look back on this time and resent (for her) how much she did. Dad was lazy and could have done so much more. It was far from equal."
> – Men's Survey 2017

A wise man once told me that many women have a misunderstanding about a man's enthusiasm for having sex with the woman he loves. He argued that the closest place a man can get to the woman he loves, is the point of ejaculation inside her. This is a place of complete surrender – a place that many warriors find difficult to embrace in a world that says men are supposed to be the stronger sex. It is interesting food for thought.

Our challenge in today's modern world – which is full of consumerism, has a focus on self, and allows a distortion of a sexualised culture – is to teach boys how to grow up to be men who can nurture a mutually beneficial relationship with the person they love, over time, with understanding and compassion.

> "I wish my mum hadn't stayed with my dad for as long as she did 'for the sake of us kids'." – Men's Survey 2017

Willingly committing oneself to another human being in a relationship can happen in many forms and ways that do not require a legal document. However, I am an authorised marriage celebrant in Australia and I have conducted more than 1030 marriages over the last 21 years (I only do this for family members and close friends now!). It has been an incredible privilege to witness the joining of two lives in a formal sense. Being right beside two people making a public commitment to each other in front of the people who matter to them the most, I have witnessed love in its purest form and I know how deeply both men and women can love. Over the years I have noticed how much more open men have become to showing how powerful this moment is, regardless of the public setting. It is not just at weddings that I have witnessed an increase in emotional honesty. It happens around funerals, sporting events, and community happenings. I see this as a hugely positive sign indicating that we are moving into a better world for our boys and men by allowing them to be emotionally honest when it really matters. Emotional honesty – yup, the amazing, the good the bad and the bloody awful – in our intimate relationships is the surest way that we can stay better connected and stay in love.

> "My DB (2) came home grumpy and tired from daycare and plopped himself on his chair. With my husband's help, I looked my son in the eye and announced, 'I love Daddy'. My son is very competitive so his response was, 'No, I love Daddy!' This continued with us both shouting, giggling and kissing Daddy on the cheek to show our love." — Learning Mum

TOP TIPS

- ✓ Human relationships can be difficult at times even when they are still healthy.
- ✓ Parental relationships can change when babies and children arrive.
- ✓ The roles of key provider and key caregiver are now much more flexible.
- ✓ In the most effective long-term relationships, couples work as teams.
- ✓ Teaching boys about personal boundaries and consent needs to start early in life.
- ✓ Being honest and open about sexuality from an early age is really important.
- ✓ Puberty can be a really confusing time for boys.
- ✓ Early adolescence can be a time of high risk for our boys becoming creeps.
- ✓ Helping our boys develop emotional honesty will help them later to be emotionally honest men in their intimate relationships.
- ✓ There has been a shift around men displaying emotional honesty publicly over the last 20 years.

CHAPTER 18

Five **SECRETS** I have learnt about **MOTHERING SONS**

> "As a mum of three girls, how lucky am I to now have four grandsons. The word 'different' is an understatement! Sitting quietly, walking not running, using your inside voice inside, fighting, wrestling, arguing, playing, boys. Nannie has had to readjust to little boys and, would I change them? Never in a million years."
> — Mum of Girls, Nannie of Boys

1. If your son has genuinely found he has your unconditional love, he will quietly always worry about you. Even though he may forget your birthday, Mother's Day and he will forget to stay in touch or call – and even when he has his own family – he will always in his quiet thoughts wonder if you are OK. So, reassure him that you are OK – often.
2. Your son will watch and observe **both** men and women throughout his childhood and adolescence, working out who he wants to be. He will copy the attributes he admires and respects the most, and he will do this quietly, in his own way and his own time. So model greatness intentionally.
3. Your son will find a woman to love who will have aspects of you – sometimes your good aspects and sometimes some of your faults. If your son is in a same-sex relationship, the same thing can also be said – he will have attracted an intimate partner who is like you in some way. This is both scary and kinda nice!

4. Your son can learn to parent not just from how his father fathered but also from how his mother mothered. I found this discovery quite mind-blowing, especially with my rooster sons!
5. Your son will love you more than you can imagine possible when you genuinely let him be free to find his own pathway in life – regardless of whether you agree with him or not. Reassure him it is his life and you will love him no matter what. This is such an irony – letting them go to fly free is the best way to keep the loving bond alive and well when they become men.

Technically, I have one more secret about mothering sons, but this one applies solely to those mums who only have sons. I have put that secret at the end of the next chapter about letting go.

"First, to be fair, I do actually have to think hard to find a way in which either of my parents could do better. That being said, when I was a teenager – like most other teenagers – I was actively trying to differentiate myself from my parents and find my sense of self. Which usually leads to a large amount of bullshit, but also some things that are going to be a foundation of who you are as you grow. I found that half the time when mom was writing off something I said as teenage bullshit, I was actually being serious, actually reaching out, actually making a grounded, well-reasoned point. It's not something that frustrates me today at all, but it is definitely something that I wish happened differently." – Men's Survey 2017

CHAPTER 19

LETTING them **GO** on the bumpy ride to **ADULTHOOD**

> "My DB (5) was a few days into a new year of pre-primary and was a bit sad when I went. At pick-up I asked if he was ok after I left and he said, 'Yes Mummy, I felt sad but I held it all in as I didn't want everyone to see my soft bits'. Resilience being built, Mum's heart strings being pulled!" — Loved Mum

To be honest, as mums of sons, we are in a process of letting go of our boys from the moment they are born because they are destined to go on a different journey than us as women. It is such an interesting journey of separation because every mother is different, every son is different, and every family and environment is different. So, there is no one right way of letting your son go.

> "I wish my mum had not been awful to my then fiancée (now wife)."
> — Men's Survey 2017

Sons leaving home 18+

It's a tricky window for mums of sons to understand what happens when their son becomes a legal adult — as he steps onto the launch pad to a fully adult life. Technically, this starts happening at 17 years of age when boys are legally able to drive a car! While many boys are keen to leap into driving, research has shown that boys tend to be a little slower than girls in their readiness for the leap into the real world of being an adult. Indeed, boys who have been raised in a screen world might find that the transition point at which they are ready to manage their own lives seems to have stretched even further into their early 20s. We need to be clear that the final growth of our mature brain — the prefrontal cortex — has been shown not to be complete for our girls until around age 22 to 24, and for our boys it is anytime from 25 onwards. With my tongue in my cheek and with great love I say that a boy's prefrontal cortex tends to mature somewhere between 27 and 82!

> "One day my DB (7) was sitting with me — he is very literal — one of his many beautiful autistic traits. He looked at me and out of nowhere said, 'Mammy I love you'. I jokingly said, 'Can I have that in writing?' He got up and after a few minutes returned with a piece of paper with, 'Mammy I love you' written on it! He's a lamb." — My-heart-just-melted Mum

Those lads who have spent endless hours in their bedrooms or on their couches gaming rather than participating in the real world with real people, are arriving at this point of launch very underprepared. To avoid this happening, we need to stop doing for our boys things that they can do for themselves. Seriously, it is an interesting irony that as boys get older mums tend to do more for them than they do for their daughters. Lazy boys who know that their mum will do their washing, their chores and get their lunch will simply sit back and let it happen.

Respected paediatrician and author Meg Meeker, highly regarded social justice advocate and author Celia Lashlie, and I all sing from the same song sheet and believe that when mums don't make boys do things for themselves we are disabling them on so many levels. This is why a son benefits from having a mean and loving mum — in a type of balance! If we don't expect boys to learn to do things for themselves, we are teaching them that they don't have to be responsible or accountable. We are also teaching them that housework and chores are women's work and that is simply very unhelpful for when they are in a committed relationship later in life. How can we teach fairness if we don't ensure they play a responsible part in the family? How can he learn how to be an effective partner in an intimate relationship?

Meeker puts it simply:

> **"Love is gritty. Saying no and keeping clear boundaries and solid rules makes sons feel loved."**
>
> — Meg Meeker, *Strong Mothers, Strong Sons: Lessons mothers need to raise extraordinary men* (2014).

To help you ensure that you keep building skills and abilities in your sons from the age of 10, check out my life skills posters, which you can find on my website.

> *Mums must keep reminding their boys that we are helping them become good, capable men who are responsible and not useless jerks! Building these vital life skills both before and during the teen years is incredibly helpful.*

The post high-school hole

I hear from many parents who have an incredibly unmotivated 18-year-old boy lounging around their house, lost and appearing lazy. Indeed, he is lost, however, his lack of motivation is partly developmental and he will need tiny steps of encouragement to help him move towards a more positive outcome. Shouting, criticising and shaming him for being unmotivated will make him retreat further. He is terrified of failure and doing nothing is a way to avoid failing. Many of these lads' parents have talked to me about how their sons have turned to alcohol or serious risk-taking behaviour to soothe their sense of inadequacy and separation from their friends after high school has finished.

> "I wish my mum had not stopped me from moving out of home when I wanted to and was ready to." – Men's Survey 2017

I am a firm believer in gap years where young people work, travel or both – especially boys. In a way, a year to 'grow up' a little and gain some life experience can be deceptively advantageous. Hopefully, boys who choose a gap year – if they spend time away from the safety of home and stretch their wings – learn to make some sound choices around managing money, accommodation and living with others. Many have experiences during that gap year that change their perception of what they want to do, and experiencing mild financial challenge or unexpected travelling setbacks all help to develop a stronger sense of character and resilience for when they are finally ready to plot the journey of the rest of their lives.

Many boys simply follow what their parents advise to keep the peace, and later on they can come to resent the path chosen by their parents. This window can take some time and as long as your son is actively participating in life – even if it is delivering pizza, or working as a dishwasher in a café or restaurant – every day will be taking him closer to developing the maturity to make good choices about what he wants to do with his life. I have counselled many young men who struggled during this transition and who finally realised what they wanted to do when they were around 27-30 years of age. In a way, having more time to bloom at this point in life can be as helpful as having a little bit more time to bloom in the early years. In our hurry-up world, taking this time out is becoming harder to achieve.

Constantly reaffirming your unconditional love for your son when he has his muck-up moments in late adolescence will help him enormously when the world becomes uncertain and confusing. It can be an incredibly frustrating time. Remember:

> *So often our young lads need our love and encouragement when they deserve it the least.*

As our boys keep stepping away from us, as they need to, unfortunately life can throw them unexpected moments of significant adversity that can tip them into a world of emotional turmoil, and they often have few tools to manage in the fallout. A teen boy can find himself dealing with the end of his parents' relationship, death, a natural disaster, serious illness or accident, a broken heart or significant bullying that is threatening his sense of safety in the world. Every child needs to have a safe grown-up that they can turn to — a lighthouse figure who will always hold a welcoming and safe space for them while the turmoil rages around them. The time of 18+ can actually be more risky than the earlier years of adolescence. This is why I humbly ask all mums to watch out for all their son's mates and friends on this final journey to adulthood, because mother figures can have such an enormously positive influence. Traditionally boys have been less forthcoming seeking help from others when they are feeling vulnerable and we need to change this so more of our beautiful boys can grow up to be healthy, happy, loving men. *Every gesture* of kindness and compassion will make a difference to our boys during their final stage of letting go of their mums.

> "There is nothing like the love between a mother and her beautiful boy — when my DB (16) was a gorgeous, chunky toddler he held my face and said to me with such intensity, 'Mummy, when I look at you, I have love hearts coming out of my eyes.'" — Liverpool Mum

As my sons grew in assertiveness and confidence, having an in-depth conversation about something that concerned me became more difficult. It took me a while to realise that they no longer needed me to have the mother-child relationship because they felt they were now adults. Of course, they were not complete adults, however, only parts of them were. They were also very sensitive to feeling criticised if they had made a poor choice, and

I know many mums who feel they tiptoe around their sons and are not sure how to communicate when they are genuinely worried.

The mum letter revisited

This where a 'mum' letter can be really helpful. As I explained in more detail in Chapter 10, effective communication requires a person to really listen to the message being given. For boys who are very sensitive to being judged, criticised and even accidentally shamed, listening to verbal communication can be really difficult. With a written note, a boy has a chance to read the message several times to ensure he understands the meaning of the message, rather than jump to unintended conclusions. There are times we do need to ask our boys if they are struggling, and in a way that they can hear us.

So, if you are worried about your son or you need to explore something else that is worrying you, simply modify this technique of the mum letter (see the sample mum letter I included in Chapter 10). The mum letter does not require a response of any kind – and this expectation needs to be respected. We are simply giving them some information that we want them to seriously think about and then we will trust that they will make appropriate choices as a consequence of what they have learnt.

For my own boys, there were many challenges in their bumpy ride after the safety of home: failed exams, crashed cars, funerals for mates, cousins who died tragically young, cars vandalised, sporting injuries, knee reconstructions and frequent mismanagement of money. These were life-enhancing experiences because my young men gained wisdom, learnt skills, and discovered how to walk through the dark nights of the soul and reclaim life in the sun. There have been many brilliant moments too, such as shared surfing holidays, endless games of backyard cricket, golf, parties – lots of parties – new friends, falling in love, concerts, football games and graduations.

Each of my boys had to work out their own unique way of managing their lives. My extrovert sons were often pushing the edges of life and endured weeks eating boring sandwiches because they spent too much on beer over the weekend. My introvert son needed extra support and encouragement through the pressures of exam time when he lacked self-confidence; however, he never ate boring sandwiches and never ran out of money.

These lessons helped develop each boy's character and their appreciation of a good salary and a worthwhile job to allow them to enjoy a good life. Raising sons to be good men is not for wimpy mums. There will be so many times you will worry like mad, cry into your pillow in the dark and pray lots. However, I am sure there are many mums of daughters who have had to do the same – maybe less frequently!

Letting go, even when you want to hold on tight

As I was putting together this chapter, I found this message which I wrote in my newsletter when my second son left home in 2003 and I felt compelled to include it as it took me right back to that time.

> For those of you who do not know, I am the proud mum of four sons. Needless to say, over the last 20 years I have cooked, cleaned, run around after, laughed with, cried with and worried about these wonderful lads in every permutation possible. My eldest left to go to the city for uni two years ago. I found it hard for the first week and cried a few tears. He was very confident and ready to go.
>
> Last Sunday, I had to let my second six-foot baby leave home. I thought because I had done it once, it would be easy. Not so. Number two son was the placid baby, the understanding, patient child, the nature lover with the unexpected sense of humour, the thrillseeker up trees and in the waves of the ocean he loves. So much harder to let go ...
>
> He is the one who calls work to see what he can cook for dinner, brings the washing in without being asked – mostly folded – asks if you want a coffee and generally asks if it's OK to do things even when he knows he can make his own decisions. So much harder to let go ...
>
> He is the one who is the animal lover, feeds the cat, eats his breakfast with her on his lap ... the good friend who stays loyal and supportive no matter what. Not afraid to hug lingeringly and to chat to family friends warmly ... the one who was there for his mate when his mate's dad died suddenly ... so much harder to let go ...
>
> But I have and my heart is still heavy ... and it tugs when I call to say hi.
>
> Being a mother whether biological, step or surrogate, was always going to have its moments and I am sharing this with you to remind you to be grateful for every moment in your son or daughter's lives while they are there in the family home. Don't waste time on the nagging, the growling. Let it go and love more often. Laugh with them and stand beside them as they discover who they are, independent of you. Above all this is my final message when they choose to leave – let them go, no matter how much you want to hang on and keep them. It may very well be the hardest and kindest thing you will ever do for them.

When, eventually, all four sons had left to study in Perth I pretended to them at times I was fine, and other times I told them I missed them. I saw them on a journey of transformation away from childhood and towards adulthood and one away from me. Just because I knew they needed space to stand on their own didn't make it easy! *It was hard*. I knew they had to work out how to manage money, relationships, food and the rigours of university study without me beside them. *It was hard*. I wanted to call them so often just to remind them of things or to check how they were going, and I resisted. *It was hard*. Instead, I looked forward to their calls and their visits back home. There were nowhere near enough of those. We survived. And so will you. Please step back ... let them go.

The ultimate letting go is when our boys find another person to love deeply instead of us. I have joked with one of my sons who was very late in finding that woman that I needed to hand the baton over to – she needed to matter more than me. There is no better way to explain this than this poignant and beautiful letter written by the wise and amazing family therapist and educator – Claire Orange – also a mum of four sons (and no daughters).

An open letter to the future heartbreakers of my sons

Let me tell you the truth about boys and their hearts – and what to do when relationships get rocky

Dear Future Heartbreaker,

We haven't met yet – but somewhere out there you're living your life, learning about relationships and at some undefined point your path is going to cross that of one of my sons. And I want you to know right from the very bottom of my mamma's heart the truth about boys and love and the ways that they want and need to be loved, and the ways that they express their love too.

So, there are some things that I want you to know – that perhaps you don't know about boys and their hearts because, as a society, we pigeon-hole boys. The bad and over-sexualised behaviour of some boys and some men is put front and centre in the news (you have a lot to answer for the Harvey Weinsteins of this world) – and somehow it filters into our thinking about all boys and men. It's not true – and it's certainly not true of my sons.

Lesson # 1 – Little boys are the most affectionate creatures – I know this because of my son who will one day give you his heart like he gave me his heart first. He was so eager to please, to be noticed, to be loved – to be at the very centre of my world. He loved a snuggle, he wanted me to laugh with him and at him and he went to all sorts of crazy lengths to make that happen. Please help my son to show you affection in ways that sit well with you because he's mostly likely going to want to fix things and do things – and he might not be all that good at reading your language of affection. My little boys expressed their love by sharing noisy wind on my lap (very gross but the boy gift that keeps on giving), flowers from the tops of weeds on the way to school, a very special rock and a prize stick. This was their language of love. It can get messy, noisy and sometimes a little boisterous but the intention is to show you just how deserving you are of their love and affection. Help my sons to shape this so that they continue to grow into good and respectful men.

Lesson #2 – Be gentle with his heart – If you find that your paths diverge, as sometimes paths do, please remember that what might look 'together' and OK on the outside is crying and wounded on the inside. Please don't use on-again-off-again manipulations to push him away and then draw him in. He's fragile on the inside – far more fragile than you know. The heart of a boy once given is as vulnerable as any heart that risks love. So, when it gets bruised or even broken try to remember that healing takes time. All of the signals you might have given him about not feeling the same way – the ones you thought he might be reading which might help him prepare for the end – let me tell you this – he missed them all. No, not because he's silly but because he's a boy and boys don't read those subtle emotional messages very well (or often at all). So, when he looks surprised and takes time to process his hurt – give him space to do it. It might take some time to be friends again – and that's going to depend on just how long it takes his heart to heal.

Lesson #3 – Subtlety doesn't work. The passive aggressive moves meant to communicate being unhappy, feeling let down, not getting what you need will almost always be misread by each one of my sons. When you say, "I need some space – leave me alone". – that's what's going to happen. Now, if you mean, "Try harder and pay me more attention", simply say that. When you ask, "How does this top look?" and you get the response, "Like a pumpkin", be prepared that he's saying what he thinks – sometimes without having considered how hurtful it might sound (yes, this is right from the mouth of one of my sons). I asked for an opinion and it was given – no hurt intended – just missing some grey, some massaging of the truth to make it softer and acceptable.

The truth about most boys is that they struggle to read us girls. "Why don't you just say what you mean?" – heard that before – accompanied by a look of genuine confusion, a feeling of great frustration and a deep desire to be able to interpret the **secret** language of girls. I sure have – even when I've been certain that my demeanour has communicated my unhappiness. Sigh. When there's the choice between subtle and sledgehammer – choose the latter.

So, future heartbreakers of my sons, learn well the secrets of boys and their hearts. Let go of those clichéd notions of boys being less sensitive and less emotional — they're simply not true. One day, when my son gives you his heart, hold it gently, know that you will become his world and even though he may not always speak or understand your language of affection — he will do anything to see you smile and to know that he is loved. It's a heart that has been loved and shaped and although it might be housed in the body of a brawny and deceptively tough body — it is infinitely breakable.

— Claire Orange.

The Sixth Secret — for mums of sons only

Claire's beautiful message holds the clue to my final secret. If your son falls in love with a special woman, you will finally — if you are lucky like me — get to know life as a mother of a daughter. I am blessed with four 'daughters from other mothers' who I love and respect deeply. Finally, I get to talk about 'girl' stuff like really good books to read, recipe sharing, chatting about sewing and fashion, and cooking together. At last, I have enthusiastic participants to go to musicals with — shows that begin with dining out and celebratory champers. I know I missed these opportunities as a mum to my sons. It reminded me how lucky I have been to have so many special biological and non-biological nieces, also from other mothers. I hadn't really missed out as much as I thought and I know that I matter deeply to lots of beautiful daughters that have other mothers. For even though you may be a mum of sons only, look around you because there will be beautiful girls who will welcome you into their lives and their hearts and it will prepare you for the absolute magic that can happen later, when your sons' partners deliver your precious grandchildren. So, the last secret is that you don't have to miss out on having special relationships with girls who can be like daughters — open your heart and let them in. Your boys won't mind. You can have daughters, even as a mum of sons only.

> "I dropped my DB (10) boy off to a birthday party and drilled him with the usual manners lecture. Me (admittedly sounding like a broken record): 'What do you say to the parents when you leave the party?' Him (insert a pause and a cheeky grin here): 'I think I say ... DROP DEAD, SUCKERS!!' My immediate horrified reaction was to go back over the manners lesson, until we both cracked up laughing!" — Manners Mum

TOP TIPS

- ✓ Your son needs to leave home.
- ✓ If you do everything for your son he won't learn the necessary life skills to live away from home successfully.
- ✓ Some sons are harder to let go of than others.
- ✓ Your son needs you to be strong and make him become capable and responsible.
- ✓ Your son needs to leave his mother to find himself.
- ✓ Your son will love someone else deeply one day.
- ✓ You can still experience life with daughters if you only have sons.

CONCLUSION

As I write the final words of *Mothering our Boys*, I need to make two apologies to you. Firstly, I am sorry the book is such a big book, knowing how little time busy mums have to read. Remember there is a great index that can help you find something you may need in a hurry. Secondly, I am sorry I cannot include an in-depth exploration of mothering sons right through adolescence as that would take another 100 pages.

There is no question, positive changes are happening in the Western world for both genders and it can only happen when everyone takes a part – no matter how small. There are going to be some uncomfortable moments as individuals realise that they, too, have supported an unhelpful perception around our gorgeous boys and our beautiful girls.

I see and hope for a better future where people will embrace every child as a unique miracle – a blend of the masculine and the feminine, with a mind, body, heart and soul that needs to be cared for, nurtured and guided so that every child can shine – at times.

In these final pages, I am including the voices of three of my favourite boy champions:

> **"Society has the choice of whether to fight our natural and inherited abilities or channel them effectively. When we use the common sense of nature in our upbringing of boys, we work with boys not against them and give them the love, structure, discipline and wisdom that they, as boys, need. In our lives as parents, mentors and educators we stop feeling as if we are fighting against boys and masculinity; we start realising how to work with boys and maleness. Consequently our homes, schools, streets and bedrooms start looking very different."**
>
> – Michael Gurian, *The Wonder of Boys* (1996).

> **"My research shows that the absence of a close relationship with a loving mother puts a boy at a disadvantage in becoming a free, confident and independent man who likes himself and can take risks and who can form close and loving attachments with people in his adult life. In the early years as well as adolescence I think boys benefit enormously from spending time in the loving environment created by his mother and her friends — the happy nurturing world of women."**
>
> – Dr William Pollack, *Real Boys* (1998).

> **"Right now, the world badly needs good men. There are some awful ones needing to be put in their place. Your boy can be one of those who grow up to help heal this sad and sometimes frightening world. Thank you for joining the boy revolution. As the 21st century rolls on, it's badly needed. Enjoy your boy, love him well and watch him fly in his own special way."**
>
> – Steve Biddulph, *Raising Boys in the 21st Century* (2018).

Raising our boys to be respectful of themselves, others and the world around them takes much more than encouraging boys to talk about their feelings. There are so many possible contributing factors that lead to boys being oppositional or aggressive and violent. Nature versus nurture is only one part of the puzzle. We need to look wider into male biochemistry, epigenetics, physical and emotional nurturing in childhood, the negative influence of the digital world and the value of strong, positive norms around masculinity.

My main purpose in writing this book is to help mums develop a better understanding of how our boys see the world, to realise how many of the stereotypical perceptions of boys are incorrect and very unhelpful, and to look at how we can make things better. Our boys need us to be firm, fair and fun, and to reassure them we love them unconditionally – no matter what poor choice they may have made.

We want all of our children to grow up to live a life of meaning and purpose, and to somehow make the world a better place because we have lived. With emotional, social and psychological competences this is more likely to happen.

Let's all become positive influences in our boys' lives – as mothers, aunties and wise grandmothers – so that every boy will always have a metaphorical, safe place to land and rest when the going gets tough. Let's choose every day to make good things happen for today's boys.

– Maggie Dent, July 2018

And a **FINAL WORD** from the men ...

As I mentioned at the beginning of this book, 66% of the 1600 men I surveyed reported having either 'respectful and loving' relationships with their mum, or they 'generally get on well'.

While 16% reported that their relationship is 'challenging, however, still worth it', 18% of men said they either 'only relate out of obligation' or are 'completely estranged' from their mother.

So that we as mums can be mindful of what NOT to do – and to see how sometimes our habits and choices and even well-meaning traits can be unhelpful to our boys – I wanted to leave the final word to these men.

In your life, what is one thing you wish your mum hadn't done?

Sacrificed so much of her time and health for her job.

Feminised me.

Been abusive.

Been so intense sometimes. Sometimes her love of me feels overwhelming.

Been so traditional.

Talked about finances and relationships when I was younger.

I wish she could have been a bit more approachable.

Didn't let me come home (to my home town) from boarding school for a friend's parent's funeral.

Made me go to church. It pushed me away.

Doing too much for me and not making me do things for myself.

Had issues with alcohol.

Spent so much time at work. Tough I know, as I can thank my mum for the blessed life I lived, but it was difficult to develop without her around at important times.

Send me to an Aunt's in another state when I was a kid and then send a telegram to me saying she couldn't take me back and that my things had been taken and left at my father's.

Failed to relocate me out of a high school where I was being physically bullied.

Bought so many toys when I was a child.

Hid her negative feelings, i.e. she was only ever happy around us.

Do so much for me. I would have like to have been made to cook and clean – but I wasn't!

Said things like, "I worry you're going to grow up to be a wife beater" when me and my little sister would fight. I now react really badly to my 5-year-old son being physically rough with his younger siblings, and sometimes I wonder if there's more to it than the obvious frustration and disappointment over such behaviour ...

Physically and emotionally abused me. I wish she hadn't been so violent.

Been so controlling.

Told me I'm not good enough.

I wish she would have taught me more home life skills like cooking, ironing and cleaning. She tended to do this herself as she was a home maker. This didn't prepare me for living away from home and also instilled more traditional values in me, which influenced my expectations around whether my wife or I should take on certain responsibilities.

Done so much for my brother and I when we lived at home. When I eventually left home I really didn't have any idea how to cook, clean or do my own washing, etc., etc. Being a young bloke, it's easier to let Mum do everything for you.

Put so much pressure on me to be at her beck and call because she thinks that's my duty.

Broken our family by having an affair.

Married my stepfather. He is an abusive jerk.

Come to watch me play rugby and I was reserve.

Smoked cigarettes.

Fight with Dad.

Told my friends that we were going to see Babe (the pig movie) when I was 14.

Made my bed every day!

Been so selfless. (It's a paradox I know ... but I didn't learn to care for myself!)

Gossiped.

Kicked me out of the house.

Let me do what I wanted.

Said some emotionally hurtful things.

Force herself into my life and not respecting my wishes.

Not encouraging me enough to have a relationship with Dad after splitting.

Left me!

Made some insults about my appearance.

Done everything for me. Cooking, cleaning, etc. growing up.

Had favourites.

Died.

Tried to keep me as her baby boy, not letting me grow and make my own decisions.

Bottled her emotions.

Embarrass me on many occasions.

Smoked around us as kids.

Told people my personal business.

Crushed my soul.

Smoked and drank too much wine.

Ignored signs of sexual abuse.

Blamed everyone else for her issues.

Nag me all day, every day.

Spoiled me.

Degraded and belittled me, and not accepted my choices about who I am with.

Been so lazy.

Belt me with no reason.

Misunderstood my boyhood sense of wonder and adventure as being difficult and misbehavior.

Worried so much about us – she's a stress head.

BUT let's end on a positive note (remember the majority of men have good relationships with their Mums) ...

"What would I change? ... Nothing. I would not change a thing."

NOTES

INTRODUCTION

Page 17 'In another disturbing recent phenomonen, young boys — some as young as eight — are being diagnosed with eating disorders and in a recent study that included Australia and the UK there has been an alarming increase in the number of boys who are self-harming ...' Mitchell, R.J., Seah, R., Ting, H.P., Curtis, K., Foster, K. (2018). Intentional self-harm and assault hospitalisations and treatment cost of children in Australia over a 10-year period. *Australian and New Zealand Journal of Public Health*. Online. doi: 10.1111/1753-6405.12782.

Page 17 'In Australia there has been a huge increase in the number of 4- to 5-year-old students being suspended and even expelled ...' Wood, A. & Crawford, S. (1 November 2014). Kindy crisis: Over 400 children aged four to six suspended in past year as unruly behaviour soars to its highest level. *The Daily Telegraph*. Retrieved 15 May 2018, www.dailytelegraph.com.au/news/nsw/kindy-crisis-over-400-children-aged-four-to-six-suspended-in-past-year-as-unruly-behaviour-soars-to-its-highest-level/news-story/6ed37be9c48a97971faa8945c7e916c5.

Page 17 'According to the annual Mission Australia Youth Survey ...' This is Australia's largest online youth survey, running since 2001, surveying young people aged 15 to 19 about issues that concern them. 24,000 young people participated in the 2017 survey. Retrieved 1 May 2018, <https://www.missionaustralia.com.au/what-we-do/research-evaluation/youth-survey>

Page 18 'In the UK between 2013 and 2016, 70% of all victims of domestic homicides were women ...' Flatley, J. (23 November 2017). Domestic abuse in England and Wales: year ending March 2017. Accessed 1 June 2018, www.ons.gov.uk/peoplepopulationandcommunity/crimeandjustice/bulletins/domesticabuseinenglandandwales/yearendingmarch2017.

CHAPTER 1

Page 28 'The effect of the neurotransmitter vasopressin... territoriality and competitiveness ...' Young, L. J. and Flanagan-Cato, L. M. (2012). Editorial comment: Oxytocin, vasopressin and social behavior. *Hormonal Behavior*. March. 61(3): 227–229. doi: 10.1016/j.yhbeh.2012.02.019 ... and Insel T.R., Winslow J.T., Wang Z., Young L.J. (1998) Oxytocin, Vasopressin, and the Neuroendocrine Basis of Pair Bond Formation. In: Zingg H.H., Bourque C.W., Bichet D.G. (eds) Vasopressin and Oxytocin. *Advances in Experimental Medicine and Biology*, vol 449. Springer, Boston, MA. https://doi.org/10.1007/978-1-4615-4871-3_28.

Page 29 'Gurian believes that the invisible drive at the biological core of manhood is the pursuit to prove self-worth ...' Gurian, M. (1996). *The Wonder of Boys: What parents, mentors, and educators can do to shape boys into exceptional men*. New York: Putnam.

CHAPTER 2

Page 33 'I again wish to acknowledge and respect the work of Alison Armstrong ...' Armstrong, A. (2005). 'The Amazing Development of Men: How men change from birth to seniority and the most common mistakes to avoid'. CD-Audio. Duarte, CA, United States: Pax Programs, Inc. More from Alison at www.understandmen.com

Page 34 'Pastor and motivational speaker Mark Gungor has a great way of explaining the differences in the way men and women think ...' www.youtube.com/watch?v=0KrOZe2SxoQ

CHAPTER 3

Page 47 'Research has shown that parents treat their boys and girls differently right from infancy ...' There are a range of studies that show people interact differently with babies according to whether they think they are male or female including: Seavey, C.A., Katz, P.A. & Zalk, S.R. Sex Roles (1975) 1: 103. https://doi.org/10.1007/BF00288004.

Also: Eliot, L. (2009). *Pink Brain, Blue Brain: How small differences grow into troublesome gaps – and what we can do about it.* Boston: Houghton Mifflin. Further, this article contains a good summary of this work: www.jezebel.com/5352031/do-parents-create-gender-differences

Also: Sidorowicz, L., & Lunney, G. (1980). Baby X revisited. *Sex Roles*, 6 (1), 67-73 DOI: 10.1007/BF00288362.

Also: Seavey, Katz, and Zalk (1975). Baby X: The effect of gender labels on adult responses to infants. *Sex Roles*, 1 (2). And Lewis, M. and Weintraub, M. (1979) 'Origins of early sex-role development', *Sex Roles*, 5, 2.

Page 48 'Male vulnerability in terms of health and wellbeing has been well-researched ...' Kraemer, S. (2000). The fragile male. *The British Medical Journal.* Dec 23; 321 (7276): 1609-1612. Retrieved 5 May 2018, www.ncbi.nlm.nih.gov/pmc/articles/PMC1119278/

Page 49 'On top of the influence of hormones and social experience, Schore presents evidence ...' Schore, A. (2017). All our sons: The developmental neurobiology and neuroendocrinology of boys at risk. *Infant Mental Health Journal*, 38(1), pp.15-52.

Page 49 'Statistically boys die in utero at a higher rate than girls ...' Pera, G. (2018). Male entitlement and male fragility. *ADHD Roller Coaster.* Retrieved 25 May, www.adhdrollercoaster.org/essays/male-entitlement-male-fragility/

Page 50 'If you take a look on YouTube at videos from the Center on the Developing Child at Harvard University ...' 'InBrief: The Science of Neglect' from the Center on the Developing Child at Harvard University on 'serve and return' between a child and adult informs part of this chapter. www.youtube.com/watch?v=bF3j5UVCSCA&feature=youtu.be

Page 50 'This new review of interdisciplinary research by Schore supports the major premise that Biddulph made 25 years ago ...' Schore, A. (2017). All our sons: The developmental neurobiology and neuroendocrinology of boys at risk. *Infant Mental Health Journal*, 38(1), pp.15-52. cited in Biddulph, S. (2018). *Raising Boys in the 21st Century*. Sydney: Finch.

Page 50 'This is also supported by research that shows male adolescent violence is now strongly linked to neglect in early childhood ...' see Brown, S. with Vaughan, C. (2010). *Play: How It Shapes the Brain, Opens the Imagination, and Invigorates the Soul*. New York: Avery.

Page 51 'Certainly, research has linked postnatal attachment trauma to being predisposed to a range of personality and psychiatric disorders ...' Schore, A. (2017). All our sons: The developmental neurobiology and neuroendocrinology of boys at risk. *Infant Mental Health Journal*, 38(1), pp.15-52.

Page 52 'On reading Goddard Blythe's book ...' Goddard, S. (2008). *What Babies and Children Really Need*. UK: Hawthorn Press.

Page 52 'The former Governor General of Australia, Quentin Bryce – herself a mother of five children – said that indeed we can "have it all, but not all at the same time" ...' retrieved 15 May 2018, www.smh.com.au/national/youve-got-to-deliver-goals-and-targets-20100604-xklw.html

Page 52 'In my book, 9 Things ...' Dent, M. (2014). *9 Things: A back-to-basics guide to calm, common-sense, connected parenting birth-8*. Murwillumbah, NSW: Pennington Publications.

Page 53 'Girl babies are much more likely to focus on a face, whereas boy babies are much more likely to focus on something beyond the face ...' Connellan, J., Baron-Cohen, S., Wheelwright, S., Batki, A., & Ahluwalia, J. (2000). Sex differences in human neonatal social perception. *Infant Behavior And Development*, 23(1), 113-118. doi: 10.1016/s0163-6383(00)00032-1

Page 59 'Michael Gurian writes about how males and females tend to process emotion differently in the brain ...' Gurian, M. (2017). *Saving Our Sons: A new path for raising healthy and resilient boys*. Spokane, WA: Gurian Institute Press. In the 'Notes and Resources' section of this book, Gurian points to a useful list on his website that features around 1000 primary and secondary sources in gender neuroscience, which is an excellent compilation of research into male/female brain difference. www.michaelgurian.com/Research

Page 61 'In fact, research from Perth's Telethon Institute for Child Health Research ...' Whitehouse. A, Mattes. E, Maybery. M, Sawyer. M, Jacoby. P, Keelan. J, Hickey. M, Sex-specific associations between umbilical cord blood testosterone levels and language delay in early childhood. *Child and Adolescent Mental Health*, Wiley-Blackwell, January 2012, DOI: 10.1111/j.1469-7610.2011.02523.x cited in: Retrieved 11 July 2018, www.telethonkids.org.au/news--events/news-and-events-nav/2012/january/testosterone-womb-language-problems/

CHAPTER 4

Page 65 'Some researchers suggest this can make children more resistant to being parented or educated …' this refers to Gordon Neufeld's comments in Mrozek, A. (2012, 30 August). Nurturing children: Why "early learning" doesn't help. *Institute of Marriage and Family Canada*. Retrieved 2 March 2014, www.imfcanada.org/issues/nurturing-children-why-early-learning-does-not-helpNeufeld

Page 66 'Child psychologist Dr Louise Porter, believes that children are technically unable to master social skills until around three years of age …' Porter, L., PhD., (1994). *Children Are People Too: A parents' guide to young children's behaviour.* South Australia: East Street Publications.

Page 67 'Psychologist and researcher Professor Carol Dweck researched mindsets with 4-year-olds …' Dweck, C. S. (2012). *Mindset: The new psychology of success – How you can fulfil your potential.* London: Robinson.

Page 68 'Speech pathologist Amanda Styles wrote to me …' personal email communication received Monday 26 August 2013.

Page 69 'In the The Lost Boys Report 2016 in the UK …' this report was prepared by Save the Children fund. www.savethechildren.org.uk/content/dam/global/reports/The_Lost_Boys_Report.pdf

Page 70 'Similar results can be seen on the data from the Australian Early Development Census …' The AEDC is census that is held every three years nationwide to collect data about early childhood development at the time children commence their first year of full-time school. It's accessible at www.aedc.gov.au/

Page 70 'The Longitudinal Study of Australian Children (LSAC) …' *Growing Up in Australia:* The Longitudinal Study of Australian Children (LSAC) is a major study that tracks the development of 10,000 children and families from around Australia. It is a joint initiative of the Australian Institute of Family Studies, the Australian Department of Social Services and the Australian Bureau of Statistics. <https://growingupinaustralia.gov.au/>

Page 71 'Shanker shared this message during a keynote address for the commissioner …' Shanker, S. (2014, 6 February). 'Raising Children & Self-regulation: An information session for parents'. A seminar delivered for the Western Australian Council of Social Service Inc.

Page 73 'The more words that children hear in the first three years of their life …' Medina, J. (2014). *Brain Rules for Baby: How to raise a smart and happy child from zero to five.* Second edition. Seattle, WA: Pear Press. http://brainrules.net

Page 73 'Research still tends to suggest that repeating year levels once you have started primary school does not have the success rate we would hope …' Dr Helen McGrath from Deakin University conducted a review of 75 years of research to determine the benefits of repeating a year of school and found it was not a successful strategy on many levels. The review: McGrath, H. (2006). To repeat, or not to repeat. *Words*, vol. 26, no. 2, pp. 39-46.

CHAPTER 5

Page 85 'More recent research suggests that rather than boys hearing less' ... Rowe, K. and Pollard J. 'Literacy, Behaviour and Auditory Processing: Does teacher professional development make a difference?' Background paper to Rue Wright Memorial Award presented at the Royal Australasian College of Physicians Scientific Meeting, Wellington, New Zealand, 2005, cited in Biddulph, S. (2018). *Raising Boys in the 21st Century*. Sydney: Finch.

Page 94 'There has been a significant increase in incidences of inappropriate sexual play among children under five ...' Bita, N. (29 Feb 2016). 'Porn "turning kids into copycat sexual predators"'. *The Australian*. Retrieved 14 May 2018, < https://www.sott.net/article/313403-Porn-turning-kids-into-copycat-sexual-predators>

CHAPTER 6

Page 99 'The research is significant in acknowledging that girls develop their capacity for effective communication well before boys ...' Schore, A. (2017). All our sons: The developmental neurobiology and neuroendocrinology of boys at risk. *Infant Mental Health Journal*, 38(1), pp.15-52.

Page 99 'Some of the research into the high suicide rates of men aged 40-44 years ...' These news articles give a good summary of this: www.theguardian.com/society/2016/mar/09/highest-australian-suicide-rate-in-13-years-driven-by-men-aged-40-to-44 and www.huffingtonpost.com.au/2016/09/26/lifeline-60-percent-of-aussies-often-feel-lonely_a_21479693/

Page 100 'Interestingly, there has been a lot of research on the origins and nature of same-sex friendships, nature of same-sex friendships ...' Guyer, A., McClure-Tone, E., Shiffrin, N., Pine, D., & Nelson, E. (2009). Probing the neural correlates of anticipated peer evaluation in adolescence. *Child Development*, 80(4), 1000-1015. doi: 10.1111/j.1467-8624.2009.01313.x. Cited in Cloud, J. (2009). 'Why girls have BFFs and boys hang out in packs'. *Time*. 17 July. Retrieved 16 May 2018, http://content.time.com/time/health/article/0,8599,1911103,00.html

Page 102 'Dr Joe Tucci of the Australian Childhood Foundation has reported a massive increase in inquiries about inappropriate sexual play with children under five, especially of a penetrative nature ...' Kozaki, D. (2016). 'Internet pornography causing long-term public health crisis amongst Australian children, seminar hears'. ABC News Online. 9 Feb. Retrieved 14 May 2018, www.abc.net.au/news/2016-02-09/health-crisis-looming-over-accessibility-of-porn-for-children/7153016

Page 106 'We must stop this homophobic teasing of boy friendships ...' A good article discussing this trend and its implications on men's friendships is Mark Greene's 'Why do we murder the beautiful friendships of boys'. www.goodmenproject.com/featured-content/adult-male-lonliness-megasahd/

CHAPTER 9

Page 138 '...Celia Lashlie, the well-respected and passionate boy champion from New Zealand, certainly believed this and she linked the probability of going to prison very strongly with the absence of a strong maternal figure in the Maori culture ...' Lashlie, C. (2005). *He'll Be OK: Growing gorgeous boys into good men*. Auckland, NZ: Harper Collins. Read more about Celia's work at https://www.celialashlie.nz/

Page 157 'If you are not familiar with Lenore Skenazy please check out her website ...' Lenore Skenazy wrote a column about letting her 9-year-old ride the New York subway alone and was subsequently declared by media as "America's worst mom". She went on to write *Free-Range Kids: How to raise safe, self-reliant children (without going nuts with worry)* and blogs at www.freerangekids.com

Page 157 'More and more research is showing that the modern, supposedly safe, playgrounds are diminishing our children's capacity to assess and manage risk ...' Gill, T. (2007). *No Fear: growing up in a risk averse society.* UK: Calouste Gulbenkian Foundation.

Page 159 'Again, Stuart Shanker believes that poor quality food, lack of good sleep ...' Shanker, S. & Teresa Barker (2016). *Self-reg: How to help your child (and you) break the stress cycle and successfully engage with life.* Canada: Penguin Random House.

Page 166 'Steve Biddulph cautions parents to be mindful of the unintended negative side effects around certain sporting codes ...' Biddulph, S. (2018). *Raising Boys in the 21st Century.* Sydney: Finch Publishing.

Page 169 'The link between dopamine and attention has been the subject of research for many years ...' For example: Dawei Li, Pak C. Sham, Michael J. Owen, Lin He; Meta-analysis shows significant association between dopamine system genes and attention deficit hyperactivity disorder (ADHD), *Human Molecular Genetics*, Volume 15, Issue 14, 15 July 2006, Pages 2276–2284, https://doi.org/10.1093/hmg/ddl152

CHAPTER 10

Page 174 'The wonderful and highly respected Indigenous educator Professor Chris Sarra of the Stronger, Smarter Institute writes passionately ...' New Matilda (28 January 2015). Retrieved 10 May 2018, https://newmatilda.com/2015/01/28/chris-sarra-schooling-teachers-stronger-smarter-black-education/. See also Chris Sarra's book, *Good Morning Mr Sarra* (2012) published by The University of Queensland Press.

Page 175 'A partial explanation for this change in behaviour in a significant number of our boys is due to some shifts in hormonal activity, particularly the luteinising hormone ...' Schore, A. (2017). All our sons: The developmental neurobiology and neuroendocrinology of boys at risk. *Infant Mental Health Journal*, 38(1), pp.15-52. cited in Biddulph, S. (2018). *Raising Boys in the 21st Century*. Sydney: Finch.

Page 179 'Aggression nurturance... a term coined by Michael-Gurian ...' Gurian gives a good description of this in this talk on YouTube: www.youtube.com/watch?v=gwAxxgAWfAs

Page 186 'In fact, there is more and more research coming out that links the state of our microbiome (basically the microorganisms that live inside us) to anxiety, depression and other mood disorders ...' Some useful links here include www.nature.com/articles/518S13a and www.telethonkids.org.au/search/?q=diet+and+mental+health

Page 186 'I have already mentioned the sensitivity of boys to endocrine-disrupting chemicals and this sensitivity may possibly be behind some of the poor behaviour in our young lads ...' Schore, A. (2017). All our sons: The developmental neurobiology and neuroendocrinology of boys at risk. *Infant Mental Health Journal*, 38(1), pp.15-52.

Page 187 'The World Health Organisation suggests children have no more than the equivalent of four to six teaspoons per day of sugar ...' www.thatsugarfilm.com

Page 187 'Just to give you an idea, a 600ml bottle of lemonade ...' Healthy Food & Sport: Sugar content of popular drinks: Considerations for children in sport – fact sheet. www.health.act.gov.au. Retrieved 10 June 2018, www.health.act.gov.au/sites/default/files/Fact%20sheets/Sugar%20Content%20of%20Popular%20Drinks%20-%20Considerations%20for%20Children%20in%20Sport.pdf

CHAPTER 11

Page 202 'American shame researcher Dr Brené Brown says there is an important distinction between shame and guilt ...' Brené Brown's TED talk, 'Listening to shame' has had more than nine million views. It's worth a watch: <https://www.ted.com/talks/brene_brown_listening_to_shame>

Page 202 'Brown cites a longitudinal research study of a large group of fifth-grade students ...' Brown, B. (2013). 'The Gifts of Imperfect Parenting: Raising children with courage, compassion, & connection'. Audio CD. Boulder, CO: Sounds True.

Page 205 'Dr Helen Street, a social psychologist and co-founder of the Positive Schools Conferences, has found this is similar to the empty yearning for fame ...' Dr Helen Street, 'Rewards, punishments and motivation' presentation to Positive Schools conference. May 23rd 2013, Perth.

CHAPTER 12

Page 211 'There are three types of insecure attachment ...' You can read a concise explanation of this here: www.child-encyclopedia.com/attachment/according-experts/attachment-early-age-0-5-and-its-impact-childrens-development

Page 217 'In one research study led by Wayne State University in Detroit into the relationship between sexual assault and alcohol consumption ...' Abbey, A., Zawacki, T., Buck, P., Clinton, A., & McAuslan, P. (2004). Sexual assault and alcohol consumption: what do we know about their relationship and what types of research are still needed?. *Aggression And Violent Behavior*, 9(3), 271-303. doi: 10.1016/s1359-1789(03)00011-9

Page 220 'For example, Ed Sheeran has given a great speech about how he started life with a port-wine stain birthmark on his face...' June 8 2015, 9th Annual American Institute for Stuttering. https://www.youtube.com/watch?v=K_3r3SolyDs.

Page 221 'Jimmy Stynes, the late AFL footballer ...' Watc the documentary, 'Every Heart Beats True-The Jim Stynes Story': Channel 9/Lightstream Pictures. Also Jim Stynes' memoir is *My Journey*. His co-author Warwick Green has also adapted the memoir for younger readers in a book called *Walk Tall* (both published by Penguin).

CHAPTER 16

Page 261 '... from a study of some of the American teenagers who committed mass murders in their school environments in the early 1990s ...' This information came from a lecture delivered by Gayle Gregory in early 2000. She is the co-author of: Gregory, G & Parry, T. (2006). *Designing brain-compatible learning.* California: Corwin Press.

Page 262 'Despite research findings to the contrary, play fighting has come to be seen as a disturbing facet of childhood ...' Gill, T. (2007). *No Fear: Growing up in a risk averse society.* UK: Calouste Gulbenkian Foundation.

Page 263 'This is one of the reasons why pioneering paediatrician and educator Emmi Pikler encouraged the 3Rs ...' Gonzalez-Mena, J. & Widmeyer Eyer, D. (2008). *Infants, Toddlers and Caregivers: The Philosophy of Respect based on the work by Magda Gerber and the Hungarian paediatrician Emmi Pikler.* New York: McGraw-Hill.

Page 266 'The effects of being treated fairly and with kindness have been shown in studies in neuroscience, to make a significant difference to the way the brain integrates ...' Lieberman, M. PhD., and Eisenberger, N. PhD. (2008). The pains and pleasures of social life: A social cognitive neuroscience approach. *Neuroleadership Journal.* Retrieved 20 June 2018 from www.scn.ucla.edu/pdf/Pains&Pleasures (2008).pdf

Page 267 'Medina explains the astonishing skill called 'deferred imitation' ...' Medina, J. (2014). *Brain Rules for Baby: How to raise a smart and happy child from zero to five.* Second edition. Seattle, WA: Pear Press. http://brainrules.net/

Page 271 'Fostering gratitude improves wellbeing both emotionally and physically and, in one study, the gratitude group reported being more supportive around other people ...' Emmons, R. (2008). *Thanks! How Practising Gratitude Can Make You Happier.* New York: Houghton Mifflin Harcourt Publishing Company.

CHAPTER 17

Page 286 'A really good place to start is with the picture book *No Means No!* by Jayneen Sanders ...' https://e2epublishing.info/shop/no-means-no There is also a list of books on my website about body safety and protective behaviours. https://www.maggiedent.com/blog/top-tips-resources-teach-children-body-safety-protective-behaviours/

REFERENCES & RECOMMENDED READING

Anderson, H., Angelo, F., Stewart, R. (2015). *The Secret Business of Relationships, Love and Sex*. Balwyn North, Victoria: Secret Girls' Business Publisher.

Armstrong, A. (2005). 'The Amazing Development of Men: How men change from birth to seniority and the most common mistakes to avoid'. CD-Audio. Duarte, CA, United States: Pax Programs, Inc.

Barker, G. (2013, Spring). Lost boys. *Scoop*. Vol 65. Retrieved 4 April 2014 from http://scoop.realviewtechnologies.com/?iid=81811&startpage=56

Biddulph, S. (2018). *Raising Boys in the 21st Century*. Sydney: Finch Publishing.

Bronson, P. & Merryman, A. (2009). *NurtureShock: New thinking about children*. New York: Hachette Book Group.

Brooks, B. (2018). *Stories for Boys Who Dare to Be Different*. United Kingdom: Quercus.

Brown, B. (2013). 'The Gifts of Imperfect Parenting: Raising children with courage, compassion, & connection'. Audio CD. Boulder, CO: Sounds True.

Stuart Brown, *Play: How it shapes the brain, opens the imagination, and invigorates the soul* (2009).

Campbell-McBride, N. (2010). *Gut and Psychology Syndrome: Natural treatment for autism, dyspraxia, A.D.D., dyslexia, A.D.H.D., depression, schizophrenia* (Rev. and expanded ed.). United Kingdom: Medinform.

Chapman, G. D., and Campbell, R. (2012). *The 5 Love Languages of Children*. Chicago: Northfield Pub.

Clark, E. (2017). *Love, Sex and No Regrets: For today's teens*. Mona Vale, NSW: Finch Publishing

Cunningham, H., & Morpurgo, M. (2006). *The Invention of Childhood*. London: BBC.

Dent, M. (2014). *9 Things: A back-to-basics guide to calm, common-sense, connected parenting birth-8*. Murwillumbah, NSW: Pennington Publications.

Dent, M. (2016). *A Dog's Life Wisdoms: 21 Life wisdoms from a dog called Jess*. Murwillumbah, NSW: Pennington Publications.

Dent, M. (2004). *Black Duck Wisdom: Understanding life through the wisdom of ducks*. Murwillumbah, NSW: Pennington Publications.

Dent, M. (2005). *Nurturing Kids' Hearts and Souls: Building emotional, social and spiritual competence*. Dunsborough. WA: Pennington Publications.

Dent, M. (2016, Rev. Edition), *Real Kids in an Unreal World: How to build resilience and self-esteem in today's children.* Dunsborough, WA: Pennington Publications.

Dent, M. (2010). *Saving Our Adolescents: Supporting today's adolescents through the bumpy ride to adulthood.* Murwillumbah, NSW: Pennington Publications.

Dent, M. (2017 Reprint). *Saving Our Children From Our Chaotic World: Teaching children the magic of silence and stillness.* Dunsborough, WA: Pennington Publications.

Dent, M. (2014). *Some Secrets for the Modern-Day Mammoth Hunter: Becoming and being a good man.* Murwillumbah, NSW: Pennington Publications.

Dweck, C. S. (2012). *Mindset: The new psychology of success – How you can fulfil your potential.* London: Robinson.

Dwyer, N. (2013). *Being Adventurous: An everyday learning series title.* Deakin, ACT: Early Childhood Australia.

Eady, J., & Additive Alert Pty Ltd. (2017). *Additive Alert: Your guide to safer shopping: the essential information about what's really in the food you eat, which additives to avoid and why.* 3rd Edition. Warriewood, NSW: Woodslane Press Pty Ltd.

Estroff Marano, H. (2008). *A Nation of Wimps: The high cost of invasive parenting.* New York: Broadway Books.

Farmer, N. (2012). *Getting It Right For Boys: Why boys do what they do and how to make the early years work for them.* London: Bloomsbury Publishing.

Gardner, H. (1983). *Frames of Mind: The theory of multiple intelligences.* New York: Basic Books.

Gill, T. (2007). *No Fear: Growing up in a risk averse society.* UK: Calouste Gulbenkian Foundation.

Goddard, S. (2008). *What Babies and Children Really Need.* UK: Hawthorn Press.

Goleman, D. (1996). *Emotional Intelligence: Why it can matter more than IQ.* UK: Bloomsbury Publishing.

Goleman, D. (2006). *Social Intelligence: The new science of human relationships.* New York: Bantam Books.

Grant, I. (2006). *Growing Great Boys.* Auckland, N.Z.: Random House New Zealand

Gray, J. (1992). *Men Are From Mars, Women Are From Venus: A practical guide for improving communication and getting what you want in your relationships.* New York, NY: HarperCollins.

Gray, P. (2013). *Free to Learn: Why unleashing the instinct to play will make our children happier, more self-reliant, and better students for life.* New York: Basic Books.

Gray, P. (2013, September). The play deficit. *Aeon.* Retrieved 3 October 2013. www.aeonmagazine.com/being-human/children-today-are-suffering-a-severe-deficit-of-play

Grille, R. (2008). *Heart to Heart Parenting: Nurturing your child's emotional intelligence from conception to school age*. Sydney: ABC Books.

Grille, R. (2013). *Parenting for a Peaceful World* (second edition). Asheville, NC: Vox Cordis Press.

Gurian, M. (1993). *Mothers, Sons and Lovers: How a man's relationship with his mother affects the rest of his life*. Boston, MA: Shambhala Publications Inc.

Gurian, M. (2017). *Saving Our Sons: A new path for raising healthy and resilient boys*. Spokane, WA: Gurian Institute Press.

Gurian, M. (1999). *The Good Son: Shaping the moral development of our boys and young men*. New York: Jeremy P. Tarcher.

Gurian, M. and Stevens, K. (2005). *The Minds of Boys*. San Francisco, CA: Jossey-Bass.

Gurian, M. (1996). *The Wonder of Boys: What parents, mentors, and educators can do to shape boys into exceptional men*. New York: Putnam.

Hanford Morhard, R. (2013), *Wired to Move: Facts and strategies for nurturing boys in an early childhood setting*. US: Gryphon House.

Holland, P. (2008). *We Don't Play With Guns Here*. Maidenhead: Open University Press.

Kraemer, S. (2000). The fragile male. *BMJ: British Medical Journal*, 321(7276), 1609–1612.

Kohn, A. (1998). *What to Look for in a Classroom: And other essays*. San Francisco, CA: Jossey-Bass.

Lapointe, V. (2016). *Discipline Without Damage: Hot to get kids to behave without messing them up*. Canada: Life Tree Media.

Lashlie, C. (2005). *He'll Be OK: Growing gorgeous boys into good men*. Auckland, NZ: Harper Collins.

Lieberman, M. PhD., and Eisenberger, N. PhD. (2008). The pains and pleasures of social life: A social cognitive neuroscience approach. *Neuroleadership Journal*. Retrieved 20 June 2018 from http://www.scn.ucla.edu/pdf/Pains&Pleasures(2008).pdf

Lillico, I. (2000). *Boys & Their Schooling: A guide for parents and teachers*. Duncraig, WA: I. Lillico.

Medina, J. (2014). *Brain Rules: 12 principles for surviving and thriving at work, home, and school*. Second edition. Seattle, WA: Pear Press. http://brainrules.net/

Medina, J. (2014). *Brain Rules for Baby: How to raise a smart and happy child from zero to five*. Second edition. Seattle, WA: Pear Press. http://brainrules.net/

Meeker, M. (2014). *Strong Mothers, Strong Sons: Lessons mothers need to raise extraordinary men*. New York: Ballantine Books.

Mrozek, A. (2012, 30 August). Nurturing children: Why "early learning" doesn't help. *Institute of Marriage and Family Canada*. Retrieved 2 March 2014 from www.imfcanada.org/issues/nurturing-children-why-early-learning-does-not-helpNeufeld

Perlmutter, D with Loberg, K. (2013). *Grain Brain: The surprising truth about wheat, carbs, and sugar—your brain's silent killers.* New York, NY: Little, Brown and Co.

Pollack, W. S. (1998). *Real Boys: Rescuing our sons from the myths of boyhood.* New York: Random House.

Rubinstein, A. (2013). *The Making of Men: Raising boys to be happy, healthy and successful.* Sydney: Xuom.

Sanders, J. (2015). *No Means No! Teaching children about personal boundaries, respect and consent; empowering kids by respecting their choices and their right to say, 'no!'* Victoria, Australia: UpLoad Publishing.

Schore, A. (2017). All our sons: The developmental neurobiology and neuroendocrinology of boys at risk. *Infant Mental Health Journal*, 38(1), pp.15-52.

Shanker, S. & Teresa Barker (2016). *Self-reg: How to help your child (and you) break the stress cycle and successfully engage with life.* Canada: Penguin Random House.

Siegel, D.J., MD. (2010). *Mindsight: The new science of personal transformation.* New York: Bantam Books.

Smiler, A. P. (2016). *Dating and Sex: A guide for the 21st century teen boy.* Washington, DC: Magination Press.

Stewart, R., Angelo, F., Anderson, H. and Taylor, J. (2011). *Secret Boys' Business.* North Balwyn, Vic: Secret Girls' Business Publishing.

Stiffelman, S. (2010). *Parenting Without Power Struggles: Raising joyful, resilient kids while staying calm, cool and connected.* New York: Atria Paperback.

Sunderland, M. (2007). *The Science of Parenting: How today's brain research can help you raise happy, emotionally balanced children.* New York: DK Publishing.

Tsabary, S. (2014). *Out of Control: Why disciplining your child doesn't work and what will.* Vancouver, BC: Namaste Publishing.

Wiseman, R. (2013). *Ringleaders and Sidekicks: How to help your son cope with classroom politics, bullying, girls and growing up.* London: Piatkus.

CREDITS

© Farmer, N. (2012). GETTING IT RIGHT FOR BOYS: WHY BOYS DO WHAT THEY DO AND HOW TO MAKE THE EARLY YEARS WORK FOR THEM, Featherstone, used by permission of Bloomsbury Publishing Plc.

Excerpt from SOCIAL INTELLIGENCE: THE NEW SCIENCE OF HUMAN RELATIONSHIPS by Daniel Goleman, copyright © 2006 by Daniel Goleman. Used by permission of Bantam Books, an imprint of Random House, a division of Penguin Random House LLC. All rights reserved.

Excerpt from HE'LL BE OK by Celia Lashlie © 2005. Used by kind permission of the late Celia Lashlie's family. To contribute to Celia's Legacy or join Celia's Army, please visit https://www.celialashlie.nz/

INDEX

A

B

C

D

E

F

G

Gratitude, 139, 222, 263, 266, 271-273

H

I

J

K

L

M

Q

R

S

T

U

V

W

ACKNOWLEDGEMENTS

This book has been in my heart and my mind for many years. I need to thank a few people who have helped me bring it out into the real world. Firstly, my amazing editors – both of whom, like me, happen to be mothers of sons only. Carmen Myler and Louise Shannon – you have been a complete delight to work with as always and I know this was as important to you as it was to me.

My team support me and protect me so that I may write and spend glorious times in nature pondering, questioning, dreaming and writing. Thank you so much to my amazing niece and PA Laura Browning – your bubbly presence in my life is such a joy. To my fabulous graphic designer, web Mistress, email gatekeeper and dear friend Katharine Middleton – thanks again for helping me birth another baby. Behind the scenes is my techno guru Will Ambrose and my research assistant Kelly Skinner – thank you both for all that you do.

This book began its journey onto paper while I was on an emotional tour of the battlefields of the Western front in Belgium and France in April this year. I was celebrating my grandfather's amazing contribution to the history of this country – Australia – 100 years after he had walked the sacred lands. My pop fought in four of the worst battles, excluding Gallipoli, that took place in Europe during the First World War. I offer deep thanks for the inspiration from all of those who fought in the name of peace and, as a mother of four sons, I was deeply touched by the stories of loss that I heard and very grateful that my sons arrived at a different time in history.

My growing family constantly fill my cup with laughter and joy and I'm so grateful that I was blessed with four healthy sons – and now with four special daughters-in-law and soon-to-be five grandchildren. My life is so enriched by my immediate family and my extended family scattered around Australia.

A special thank you has to go to my good bloke, my husband Steve. When I am in writing mode I am completely disconnected from the real world. So, thank you for the healthy meals, the endless cups of tea, glasses of water and occasional shoulder rubs that kept me going. We make a good team and I can only do what I do because of you and your unconditional love and support. Thanks babe.

Ever since I first stepped into the classroom in 1977 I have met so many boys who have allowed me to walk beside them and often times be a guiding presence in their lives. To every boy who trusted me and allowed me to see into your heart – I thank you dearly. To all my nephews and sons, and their special mates – you are all *my boys* – and I love you all.

I also want to thank all the mums and dads who responded to my requests – my survey for men and my anecdotes from women. Your voices make this book so much more meaningful. Finally, I want to thank all the mums and dads who have connected with me at some point over the years to thank me for helping make their homes a happier place to be. Without your gratitude and encouragement – and often beautiful stories – I am sure I would have retired years ago and this book would simply have stayed a dream.